POLITICS IS ADJOURNED

SEWARD W. LIVERMORE

POLITICS

IS ADJOURNED

WOODROW WILSON
AND THE WAR CONGRESS,
1916-1918

WESLEYAN UNIVERSITY PRESS
MIDDLETOWN, CONNECTICUT

Library of Congress Catalog Card Number: 66-14666
Manufactured in the United States of America
First edition

TO LAURA

CONTENTS

POLITICS IS ADJOURNED

THE POLITICS OF PREPAREDNESS

I

ON THE evening of October 24, 1918, President Woodrow Wilson retired to his study in the White House and tapped out on his typewriter a brief message to the people of the United States. It contained a sharp indictment of his political opponents for their obstructive behavior during the war and concluded with an appeal, almost a peremptory demand, for the election a few days thence of a Democratic Congress. The gravamen of his charge was that the Republican leaders in Congress, although pro-war, were anti-administration and thus incapable of giving him the support he needed to see him through the critical period ahead. "At almost every turn, since we entered the war," he said, "they have sought to take the choice of policy and the conduct of the war out of my hands and to put it under the control of instrumentalities of their own choosing. This is no time either for divided counsel or for divided leadership."[1]

The publication of this document the next day in the nation's press produced an appalling uproar from one end of the country to the other. It astonished a good many Democrats, enraged all the Republicans, and brought into focus a bitter political controversy that had been going on for many months despite a great amount of pretense to the contrary. In the noisy outburst of abuse and recrimination that followed the appearance of the message, the "instrumentalities" mentioned by Wilson were largely lost to sight or obscured by other issues raised by the warring parties, and the matter has escaped attention ever since. Consequently, out of this omission or neglect has sprung one of the sturdiest and most enduring myths in American history — the myth that Wilson by his appeal had revived partisan politics which had automatically and miraculously come to an end when the country entered the war on April 6, 1917.

Wilson's appeal is considered all the more opprobrious because it presumably violated the partisan truce established as a result of his famous "politics is adjourned" statement of May 27, 1918. Besides presupposing a state of affairs without parallel in American experience, this interpretation does not explain why such a truce was necessary in the first place if all partisan activity had already ceased. Nevertheless, it has remained the most popular and widely accepted explanation of the disaster which overtook the Democrats at the polls on November 5. Many otherwise reputable accounts of that critical period make it appear that the President had enjoyed the most harmonious bipartisan cooperation in the stupendous task of forwarding the war program of the government.[2] Republicans and Democrats are pictured working shoulder to shoulder in patriotic support of the Great Crusade without a thought of political advantage or disadvantage arising to mar this remarkable display of transcendent national unity, except perhaps for some welcome constructive criticism from certain quarters. Wilson's appeal, therefore, far from rallying the people to his cause, justly infuriated the hitherto loyal Republican opposition, alienated the electorate, and brought about one of the most significant political upsets in American history.

That other factors might be responsible for this denouement has occurred to a few commentators on the period, but their observations have done little to dispose of the legend of Wilson's allegedly irrational behavior. For the most part, the entire World War period has been sadly neglected on the political side. In the case of the 1918 elections, too much reliance has been placed on the official propaganda put out by both parties in the hectic closing days of the campaign. In the frenzied insults that were exchanged, neither side paid much attention to the truth; and in the post-mortems that followed the election, nothing was done to set the record straight. The victorious Republicans naturally felt called upon for no explanation of their unexpected and stunning success other than the obvious one of the appeal. The unhappy Democrats, on the other hand, beyond claiming to be the innocent victims of foul play, were disinclined to indulge in any painful public analysis of their mistakes, since it would not alter the outcome. Consequently, the pre-election image carefully fostered by Republican propaganda of selfless and wholehearted cooperation in the war effort has remained undisturbed, and statistics are frequently drawn from this source to demonstrate that as many, if not sometimes more, Republicans as Democrats voted for military appropriations and other war measures. Statistics alone, however, do not convey any idea of the bitter and prolonged struggles that preceded the adoption of many of these measures, indeed all of the major ones, and gave a strong partisan coloration to the proceedings despite all the solemn disavowals to the contrary.

Hence, too much stock cannot be put in the protestations of Republican leaders like Senator Henry Cabot Lodge, whose latest biographer accepts at face value the senator's assertion that during the war he cast no party vote and made no partisan speech until his partisan passions were unleashed by Wilson's provocative action. The little space that is devoted to the World War phase of Lodge's career is concerned primarily with trying to demonstrate that patriotism precluded any political shenanigans on the part of Wilson's deadliest senatorial foe. While true up to a point, it overlooks the wily Lodge's penchant for working behind the scenes whence he could direct, with no danger to himself, the partisan activities of his more truculent colleagues such as Senator Lawrence Y. Sherman of Illinois, a windy obstructionist of great virtuosity. When Sherman's habit of undermining public confidence in the administration at every opportunity while certifying at the same time to his own patriotic loyalty brought upon him the well-merited censure of the New York *Times*, Lodge warmly defended his obstreperous colleague as ''eminently sound in his views'' and not afraid to say ''many true things that more timid men won't say.''[3]

If politics were actually adjourned, and the Republicans including Lodge and Sherman had indeed yielded the last full measure of devotion to the common cause, then Wilson truly deserved the tragic consequences of his action. If, on the other hand, the situation was different and the President had good reason to believe that his cause stood in mortal danger from intense but crudely camouflaged political activity, the course he adopted emerges as a logical corollary. At least it was taken in response to specific conditions, and while perhaps not the wisest course in the circumstances, it was not the result of megalomania or incipient mental decay, as some of his detractors have alleged. Neither the newspaper files for the war period nor the pages of the *Congressional Record* nor the private correspondence of the principal statesmen involved reveal a suspension of political activity or indicate any serious effort in that direction. One earnest New Yorker in a pamphlet entitled ''Trifling with the War'' took his fellowcountrymen severely to task for their frailty in this respect. ''The Patriot,'' he complained, ''has not yet driven the Political Partisan out of the American's heart.''[4] Many citizens deplored this scandalous state of affairs but generally absolved their own side from any responsibility in the matter. The war, therefore, far from constituting a moratorium on politics as is so widely believed, merely presented the two parties with a different set of issues and imposed a minimal amount of restraint and caution on their behavior. There was some feeling that any undue display of partisan animus would distract public attention from the major business of defeating the foe, a thing that had happened within living memory in the congressional elections of 1862 and 1864. Instead of forcing politics into the background, however, this sentiment became the occasion for an elaborate camouflage that enabled politicians to ply their trade with little fear of public censure. Behind a smokescreen of patriotic oratory, professing loyalty and devotion to the common cause, the flag, and the boys in the trenches, candidates for office carried on much as usual in the halls of Congress and on the hustings. In the ensuing struggle for power, few punches were pulled or political tricks left unturned. Shortly after the start of the war, one newspaper was moved to remark of the debates in Congress on vital war measures that ''they have been disgraced by personal or political or sectional or factional contentions which are utterly discreditable at the same time they waste precious time.''[5]

Politics, far from being adjourned in 1918 — despite the

more or less sincere protestations of many of its leading practitioners — was intensified by the war hysteria whipped up among the people by the press and by the government's propaganda bureau. The issues were shaped by the progress of the fighting overseas and turned upon the management of the war effort at home. Post-war problems received some attention toward the end, mainly an emotional discussion of Republican fears that Wilson would make a shameful compromise peace with the Germans and then invite the unregenerate foe into his crackpot League of Nations. The Democrats relied unswervingly on their successful war record and on the President's vast prestige as a war leader and formulator of world opinion to renew their lease on office in 1918. They spent a great deal of energy and money on a campaign to convince the voters that Wilson must be supported by a Congress politically in harmony with his views and aspirations or every sacrifice would have been in vain. The Republicans, smarting from their defeat in 1916 by the narrowest of margins, were grimly determined not to be totally eclipsed by this apocalyptic concept of the President as the saviour of mankind. They labored with equal intensity and spent even greater sums to demonstrate that a voter could cast his ballot against Wilson's party and still not be a traitor to the human race.

All in all, it was a remarkable election and one of the most fiercely contested in American history because of the appreciation on both sides of the high stakes involved, not the least of which were the making of the peace treaty and the organization of the post-war world. The real story only emerges, however, after the patriotic oratory, the inspired messages, the official appeals, and the frenzied propaganda are cleared away like so many wrappings that conceal the true nature of the object underneath.

II

THE ADVENT of war found the country ill prepared, emotionally as well as militarily, for the enormous and unfamiliar task ahead. The Sixty-fifth Congress, which took the country into the war on April 6, 1917, was the product of the violent controversies that had raged over neutral rights and national preparedness prior to the 1916 presidential election. Public opinion, influenced by adroit propaganda, had divided sharply over the merits of the President's foreign policies. Whatever course he adopted only fanned the fierce antagonisms that had developed among large racial groups sympathetic to one side or the other in the European conflict. The menace from abroad had made national defense a matter of prime importance, but every move of the administration in that direction met with bitter opposition from isolationists and pacifists and, at the same time, with savage ridicule from preparedness zealots angered by the inadequacy of the measures proposed. A candidate's stand on these burning issues became a measure of his patriotism, a yardstick by which the public could judge his fitness for office not only in the melee of the 1916 campaign but to a much greater extent in the superheated atmosphere of the 1918 congressional elections.

Early in 1916, after much prodding from the President, Congress moved reluctantly to improve the state of the nation's defenses. In the process of reorganizing the antiquated military establishment, the General Staff, besides urging a substantial increase in the Regular Army to 250,000 men, proposed a plan for a Continental Army of 400,000 men under federal control to replace the unreliable state militia as a second line of defense. The more preparedness-minded Senate accepted these recommendations after a hard fight, but the House, appalled at the idea of saddling the country with an expensive armament program in an election year, rejected them out of hand. Instead it allowed for only a slight increase in the Regular Army and provided a lavish outlay of funds for the National Guard, always the political apple of the congressional eye.

After the Army bill had bogged down in conference for many weeks, Representative Julius Kahn of California, a leading Republican proponent of preparedness, sought to break the impasse with two amendments aimed at restoring the original provisions of the House bill for a Continental Army and a larger regular establishment. When this maneuver failed by a large majority, the Senate yielded unconditionally on all points. Disgusted patriots agreed with Senator William E. Borah of Idaho that the final version of the Hay-Chamberlain bill was a miserable hodgepodge of everything but military efficiency.[6] The preparedness press angrily denounced the pork-barrel features of the legislation, and the Chicago *Tribune* promised to make it hot at election time for the ten Illinois congressmen who had voted against the Kahn amendments.[7] Many other isolationist congressmen found themselves running the same gantlet, nor was the issue forgotten when the 1918 congressional elections rolled around.

During the protracted struggle over national defense, the German submarine attack on neutral shipping brought the country uncomfortably closer to the European conflict. Wilson's firmness in holding the German government responsible for the loss of American lives on the high seas had thrown Congress into a turmoil of alarm and resentment. Many congressmen considered the President's attitude unnecessarily provocative and an invitation to war. The peace-at-any-price elements rallied behind the McLemore resolution, introduced by Representative Jeff McLemore, a renegade Texas Democrat, which forbade Americans to travel on armed merchant ships in submarine-infested waters. Patriots considered it a politically inspired and weak-kneed surrender to German aggression, while to Wilson the maneuver represented an unwarranted interference with his constitutional prerogatives in the field of foreign affairs which would weaken him in dealing with the German government. Pressure from the Chief Executive quickly forced all but a handful of recalcitrant Democrats into line on March 7, when the House voted 276 to 142 to table the objectionable measure after the Senate had rejected a slightly different version.[8]

McLemore's maneuver provoked an astonishing furor throughout the country. The fact that nearly three out of four of its supporters in the House were Republicans, mostly midwestern isolationists, made the administration press smell a pro-German plot to embarrass the President and influence the coming election. Many Republican newspapers, on the other hand, railed at party members so lost to party loyalty as to follow Wilson in the matter. A Vermont representative, under fire in his local press for not hewing to the party line, retorted angrily that "I simply refused to play politics on a significant international question, whether my vote for the time being appeared to coincide with the policy of a Democratic president or not.''[9] Their votes on this issue came back to haunt quite a few congressmen in the next two elections, with unpleasant consequences for many of them.

Preparedness advocates sought to stimulate public interest in the question by staging monster parades in the streets of many principal cities. The leaders for the most part were prominent Republicans who had rallied around the banner of Colonel Theodore Roosevelt, the acknowledged champion of compulsory military service, a navy second to none, and an aggressive foreign policy to match. The peace-at-any-price partisans showed no less zeal in propagandizing their views through protest meetings, petitions, resolutions, and pilgrimages to Washington. Allied with them were the racial minority groups, principally Irish and German, who constituted the so-called hyphen vote. Although often working at cross-purposes, these groups were equally determined to keep the United States neutral and unarmed. Many midwestern congressmen solicited support from racial organizations opposed to Wilson's policies by advertising their German descent or connections or sympathies in the newspapers. The German-language press was particularly hostile to the President, only 28 of the 238 newspapers in this category favoring his re-election. The New York *Staats-Zeitung,* for example, demanded the defeat of the fourteen congressmen from the metropolitan area who had upheld Wilson on the McLemore resolution and urged the return of the eight who had deserted him.[10]

The disruption of the Progressive party worked to the advantage of Wilson's party in the West, where Charles Evans Hughes showed little astuteness in handling the formidable remnants of Roosevelt's once enthusiastic following. In such states as California and Washington the Republican candidate offended many voters by allowing himself to become entangled in the factional quarrels that still raged in the party ranks. His California defeat is generally ascribed to the apostasy of Governor Hiram Johnson, who was swept into the Senate by a tremendous majority while allowing the head of his ticket to fall by the wayside.[11] However, the same pattern of electoral preference appeared in Washington, which sent a progressive Republican, Miles Poindexter, back to the Senate while giving its electoral vote to Wilson. Disappointed Republicans also accused Poindexter of having knifed Hughes, but, as in the case of Johnson, there is no evidence to support this view.[12]

If Republican factionalism helped Wilson in the West, the sectional issue almost proved the undoing of his party in the East. The privileged position of its southern wing in the federal government and the South's demands for special consideration in the legislative field had created widespread resentment outside the confines of Dixie. Consequently, an energetic display of the bloody shirt in the Maine congressional election on September 10 cost Senator Charles F. Johnson, an administration stalwart, his seat. Colonel Frederick Hale, an ardent Roosevelt follower, won easily on a platform advocating preparedness and denouncing southern dominance in Congress.[13] The success of Hale's appeal to the voters not to re-elect a man who no longer represented New England industries but "blindly obeyed the dictates of the Southern majority" inspired the Republican National Committee to concoct a pamphlet around this theme entitled "The Great Political Crime of the Democratic Party." The Speakers Bureau sent copies to all party workers and candidates throughout the country as a sure-fire way of winning votes for the cause. "It had no little bearing on the result in the State of Maine," said the head of the Bureau in transmitting the brochure, and he was confident that it would get the same results elsewhere.[14]

Democratic national headquarters, shaken by the Maine landslide, hastily countered with a booklet of its own called "The Issue of Sectionalism," which strove to refute the canard by emphasizing Wilson's great services to the nation, while the President in his campaign speeches also deprecated the opposition's below-the-belt tactics.[15] The Republicans, however, continued to push the matter with enthusiasm, and the press of both parties erupted in a noisy warfare of abuse and reproof.[16] So vulnerable were northern Democrats on this issue that their adversaries, but for incredible bungling in other directions and despite the attraction of the "he kept us out of war" theme, might well have put their candidate in the White House. With Wilson safely back in the White House, the situation of his party in Congress was somewhat less favorable. The Democrats retained their fairly substantial majority in the Senate but saw it wiped out in the House. Twelve Senate seats changed hands, with the Republicans winning seven and the Democrats five. In addition to a pair in Indiana, the Republicans picked up seats in Maine, New York, New Jersey, West Virginia and Maryland, while losing in Rhode Island, Delaware, Utah, New Mexico, and Wyoming. This left the administration with a comfortable working majority of twelve (fifty-four Democrats to forty-two Republicans). From the standpoint of the organization of the next Congress, the administration was badly served by the defeat in Indiana of Senator John W. Kern, the able Senate Majority Leader and a strong supporter of the President. Kern's replacement by Senator Thomas S. Martin, an unfriendly old Bourbon reactionary from Virginia, proved a serious handicap to Wilson in lining up support for his policies in the Sixty-fifth Congress. The prevalence of statesmen such as Martin on Capitol Hill confirmed Wilson in the opinion, which he took no great pains to conceal, that the Senate was a "rum lot" irrespective of party.[17]

For the first time in history, elections for the House ended in a dead heat between the two major parties. Each had 215 seats, and the balance of power lay in the hands of 5 minor-party members: a Socialist, an Independent, a Prohibitionist, and two Progressives. The Republicans wiped out a Democratic majority of 28 — or a plurality of 19 counting the 9 minor-party members in the previous Congress — and might have done better but for the stigma accruing to the party from the McLemore resolution. Thirty of the isolations who voted for it failed of re-election: of these 21 were Republicans, 7 were Democrats, and 2 were Progressives. On the other hand, the sectional issue cut down many of Wilson's followers, especially in Illinois, Indiana, and Wisconsin, where Democratic losses were heaviest. To offset what might have been a rout, the Democrats did surprisingly well in Ohio. They captured five Republican districts largely as a result of the Harding-Daugherty faction's refusal to support the party ticket after Harry M. Daugherty, a notorious isolationist, lost the senatorial nomination to former Ambassador Myron T. Herrick, a Roosevelt follower, who also failed to survive the general throat-cutting.[18] Elsewhere Wilson's party managed to maintain a precarious political equilibrium and with it the ability to organize the next Congress, by winning scattered seats in New York, Pennsylvania, Connecticut, Delaware, New Mexico, Utah, and California.

III

BECAUSE the 1916 elections resulted in no clear mandate, both parties remained hopelessly divided and confused in their approach to the problems posed by the war. Congress continued to operate in a highly haphazard manner and to show itself loath to accept advice, least of all from the White House, on the course to pursue in the crisis. The lame-duck session which met early in December to hear the President's State of the Union message proceeded to ignore his recommendations with respect to the economic maladjustments brought about by the war. It manifested instead a marked preference for challenging the Executive in the field of foreign affairs, particularly in connection with the peace negotiations in which Wilson became involved as a result of the German peace note of December 12.

Wilson's reply on December 18, asking the belligerents to state their peace terms, precipitated an angry controversy. Senate Republicans blocked a resolution calling for a blanket endorsement of the note. In the House a similar resolution caused a violent explosion in the Republican ranks when Minority Leader James R. Mann unexpectedly arose in defense of Wilson as a peacemaker and urged bipartisan support for his endeavors. Die-hard interventionists of the Roosevelt persuasion hotly denounced Mann as a tool of the Kaiser and challenged his moral right to the continued leadership of the party. The Allied rejection of Wilson's proposals on January 10 gratified his enemies as much as it disheartened the President. Irritated by the Republican elation over the failure of his plan and unwilling to abandon hope for a world settlement, Wilson appeared before the Senate on January 22 to deliver his famous "Peace without Victory" speech, the reaction to which was more violent than to his original gesture.

Outside Congress a few prominent Republicans strove to calm the partisan uproar provoked by the President's address. Elihu Root, for one, essayed a qualified endorsement of Wilson's position before a monster rally of the National Security League on January 25. In sharp contrast to the other speakers who flayed the President's pacifism, Root urged his fellowcountrymen to put aside partisanship and rally behind the government in the crisis. Root's statesmanlike attitude, however, angered a great many in his party like old Senator Jacob H. Gallinger of New Hampshire, the Senate Minority Leader, who deplored the "Republican gush" over Wilson and complained that "a Republican victory two years from now cannot be brought about by exalting Wilson, and declaring that he deserves the undivided confidence of the American people."[19] Colonel Roosevelt also could see nothing but harm in the "general idiot cry" on Wilson's behalf. The next time he met his former Secretary of State, the Rough Rider "stood Root on his head" for asking the public to support "a mean creature like Wilson."[20] Nonetheless, Root ignored the Colonel's angry remonstrances and, during the early days of the war at least, continued to press for an abatement of the partisan spirit.

On Capitol Hill the spirit of partisanship ran wild. Attempts to transact the nation's business practically ceased as the roar and thunder of party oratory surged through the halls of Congress. Although war and peace were almost exclusively the topics of debate, nothing was done to prepare for the one or to advance the other. The diplomatic break with Germany on February 3, occasioned by the resumption of unrestricted submarine warfare, threw Congress into a bitter wrangle over the question of putting naval guns on American merchant ships for protection. Isolationists denounced the idea of "armed neutrality" as leading directly to the shooting war so ardently desired by the interventionists, and Wilson was loath to recommend it.[21] The fortuitous appearance shortly thereafter of the

Zimmermann note urging Mexico and Japan to ally against the United States broke the impasse, however, and galvanized Wilson into asking Congress on February 26 for the armed-ship legislation for which the interventionists had been shouting.[22] House isolationists, led by Representative Henry A. Cooper of Wisconsin, sought to hamstring the measure with an amendment forbidding American ships while so armed from carrying munitions to the Allies. Denounced by administration leaders as another McLemore resolution and blasted in the press as the last stand of the congressional pro-German pacifists, the Cooper amendment failed to rally much support and went down to defeat, 293 to 125.[23]

In the Senate the bill set off the famous filibuster which marked the closing days of the Sixty-fourth Congress. Republican interventionists, cheered on by Roosevelt from the sidelines, were already filibustering several revenue measures in an effort to force Wilson to call an early session of the next Congress to deal with the war emergency.[24] They were willing to let the armed-ship bill pass; but the isolationists, led by Robert M. La Follette and George W. Norris, immediately closed ranks against it and brought down upon their heads the wrath of Wilson. His denunciation of the "little group of willful men" and his refusal to call an early session of Congress until the Senate had changed its rules governing debate focused public indignation on the "willful eleven" but failed to save the controversial measure. The ships were armed, nevertheless, under an anti-piracy law of 1797; meanwhile the Senate removed Wilson's objections to an early session by amending its rules on unlimited debate. Although a mere gesture, Wilson considered it sufficiently conciliatory, and on March 10 he summoned the Sixty-fifth Congress to meet on April 22. Subsequent developments in the war zone, caused him to advance the date to April 2.[25]

The prospect of an early session made the deadlock in the House a matter of some concern. Fears of a prolonged contest over its organization at such a critical moment led many citizens to favor laying aside partisanship and allowing the Democrats to retain control. In response to this sentiment, Republican National Chairman William R. Willcox hurried to

Washington to urge House Republicans to drop their fight against Speaker Champ Clark.[26] Since the defeat of Hughes, however, Willcox' influence had declined sharply in party circles, and the House leaders ignored his appeal. On March 31 the caucus renominated Minority Leader Mann over the strenuous objections of the Roosevelt contingent, an opposition inspired by Mann's anti-war views rather than by Willcox' non-partisan gesture.[27]

The bipartisan movement also got little encouragement from the White House. The President remained deaf to suggestions that he bring prominent Republicans into the Cabinet or appoint outstanding industrial figures, without regard to political affiliation, to the additional agencies required to handle vital war activities such as munitions, food, and transportation. Particularly irksome to him was the newspaper clamor for the removal of Secretary of War Newton D. Baker and Secretary of the Navy Josephus Daniels from their posts before their alleged incompetence could seriously impair the prospective war effort. Joseph P. Tumulty, the President's secretary, engaged in a wordy and foolish controversy with Henry A. Wise Wood, a waspish Roosevelt adherent, who wanted Major General Leonard Wood and Rear Admiral Bradley A. Fiske, both noted preparedness zealots and foes of Wilson, appointed to the service posts.[28] After the war started, the coalition Cabinet idea was dropped for a time, only to be raised at a later date in a more formidable fashion. In the meantime, the country went hesitantly forth upon the Great Crusade with as little agreement on how to destroy the enemy as there had been on the necessity of becoming involved in such a business in the first place.[29]

CHAPTER II

THE ROOSEVELT VOLUNTEER
CONTROVERSY

I

THE PRESIDENT'S call to arms before a joint session of Congress on April 2, 1917, was one of his great state papers. His eloquence impressed even his adversaries, who were often constrained to admire Wilson's rhetorical virtuosity while doubting his sincerity.[1] With the country finally standing at Armageddon, Wilson found himself arrayed in the same cause with Roosevelt, Lodge and the rest of the war hawks, the great bulk of whom were implacably hostile to him. The alignment was purely coincidental, resulting in no meeting of the minds or growth of sympathetic understanding, as might be expected from people dedicated to a great common objective. A few prominent Republicans, like Senator Philander Knox and Elihu Root, might urge non-partisan cooperation in the war effort, but such counsels for the most part fell on deaf ears. The hatred that Wilson inspired in men like Roosevelt and Lodge and their host of followers was too intense to admit of any modification because of a shift in national policy. Under the guise of what came to be known as "constructive criticism" they let no opportunity slip to assail the administration's hastily contrived war program.

Scarcely had Congress approved the declaration of war on April 6 than Republican strategists in the Senate brought forward the first "instrumentality" designed to curtail the President's authority. On April 9, Senator John W. Weeks, Lodge's younger but no less reactionary colleague from Massachusetts, offered a resolution to create a Joint Committee on the Conduct of the War to act as a sort of watchdog over executive expenditures for the purpose of preventing extravagance and corruption. The unlimited powers possessed by the Committee to subpoena witnesses and to inquire into all phases of war activity gave it a striking resemblance to the famous Civil War body of the same name headed by President Lincoln's radical Republican foes, Benjamin Wade and Zachariah Chandler. This notorious group had, in the opinion of many, harassed Lincoln by interfering at will with the administration of the Union Army and by running roughshod over military and civilian officials alike. The bipartisan provision for five Democrats and five Republicans on the Weeks Committee meant nothing since, in view of the strained relations between Congress and the Executive, it was not likely to have a friendly majority.

When news of what was brewing in the Senate reached him, the President hastened to the Capitol to head off what he feared would be a repetition of the ordeal to which his Civil War predecessor had been subjected.[2] Contemporary evidence on this point is somewhat contradictory, but Wilson held firmly to the opinion of Gideon Welles, the Connecticut Democrat in Lincoln's Cabinet, that the Wade-Chandler Committee was a group of "narrow, prejudiced and partisan busybodies" whose "mean and contemptible activities" had seriously handicapped the war effort of his day.[3] Buttonholing Democratic members of the Rules Committee, Wilson persuaded them to bury the obnoxious resolution, and in the press of business nothing more was heard of it for the next few months. It remained nonetheless like a Damoclean sword poised over the President's head in the bitter controversy that was gathering momentum in connection with the war program.

II

OF ALL the questions crowding upon Congress for a quick decision, the foremost involved the raising of an army. The issue at stake was how to fill the pitifully inadequate ranks of the regulars and the militia to the level required for a decisive effort on the western front. The General Staff believed that colorful recruiting posters could not attract the necessary two million men because of the competition of good war jobs and rising wages. Congress, on the other hand, suffered from a deep-seated dread of conscription, to which it ascribed the ills afflicting Europe, the downfall of ancient dynasties, and the destruction of liberal, democratic principles everywhere. The bitter congressional battle of 1916 over the innocuous Continental Army scheme, in which the administration had remained benevolently on the side lines in view of the election, had resulted in the complete triumph of the volunteer principle. Sorely disappointed by the Hay-Chamberlain bill, the War Department had continued to press for the adoption of more effective measures. Consequently, when Wilson on April 5 forwarded the General Staff's plan to draft two million men with no provision for volunteers, loud cries of anguish and consternation rang through the halls of Congress.[4]

So violent was the opposition that for several weeks the success of the measure hung in the balance. Recollection of the Civil War draft riots made a great many congressmen reluctant to hazard their political prospects by rashly condoning the coercion of free Americans. In the Senate, James A. Reed of Missouri predicted that the streets of American cities would run red with blood the day the draft went into effect, and House Democratic leaders immediately deserted the President. Speaker Champ Clark took the floor to assail the draft as a travesty upon American patriotism, while Majority Leader Claude Kitchin waxed hysterical over the tyrannical invasion of American rights.[5] Chairman Hubert Dent of the Military Affairs Committee refused to sponsor the bill and left its management to the ranking Republican on the Committee, Julius Kahn of California. Fear of what the conscription of Negroes would do to the race problem panicked the South, which seethed with wild rumors of armed Negro uprisings engineered by German spies.[6] The hysteria in and out of Congress prompted the chairman of the Rules Committee, Edward W. Pou of North Carolina, to warn Wilson that conscription could not pass without a trial first being given to the volunteer system. To attempt to force its passage, said Pou, would "provoke a bitter fight on the floor with the result much in doubt."[7]

Wilson had no intention of being dragooned into an unworkable compromise on such a vital matter. Backing the War
Department with all the authority at his command, he called
in Democratic leaders repeatedly in an effort to allay their fears
and remove their objections, but to no avail. On April 18 the
Military Affairs Committee reported out a bill that ignored
the General Staff's recommendations and proposed instead the
volunteer system, the tried and true American method of waging war. The 13-to-8 vote in committee saw the South and West
combine against the East irrespective of party.[8] The administration bill now became the minority report, sponsored by a
Republican as an amendment to the majority, or anti-draft,
report. It was a ridiculous situation, reflecting no credit on the
Democratic leadership and placing the President in an awkward
position. The press, angered by the senseless defiance of the
Executive, urged Congress to forget its political worries and
buckle down to the business of preparing to win the war.[9]

Anti-draft sentiment was less intense in the Senate, which
in the past had shown some interest in a mild form of universal
military training. The Military Affairs Committee therefore
spared the administration further humiliation by reporting out
the Army bill on April 18 in approximately the form recommended by the General Staff. The ten Democrats on the Committee split evenly on the question, while the Republican members divided 5 to 2, a circumstance that enabled the minority
party later to claim all credit for allowing the country to organize an army. The chairman, George E. Chamberlain of
Oregon, had for years championed compulsory military training,
but the next ranking Democrat, Charles S. Thomas of Colorado,
struck a heroic pose on the volunteer principle — "the system
of free men, not of slaves" — and announced that "opposition
to compulsory military service is characteristic of every government fit to be called a democracy."[10]

But for certain complications the Army bill would have
been ironed out in conference and put into effect much more ex-
peditiously than was the case. Opposition had been bipartisan,
with the onus falling on the Democrats because of the antics

of their leaders. Most congressmen, more anxious to square themselves with their constituents than to defy the President, wanted to be able to say with some truth that having fought the good fight for American tradition, they had bowed in the end to the force of circumstance and the will of the administration.[11] With the primal urge for political self-preservation satisfied, Congress might have yielded more gracefully or quickly but for the injection of a partisan factor that turned a typical congressional face-saving gesture into a knock-down, drag-out fight between the President and one of his illustrious predecessors. The occasion was Colonel Roosevelt's desire to raise and lead a division of American volunteers for service at the front.

Dreams of military glory had always haunted the Rough Rider's mind. To the German Emperor, who could presumably sympathize with such aspirations, he had confided some years before that in the event of a "big war," he would try to get permission to raise a cavalry division.[12] Although the Mexican crisis of 1916 hardly fitted this category, he had offered to do so, but to no avail. Since the diplomatic break with Germany on February 3, he had been busy organizing his division, on paper at least, amid a gratifying amount of publicity. The size of the division was elastic, with President Wilson learning in March that "good authority" placed the number at 54,000.[13] Press accounts ran the total to 200,000, but this was after Roosevelt had expanded it to an Army corps. Applications poured in to Oyster Bay from all over the country, and to handle the press of business Roosevelt set up an office on Fifth Avenue. Most of the volunteers wanted to be officers, and the Colonel heartily endorsed friends, relatives, old acquaintances, and anybody else he considered socially acceptable. His close friend Major General Leonard Wood, who was handily situated on Governors Island as commandant of the military Department of the East, passed upon the qualifications of all officer material.[14] Wood undertook this task in addition to his ordinary duties until the War Department on March 26 suddenly transferred him to the less convenient and less important Department of the Southeast at Charleston, South Carolina. The abrupt removal of his quondam

chief of staff enraged the Rough Rider and led to endless recriminations about the petty partisanship animating the administration.[15]

The Colonel's military ambitions envisaged no ordinary fighting force. His division was to epitomize the finest the United
States had to offer in the way of distinguished ancestry, business
acumen, racial selectivity, and military prowess. His staff glit-
tered with names famous in American military annals. It included able-bodied descendants of Generals Albert Sidney
Johnston, Fitzhugh Lee, Stonewall Jackson, Philip Sheridan,
Henry Wise, and Simon B. Buckner, all of Civil War fame.
Staff appointments were also offered to scions of the French
nobility in gracious recognition of the services of Lafayette.
Typifying the unity of spirit and solidarity of democratic forces
opposed to Prussian autocracy were regiments composed wholly
or in part of men of German descent and a regiment of Negroes
officered by white men.[16] To whip into shape this romantic hodgepodge of fighting men he was gathering under his banner, Roosevelt had no hesitancy in raiding the regular army for competent
younger officers. For his chief of cavalry he picked a Regular
Army colonel whose exploits on the Mexican border had pleased
him and whose theory on the training of cavalry ''exactly agrees
with my own.''[17] Roosevelt intended to assemble his division at
Fort Sill, Oklahoma, where it would be outfitted from War Department stocks at his own or his friends' expense. After a
brief period of preliminary training, estimated at from sixty to
ninety days, it would enter the trenches and vindicate the
national honor so shabbily traduced by the pusillanimous policies
of Wilson.[18]

Roosevelt was supremely confident that such a gesture would
not only bolster the sagging morale of the Allies but strike
terror into the military hierarchy at Potsdam. It would also
remove all uncertainty about the course to be followed by the
United States, where a great many citizens, among whom Roosevelt included the President and his advisers, hopefully expected
that in the unpleasant event of war, American resources would
tip the scales without resort to participation in the European

blood bath — or, at worst, that hostilities could be confined to naval operations in defense of American shipping, where the loss of life would be less spectacular. "So far as I am able," he informed his friends, "I shall endeavor to free this country from the disgrace of seeing it embark in a war without fighting, for such a war can only be ended by a peace without victory."[19] It was an offer the War Department could not lightly dismiss because of the Rough Rider's hold upon the loyalty and affection of a great many people. His proposal had the support, moreover, of a good many politicians in both parties; and the pressure brought upon the White House to gratify his whim was tremendous.

The administration naturally scoffed at the idea that the sort of demonstration planned by its archenemy would improve the desperate military situation abroad. Moreover, it could not afford to divert men and supplies from the ill-equipped regular establishment to an expedition that might prove difficult to control in view of the personal eccentricities of the self-appointed commander. Nevertheless, the situation called for tactful handling. To Roosevelt's contention that he could have his division in the trenches by September 1, Secretary of War Baker returned a polite reply, expressing his appreciation of the offer but indicating that his Department intended to rely exclusively on conscription and that the President would recommend this method in his forthcoming message to Congress.[20]

Far from discouraged by his initial rebuff, the Colonel went off on a fortnight's fishing trip to Florida and left matters in the hands of his political friends in Washington. "Do see," he directed Lodge, "that no Army legislation is so framed as to leave me out."[21] Lodge worked energetically to enlist support in various quarters, extracting from Secretary of State Robert Lansing, among others, a promise to discuss the project with Baker at once.[22] On his return, the Rough Rider stopped off in Washington on April 3 with the intention of seeing the President in person to plead his cause. Unable to arrange an interview on such short notice, he discussed the prospects for his division with congressional leaders at the home of his son-in-law, Representative Nicholas Longworth of Ohio. A week later he was back in the Capital, this time with a definite appointment at the White House.

Despite the attitude of false heartiness Roosevelt assumed for the occasion, a rather strained atmosphere pervaded the hourlong conversation in the Red Room. Rarely since the era of Andrew Jackson, when spectacular personal feuds were more the fashion, had feeling run so high between two eminent statesmen. Both were self-righteous moralists, alike in their unlimited capacity for self-deception, and hence acutely uncomfortable in each other's presence. Wilson listened with chill politeness as the Rough Rider condescendingly explained the nature of his visit. Roosevelt found ''great confusion'' in the President's mind, he later confided to a newspaper friend, and had to explain everything in great detail, from the volunteer division's importance to the Allied cause to the reasons why it would not interfere with the government's war preparations.[23] Wilson's reaction was not quite what the Colonel had hoped for. The President apparently evaded the main issue and replied with what his caller took to be an apologetic defense of the administration's failure to prepare the country adequately for war. Roosevelt thereupon magnanimously agreed to forgive all past errors of that sort provided Wilson would push the war with all vigor and sincerity. In that case he would behave toward the Chief Executive as Light-Horse Harry Lee would have acted toward Thomas Jefferson had war with England come during Jefferson's presidency at the time of the *Chesapeake* affair.[24]

Wilson's response, if any, to this odd proposition is not known. In Roosevelt's books, Jefferson, next to Buchanan, was the worst President in American history, and the allusion was hardly flattering or tactful, although the President may have found something wryly humorous in the aging Roosevelt's romantic identification of himself with the handsome, dashing cavalry leader of a bygone era, who was also greatly ''enamored of war.'' From the accounts of his partisans who were either present at the interview or immediately put in possession of the facts, the President appears to have treated his caller like a lovable but backward schoolboy and to have convinced him by patient reasoning of the impracticability of his scheme.[25] The Rough Rider, however, carried away no such impression of Wilson's remarks. It was the Colonel's belief, possibly induced by the intensity of his self-deception, that the President had remained politely noncommittal. For that reason, his optimism continued undiminished.

Before returning to Oyster Bay, Roosevelt again urged Lodge most emphatically not to allow his interests to be neglected when Congress acted upon the Army bill. Lodge showed the message to members of the Senate Military Affairs Committee and used his influence with House leaders to the same end. The Colonel also sent the two service committees transcripts of his military record and qualifications, based upon his Spanish-American War experience and upon the seven presidential years when he had doubled under the Constitution as commander-in-chief of the nation's armed forces. Three major generals of the Regular Army signed this remarkable testimonial to the Rough Rider's military prowess and proficiency. To clinch his case he threw in the airy assurance that he could get his volunteer division to the front with War Department cooperation in less than four months, compared to the year or more it would take to ready a draft army for foreign service.[26]

By now the first ominous rumblings of congressional opposition to conscription were echoing around Capitol Hill, and the Roosevelt scheme afforded a welcome rallying point for anti-draft congressmen of both parties.[27] The administration, threatened with the collapse of its first major war measure, had to act quickly to overcome the popular and demagogic appeal of the Roosevelt plan. The War Department, unable to equivocate any longer, now flatly rejected his application and curtly dismissed the sentimental value of his division for the Allied cause. Baker's letter, informing the Colonel that his agitation was delaying enactment of the selective service law and by inference asking him to desist, effectively served to dispel any illusion Roosevelt might have entertained as a result of his White House visit and of Wilson's apparent disinclination to face the issue squarely at that time.[28]

Incensed by his blunt dismissal, the Rough Rider penned a

furious rebuttal of Baker's arguments. "You forget," he wrote, "that I have commanded troops in action in the most important battle fought by the United States army during the last half century, and that I have commanded a brigade in the campaign of which this battle was an incident."[29] Vigorously he refuted the charge that his plan interfered with the draft, which he had favored for years and which, but for the incredible folly and stupidity of the War Department, would have been adopted long ago. Angrily he defended the "moral effect" of sending him to France with a field command and cited numerous pleas from representatives of the French and British governments, urging his immediate appearance on the battlefield at the head of such a force. Scornfully he ridiculed Baker's proposal to pay the Allies billions of dollars to continue fighting until an American army could be trained in comfort and safety at home. The Colonel concluded his philippic with a scathing denunciation of the hide-bound, wooden-headed "military men of the red tape and pipe clay school" who constituted the General Staff and who had been instrumental, he thought, in advising the Secretary of War not to accept his application.

III

REJECTION BY the War Department threw the issue squarely into politics, since the Colonel had no intention of taking Baker's word as final, and the Rough Rider's friends on Capitol Hill were both numerous and powerful. While his application had been pending, he had refrained with great delicacy and considerable effort from publicly criticizing the administration, a punctiliousness he mentioned frequently to friends overtaken with amazement at such unusual self-restraint.[30] Privately he had continued to excoriate Wilson and to urge his admirers, particularly in the South, to get their congressmen to back his volunteer project. It was the right thing nationally, he declared, "and I believe it would be the right thing politically."[31] Now that the bars were down, he threw caution aside and marshaled his forces in Washington for a fight to the finish.

In a move to gain wider popular support, Roosevelt expanded

his division into an Army corps under Major General Leonard Wood, with the Rough Rider modestly relegated to command of one of the three component divisions.[32] The other two divisional posts he assigned to Major General Thomas H. Barry, an old personal friend, and Brigadier General John J. Pershing, an able professional soldier. This arrangement, besides modifying somewhat the glory-seeking aspects of the original scheme, gave it an appearance of greater military competence in answer to critics who doubted the Rough Rider's ability in the field, despite the importance he attached to his charge up San Juan Hill. It also took care of Wood, whose shabby treatment by the administration had become a Republican *cause célèbre*.[33] With Lodge, Wood, and Roosevelt united in opposition to the administration's draft legislation, or at least bent upon modifying it to suit their personal or political whims, the battle on Capitol Hill became a test of Wilson's ability to control the war effort against terrific popular and political pressure.

A conference of Republican senators and representatives on April 23 decided to put the Roosevelt project in the form of amendments which would force Wilson to veto the draft act and thus incur the onus of further delay. Lodge supervised the preparation of a Senate amendment directing the War Department to authorize Roosevelt to raise and command a force of 100,000 volunteers. After Lodge declined to sponsor the resolution, lest his close friendship with the Rough Rider prove an obstacle to rallying non-partisan support, the honor went to Warren G. Harding of Ohio over Hiram W. Johnson, Roosevelt's preference. Once a bitter enemy but now nursing presidential ambitions and eager to conciliate all the factions, Harding had offered his services to Lodge, who felt that the Ohio senator would give less offense to the party in view of the strong feelings against the California Progressive engendered by the 1916 election.[34] In acquainting Roosevelt with the reasons for Harding's selection, Lodge was not at all optimistic about the outcome, and he warned his impulsive friend that everything depended upon getting a few Democratic votes.[35]

Harding managed the Roosevelt amendment with great skill. Despite Lodge's pessimism, enough Democrats deserted the

President to secure adoption of the motion on April 28 by the substantial margin of 56 votes to 31. The Republicans lined up 36 in favor, 4 against, and 2 not voting. Democratic leaders failed utterly to hold their party in line: 20 Democrats voted for the amendment, 27 against it, and 7 were not recorded. In addition to the usual anti-Wilson clique of Thomas P. Gore, James A. Reed, Thomas W. Hardwick, Gilbert M. Hitchcock, and James K. Vardaman, who generally sided with the opposition on all major issues, a number of administration stalwarts supported the Roosevelt cause.[36] Henry F. Hollis of New Hampshire, Atlee Pomerene of Ohio, Paul O. Husting of Wisconsin, and William H. Thompson of Kansas came from areas where the Roosevelt influence was strong, and giving the Rough Rider a commission was for them the simplest way of disposing of a thorny political problem.[37] Harding's performance won a telegram of hearty commendation from Roosevelt, who praised the senator's ''patriotic work'' and asserted that opponents of the amendment did not have the best interests of the country at heart. He urged Harding to rally ''our friends'' to use their influence with the House, where ''opposition is, of course, merely political. This ought not to be made merely a political war.''[38]

The somewhat paradoxical situation in the House saved the President's cause from complete disaster. The reactionary Republican leadership was weak and entirely out of sympathy with Roosevelt's objectives. The preparedness, or pro-Roosevelt, faction had never been large; and the rift between it and the dominant isolationist bloc led by Mann and his midwestern lieutenants, who were smarting under the Rough Rider's public vilification of them as pro-German pacifists, augured poorly for his chances. Medill McCormick of Illinois, a former Bull Moose adherent, was eager to offer the amendment; but again in order to avoid the personal connection, the privilege went to another prominent standpatter and former critic, Richard W. Austin of Tennessee. The amendment was promptly defeated, however, by a standing vote of 170 to 106.[39] The Democratic lines held firm, and less than half the Republican membership responded in favor. The House then reversed itself completely on the draft. After rejecting the Committee report in favor of the Kahn amendment by a vote of 313 to 109, it approved the Army bill, 397 to 24, in approximately the form desired by the General Staff.[40] This bewildering *volte-face* followed a week of feverish oratorical effort aimed at demonstrating congressional devotion to American principles and traditions, printed evidence of which was franked in vast quantities into congressional districts as insurance against any possible political backfire.[41]

On the same day, April 28, the Senate adopted the Army bill, 81 to 8, after the anti-conscriptionists had failed, 69 to 18, in a final effort to defeat the War Department version.[42] The bill then went to conference, where the principal differences to be ironed out were the Roosevelt amendment and the draft age. The General Staff wanted to take all men between nineteen and twenty-five; Congress, however, amid hysterical protests at robbing the cradle and nipping the flower of American manhood in the bud, quickly fixed twenty-one as the minimum but could not agree on a maximum. For the next two weeks the conferees wrangled over these details, while the country impatiently awaited a decision. Public irritation at the delay found vent in a flood of petitions urging Congress to stop paralyzing initiative at home and hurting Allied morale abroad.

Since the Roosevelt amendment was chiefly responsible for the deadlock, the Rough Rider's popularity ebbed rapidly. Many erstwhile supporters now assailed him for projecting his personal ambitions athwart the progress of the war at a very critical moment. The Colonel angrily denied that his scheme impeded vital war legislation, since his volunteers would come from age brackets not subject to the draft. When the jingoistic Army League of the United States, of which he was an honorary vice-president, publicly asked him to withdraw his controversial amendment so as to expedite passage of the draft, Roosevelt's blood pressure rose dangerously. He furiously asserted that "the course I have advocated, and now advocate, is the only wise and patriotic course," and he told an audience in Chicago on April 28 that "to regard my attitude as unpatriotic because of a fancied interference with the President's recommendations is mere hysteria."[43] On May 8 he resigned publicly from the League after another fierce blast at the petty partisanship that

denied him an independent command in France.[44] This display
of temper cost him more public support and strengthened the
position of the President in what was fast becoming a national
scandal.

In the meantime the Rough Rider left no stone unturned
that might help his cause. He bombarded the Republican conferees with telegrams begging them to remain firm at all costs.
He renewed his frantic appeals to friends in all parts of the
country to work upon their senators and representatives to
support the Harding amendment.[45] Senator Lodge, much less
confident of the outcome, reminded his excitable friend that
while the Republicans were doing all in their power on his
behalf, the opposition of the President made things very difficult
and might sway a number of Democrats otherwise sympathetic
to the amendment.[46] Of the Senate conferees, James H. Brady of
Idaho and Francis B. Warren of Wyoming would, in Lodge's
opinion, stand firm, as would Hitchcock of Nebraska, an anti-
administration Democrat; but the House conferees were much
more susceptible to political pressure.[47] Moreover, said Lodge,
the growing public restlessness over congressional tactics made
it inadvisable to allow the impasse to drag out much longer.

On May 10 the conferees finally reached agreement by approving the higher age limit and rejecting the Roosevelt amendment. Three Republicans — Senators Brady and Warren and
Representative Kahn — spiked the Rough Rider's military aspirations by switching their votes. Greatly embittered by the
"treachery" of these men,[48] Roosevelt wanted to press for
further changes in the conference report but reluctantly agreed
to let the matter stand because of the risk that the additional
delay might react unfavorably on the war effort and injure
the party.[49]

At this point the House, to everyone's amazement, once more
reversed itself. A surprise motion, presented by Daniel R. Anthony of Kansas, to recommit the conference report with in-
structions to support the provision giving Roosevelt an independent command carried by a 215 to 178 vote.[50] This
extraordinary performance occurred while the members were
still receiving messages from all over the country congratulat-

ing them on their farsighted and courageous statesmanship in passing the Army bill. The heavy Republican majority (170 to 30) in favor of the amendment indicated some effective back-stage work by the party leadership. Administration forces, caught flat-footed by the maneuver, could rally only 148 Democrats against the motion. Forty-three lined up with the Republicans and 2 independents; most were from the South and West, where the draft was highly unpopular. One of the handful of Republicans to put military considerations ahead of party loyalty in voting against the motion disgustedly characterized the affair as "plainly politics and partisanship and nothing else."[51]

The House action took even Lodge and Roosevelt by surprise. The Massachusetts senator, however, had no further heart for the fight; and Roosevelt, though gratified by the demonstration on his behalf, was not sanguine about its significance. Back went the Army bill to conference, where another week of wrangling elapsed before the conferees decided on May 17 to make the raising of a volunteer force under Roosevelt's command permissive rather than mandatory upon the administration. In this form Congress quickly enacted the legislation, which left Wilson free to dismiss his rival's application for high rank, call upon General John J. Pershing to command the American Expeditionary Force, and proceed with the organization of a National Army along the lines laid down by the General Staff. Volunteer enlistments continued until December, but in such small numbers as to confirm the War Department's view of the impracticality of raising a modern army in that fashion.

Congressional motives are generally mixed, and there may have been a few sincere souls to whom the Rough Rider was the answer to the nation's military problem. To many citizens, however, the weeks wasted in wrangling over the draft represented partisanship in its worst form. Even the New York *Tribune,* a vociferously pro-Roosevelt organ, was moved to remark of Congress at this stage that "its mind is on petty politics, not on earnest, patriotic preparations for war."[52] The Republicans, by somewhat overplaying their hand with respect to the Roosevelt volunteer division, lost some of the political advantage that they had gained from the earlier Democratic desertion of President Wilson on the draft issue. Nevertheless, the Republican gesture on Roosevelt's behalf served to restore a certain degree of party unity and marked the beginning of a factional reconciliation that was to draw together all but a small handful of extreme pacifists.

The Rough Rider himself accepted defeat with very poor grace. His fierce hatred of Wilson was fanned by the conviction that the President had tricked him out a European command by deceiving the public into believing that his plan was antagonistic to the draft. The State Department, he believed, had participated in the plot by barring him from the official receptions held for the French and British War Missions, which had reached Washington in late April, because Marshal Joffre and Foreign Minister Balfour were known to favor the morale value of sending him to Europe at the head of an American contingent.[53] The administration, he bitterly complained, would rather "make this a paper war if possible, but if not that then they want to make it a Democratic war. They are much more anxious to spite Leonard Wood and myself than to uphold the honor of the nation or beat Germany."[54] "The real truth is," he told his friends, "that Wilson is bent upon making this merely a war to advance his own personal fortunes from a political standpoint."[55]

Wilson, not surprisingly, entertained similar views about his opponents and on occasion said as much. On May 17 a self-appointed emissary of the Rough Rider appeared at the White House and denounced the President to his face for playing politics with the war by not giving the Colonel a European command. Overcoming an impulse to kick his brash caller out of the door, Wilson coldly informed him, "As for politics, it is not I but the Republicans who have been playing politics and consciously embarrassing the Administration. I do not propose to have politics in any manner, shape or form influence me in my judgment."[56]

This lofty resolve was sheer hyperbole, of course, for Wilson was constitutionally and temperamentally incapable of such Olympian detachment. The very day after the White House incident of the obnoxious caller, Wilson refused to consider the appointment of Charles B. Warren, a prominent Detroit lawyer and the Harding administration's ambassador to Japan, to an important post in the judge advocate general's office because Warren, as Republican national committeeman from Michigan, was "viciously partisan."[57] Shortly thereafter the question arose of sending an officer to the American embassy in London to act in a liaison capacity with the British Intelligence Service. When Major Henry L. Stimson, Taft's Secretary of War, was suggested, the President declined to appoint him because "his attitude has been anything but helpful and I think his influence on the other side would be distinctly bad."[58] Wilson's capacity for self-deception in this respect worried his friends, exasperated his enemies, and added appreciably to the bitterness of the 1918 congressional campaign.

CHAPTER III

THE POLITICAL POT KEEPS BOILING

I

SCARCELY had Congress disposed of the selective service act than a furious controversy developed over the next piece of major legislation submitted by the White House. This was the so-called omnibus bill, which, among other things, set up a censorship of all publications and gave the President very wide powers of enforcement. The government could also exclude treasonous materials from the mails, control exports to foreign countries, and establish safeguards against spies and saboteurs. There was little objection to the anti-subversive provisions, but the latitude allowed the President or his subordinates to detect and punish violators of the newspaper censorship, as well as the harshness of the penalties imposable at executive discretion, aroused violent opposition in the press and in Congress. The Republicans rallied in defense of the First Amendment and earned the gratitude of the publishing fraternity by pillorying Wilson as a despot in quest of absolute authority to promote his political fortunes. Despite the lukewarmness of his own party toward the measure and the strong feeling throughout the country against it, the President remained inflexible in his determination to force this Draconian code upon the profession.[1]

An informal censorship had been in effect since the Mexican troubles of the previous year.[2] Based on a gentleman's agreement with the press on what to publish with respect to naval and military movements, the arrangement appeared to work with a minimum of friction and bad faith. Nothing, however, could alter Wilson's low opinion of the fourth estate or his fear of irresponsible reporting. Not only did he ask Congress for stiff legal penalties to keep the profession in line during the European war; he also gave complete authority over all war news to a Committee on Public Information directly subordinate to his control and supported out of a special fund of $100 million for which no accounting to Congress was required. To head this hastily organized super-news and -propaganda agency the President picked a hero-worshiping admirer, George Creel, a former Denver newspaperman who had handled publicity for the Democratic party in the 1916 campaign. In many respects he was one of Wilson's most unfortunate wartime appointments. Despite extraordinary energy, good intentions, and considerable journalistic ability, Creel possessed neither the judgment nor the temperament for such an exacting and delicate post. The chairman's exalted view of his mission, his penchant for playing politics at every opportunity, and the intense irritation which his tactless methods aroused soon made the Committee a storm center that, in the opinion of many, greatly circumscribed its usefulness and hurt the administration.[3]

While the war powers of the President sufficed to create the Creel Committee, as it was popularly known, the legal basis for censorship was provided in the espionage act, prepared in the War Department and submitted to Congress on April 13.[4] The next day the Senate Judiciary Committee ordered a favorable report; but as soon as the senators had grasped its import, a score of Republicans, with Borah, Lodge, and Albert B. Cummins in the van, arose to assail the gross infringement on the right of every newspaper to print what it liked about the war.[5] The New York *Times* voiced the journalistic consensus by blasting it as a "tyrannous measure" that would undermine democracy in the country. On April 22 Congress sidetracked the so-called spy bill in order to devote full attention to the problem of raising an army. The matter did not come up again until the bitterness engendered by the Roosevelt volunteer scheme lent additional zest to the efforts of Wilson's critics to defeat his alleged conspiracy against free speech and unregulated publicity for the war effort.[6]

In view of the storm that was brewing, Wilson's advisers urged him to consult with leading members of the profession for the purpose of creating a censorship board. Under no circumstances, however, would he consider such an arrangement. His trust in journalists was no greater than his confidence in the Republican party, and from these prejudices he could not be moved. Moreover, several Cabinet members — including Attorney General Thomas W. Gregory, Secretary of State Robert Lansing, and Postmaster General Albert S. Burleson — shared his views and encouraged his phobia for their own ends. All three were feverishly engaged in building up super-security organizations within their respective Departments, and exhibited the keenest rivalry in extending controls over public opinion.[7] The administration's case might have had a better hearing but for a State Department order, issued at the height of the controversy, forbidding employees under pain of dismissal to give out information of any sort to newspapermen.[8] The uproar occasioned by Lansing's arbitrary action consolidated the opposition in Congress and helped seal the fate of the censorship proposal.

Although the Senate achieved a greater range and dialectical profundity in debating the constitutional issues involved, opposition was equally strong in the House. A Republican member of the Judiciary Committee, George S. Graham of Pennsylvania, led the attack and was ably supported by most of the Republican leaders, including James R. Mann of Illinois, Frank P. Woods of Iowa, Ebenezer J. Hill of Connecticut, and Irvine L. Lenroot of Wisconsin. When the measure came to a vote on May 4, Graham's motion to strike out the censorship provision in its entirety carried 220 to 167. Despite energetic lobbying by Burleson and his lieutenants, 52 Democrats abandoned the President's cause to join with 165 Republicans and 3 independents.[9]

Democratic leaders acted quickly to retrieve the situation with a compromise amendment that limited the powers requested by the President to certain specific violations and provided jury trials for violators. Under administration pressure enough disgruntled Democrats reversed their positions to secure passage of the Gard amendment by a close vote, 191 to 185. The Republicans, caught by surprise while they were still congratulating themselves on having stopped the President in his tracks, angrily denounced Wilson and Burleson for their brazen lobbying tactics. The Democratic ranks held firm, however, and the bill went to the Senate with censorship still intact, though in a somewhat watered-down form.

Lee S. Overman of North Carolina, an administration stalwart, undertook the task of steering the measure through the Senate, but he proved incapable of coping with the intransigents in his own party. With the majority leader, Martin of Virginia, and the party whip, James Hamilton Lewis of Illinois, voting consistently against censorship in any form, the President's cause proved hopeless. Southern Democrats, fearful that export controls on shipments to neutral countries might lead to an embargo on cotton, quickly got this feature stricken from the omnibus bill. A motion by Hoke Smith of Georgia carried 40 to 30, despite Overman's efforts to make its defeat a vote of confidence in the President.[10] Fourteen Democrats joined with 26 Republicans in the affirmative, while 24 Democrats and 6 Republicans supported the administration. Although export controls were later restored in a modified form, Wilson's program had suffered a serious setback, and worse was to come.

The foes of censorship, led by Harding of Ohio, attacked its constitutionality with such fervor that the Senate on May 12 eliminated the offensive proviso entirely. Senator Hiram Johnson's motion carried 39 to 38, when 15 of Wilson's followers sided with 24 Republicans against 27 Democrats and 11 Republicans.[11] In a valiant effort to save the day Overman offered an amendment restoring the original provision *in toto,* but sentiment had crystallized against regulation of any sort, and his motion was decisively rejected, 48 to 34, with the Democrats dividing 21 to 26 and the Republicans 27 to 8 against it. Senator Lodge, who had favored a modified form of censorship, now switched to the opposition on the ground that the activities of Creel's Committee had convinced him of the unwisdom of giving the President or any of his minions the power to exclude anything from the press.[12] The emasculated bill was thereupon adopted, 77 to 6, and sent to conference on May 16, where another prolonged deadlock ensued.[13]

After a week had passed, with the senatorial conferees unshaken in their opposition, a report gained currency that the White House would yield on the censorship question rather than delay further the essential security provisions of the act. Wilson promptly quashed this rumor in a public statement to Edwin Y. Webb of North Carolina, chairman of the House Conferees. The President emphasized the absolute necessity to the national safety of the powers he had requested to deal with persons who could not be trusted to show patriotic reticence in publishing war news. Angered by the uncompromising tone of this communication, House Republicans threw down the gage of battle to the administration by agreeing in caucus to oppose any form of newspaper censorship and by making the caucus decision binding on all members.[14]

Democratic journals deplored the House action as giving partisan coloring to a question that had no relation to politics, while the Republican press fulminated against Wilson and the Cabinet clique bent on gagging the fourth estate. All reputable newspapers, however, united in denouncing Attorney General Gregory for circulating to the conferees a Department of Justice memorandum revealing the extent of enemy influence in journalistic quarters. The great organs of public opinion, most of which had done their utmost to get the country into the war, found it particularly galling to be bracketed with the foreign-language press and the Socialist sheets noisily agitating for an immediate end to hostilities. Gregory's maneuver, however, resulted in the conference's agreeing to a modified form of censorship with the President's powers considerably circumscribed. In this form the bill was reported back on May 29.

Despite heroic efforts to keep administration forces in line, the House rejected the compromise 184 to 144. Thirty-seven Democrats voted with 143 Republicans and 4 independents in refusing to extend the President's authority. Only 10 Republicans disregarded the caucus injunction to join 133 Democrats and 1 independent in Wilson's favor. In view of the need to get the rest of the omnibus bill adopted without further delay, the administration abandoned the fight, and Wilson signed the emasculated measure on June 15. The government was still left with ample powers, through censorship of the mails, to proceed against erring newspapers, and Postmaster General Burleson was ruthless in the exercise of this function. The Committee on

Public Information also controlled all official sources of war news and released only such items as it considered harmless or inspirational.[15] Nevertheless, the setback damaged Wilson's prestige and did nothing to improve his relations with the fourth estate. The New York *World,* one of the very few journals to support him in the struggle, regretted that he had seen fit to engage in such a controversy. It attributed the outcome to the bungling of Lansing and Gregory, and scored the Republicans for staging a partisan field day at the President's expense.[16]

II

THE EARLY DAYS of the war witnessed a few modest efforts to maintain an appearance of non-partisanship in the war effort. The administration's chief contribution in this direction was the appointment of Elihu Root to head the mission dispatched to Russia that summer to keep the new Russian government from abandoning the Allies. When the idea of sending someone first came under consideration, Secretary of the Treasury William G. McAdoo recommended a couple of well-known Republicans so that the mission would be ''composed equally of Republicans and Democrats.'' Colonel Edward M. House suggested Root's name on the ground that the Republicans deserved some recognition for supporting the administration in the bitter congressional battle over the draft.[17] Although Wilson agreed that none of the commissioners needed to be Democrats, Root was the only recognizable Republican on the list. The fact that most of the others were wealthy, conservative friends of the President aroused considerable criticism at the time, while Wilson's casual dismissal of Root's final report gave further umbrage.[18] Nevertheless, the Democratic publicity bureau never failed to mention Root's brief connection with the administration as proof that partisanship had no place in the war effort.

Partisan displays became more frequent and bitter as friction between the legislative and executive branches continued to grow.[19] Wilson's failure to invite the Senate to the official functions in honor of the French and British War Missions brought forth angry recriminations at a heated session on May 7.[20] At another session, on May 16, Republican senators staged a mass attack on the War Department for failing to itemize a $3 billion deficiency appropriation bill. They not only refused to rubber-stamp measures for which no details were furnished but threatened to send a special committee to Europe to obtain the information the War Department would not impart. Senator Lodge reproached the President for keeping all authority in his own hands or those of a few intimates and acting in general toward the war effort like a glorified college professor. The press deplored Lodge's ''unseemly exhibition'' and urged Congress to stop wrangling and begin to work together like high-minded statesmen instead of a ''pack of squabbling politicians bent on self-interest.'' One of Wilson's admirers marveled that ''the rank and file of the Republican Party, who are loyal and good citizens, would stand for the actions of some of their leaders in both houses, whose partisan spleen and bitterness is such that they would endanger the whole nation, if it were only to embarrass the President.''[21]

As a placatory gesture, Wilson called a few of his more vociferous critics to a White House conference the next day to discuss the war program. Beyond gratifying Senator Lodge that his shafts had struck home and given Wilson a healthier respect for the minority party, the meeting accomplished nothing in the way of establishing a better rapport. To Roosevelt, who had congratulated him upon the great service the Republicans were rendering the country by exposing Wilson's ''rancorous partisanship,'' Lodge confided that he did not intend to stand by and see bad legislation ''designed merely to give the President needless power, whipped through under the war cry.''[22] Political strategy, said the senator, had dictated the attack on the administration because the powerful propaganda in favor of pushing the war effort regardless of party threatened to submerge the Republicans in Congress completely and enable the Democrats craftily to reap all the credit. While resistance might provoke hostile comment and could not be carried too far, Lodge felt that it served to stimulate the party's drooping spirits and kept alive hopes for the future. The Republicans, he said, were on the whole "acting pretty well, quite remarkably so," and thus far had made no serious mistakes.

The executive agencies hastily improvised to handle the multifold problems presented by the war furnished handy targets for uninterrupted partisan sniping. Conservatives feared them mightily as forerunners of a planned economy and socialism, while Congress and the press kept them under close scrutiny for signs of mismanagement and extravagance. Wilson's enemies sharply questioned the ability of the people he placed in charge and frequently accused him of putting personal or political considerations ahead of governmental efficiency by naming incompetent camp followers to posts of great wartime responsibility. Early in the game the Council of National Defense and the Shipping Board came under heavy hostile fire for suspending the law requiring competitive bidding in the letting of war contracts. With billions of dollars at the disposal of a few insiders in control of such agencies, the Republicans clamored for closer supervision and renewed their agitation for a Joint Committee on the Conduct of the War as the best way to safeguard these huge expenditures. Rumors began to circulate that the Senate intended to call up the Weeks resolution despite Wilson's objection unless more information was forthcoming on the manner in which the money was being spent.[23]

Wilson reacted to the incessant badgering of his critics by turning to trustworthy people of his own political faith upon whose loyal help in directing the war effort he could rely implicitly. Among others, he summoned to Washington the chairman of the Democratic National Committee, Vance C. McCormick, to head the administrative committee of the Export Council (later the War Trade Board). Authorized under the export embargo provisions of the Espionage Act, this agency controlled the country's entire foreign trade through a system of export licenses and bunkering permits for merchant vessels. It was a position of great influence and importance, and McCormick offered to resign his political post to devote his entire time to the work. Wilson, however, saw no incompatibility and told McCormick that his official duties would in no way interfere with his inter-election activities as national chairman.

McCormick's presence in Washington was expected to have a salutary effect on faint-hearted Democrats in Congress, but primarily his function was to screen applicants for high office. Those not in sympathy with the administration's policies were summarily excluded "in order to create a wholesome atmosphere and to check in some measure the propaganda being carried on by many of the so-called patriots of the Republican party, who have volunteered their services in Washington and who are doing all they can to discredit the work of the Administration."[24] Since McCormick functioned more or less behind the scenes, his activities did not attract the attention or raise the outcry that greeted other wartime operations of the government.

III

POLITICS was not confined to the nation's capital, where its manifestations occupied the limelight during the sessions of Congress, but permeated war agencies throughout the country at every level. For the most part, the machinery required to administer the draft and, later on, the Food and Fuel Administrations was constituted on a voluntary basis. Top officials in each state received their appointments from Washington generally on the recommendations of the various governors, while the administrative staffs were recruited from the local citizenry. Because in one way or another these agencies reached almost every citizen, they offered an unparalleled opportunity for intensive if surreptitious political work. The top positions, moreover, carried a good deal of influence and prestige, and competition for them was very keen. In making appointments the federal government tried to preserve an equitable balance between the parties, but senators and governors alike watched their distribution jealously. It proved impossible to satisfy everybody, and the appointments engendered a great deal of political animosity. The relative number of Republicans and Democrats named to local and national agencies became a hot issue in the 1918 campaign, with each party manipulating statistical information on the subject in its campaign literature.[25]

The most sinister aspect of this activity occurred in connection with the organization and operation of draft exemption boards. Compulsory military service was unpopular everywhere, and local politicians were seldom above doing favors for constituents who preferred a soft war job to a berth in the Army.[26] There were some 4,600 exemption boards with a total of 20,000 members, and a board of review for each federal judicial district. Filling these jobs precipitated such a mad scramble among congressmen and state officials that the press urged the government not to permit a political hash to be made of a very serious matter.[27] Federal district attorneys reported tremendous pressure for exemptions, often running as high as 60 per cent of the men registered. Frequent complaints reached Washington of gross favoritism shown by many boards in granting exemptions.[28] The War Department investigated such complaints and summarily removed a number of corrupt boards in the most flagrant cases. Nevertheless, the laxity with which many boards performed their duty gave rise to strong resentment against the government, which harshly punished overt resistance to the draft but showed great leniency in the matter of exemptions to the politically favored.

The consequences of political manipulation or interference were less harmful in other agencies. Following the establishment of the Food and Fuel Administrations early in the war, the chairman of the former, Herbert Hoover, submitted a list of state food administrators to Vance McCormick, who approved those he knew or felt would not be politically hostile to Wilson.[29] He also discouraged all attempts to subordinate state food administrations to local political machines, especially if the latter happened to be under Republican control. Appointment of a Delaware food administrator was delayed for months by the struggle between the Republican governor and the Democratic senators, with the latter finally prevailing to the intense annoyance of their adversaries.[30] The Democratic governor of Utah made an issue of the appointment of a fuel administrator until his own man secured the post instead of a Republican coal dealer backed by Senator Reed Smoot's organization.[31] While the political maneuvering that accompanied the organization of these agencies did not seriously impair the patriotic work they subsequently performed, it served to keep the fires of partisanship crackling merrily.

If the national war agencies were infiltrated by politics, such activity completely dominated the state Councils of Defense. Created under the auspices of the Council of National Defense to forward the war effort on the home front in ways beyond the competence of the federal government, these Councils — or Committees of Public Safety, as they were called in some states — derived their powers and funds from their respective legislatures. Although each Council was theoretically non-partisan, the chairman was usually the governor or one of his henchmen, so that the party in power determined the political complexion of the Council. Organization of the Pennsylvania Committee of Public Safety had to await the outcome of a bitter struggle between the Vare and Penrose factions of the Republican party over control of a $2 million legislative appropriation for the Committee's use.[32] Deposition of the Vare-dominated governor ultimately gave both factions equal representation on the Committee under a neutral chairman and an equal share of the spoils. Since it supervised all volunteer war work in the state, including Red Cross activities, Liberty Loan drives, and the like, Pennsylvania Democrats received scant recognition; and the Wilson administration suffered accordingly from the type of propaganda disseminated by this agency.[33]

Generally throughout the East, state Defense Councils had no legal powers; their work was chiefly advisory and educational. They stimulated among the people a greater understanding of war aims and cooperation in the government's policies and programs, provided comforts and conveniences for soldiers in camp, looked out for their dependents at home, and sought to promote the welfare of citizens amid the unfamiliar conditions imposed by the war. Throughout much of the West, however, it was a different story. Many western states gave their Councils wide discretionary powers which permitted them to do everything not inconsistent with state or federal law, a limitation that proved quite flexible under the rubric of promulgating and carrying out "such measures as may be necessary to meet the exigencies of all situations occasioned by the war."[34] Hence, idle persons could be compelled to work, and such persons could be classified and assigned according to occupations suffering from a shortage of labor. Councils so endowed were able to regulate not only industrial and agricultural relations but educational and religious affairs as well, and to suppress whatever in their estimation appeared unpatriotic or subversive.[35] Such Councils were, in some instances, a wartime version or revival of the vigilantes of pioneer days, and they carried out their functions in about the same rough-and-ready manner.

Each governor named his own Council, and if his party controlled the legislature as well, he had ample funds for an impromptu political machine that could, in the name of patriotism, muzzle all opposition to his regime. Senator Andreius A. Jones of New Mexico said of the situation in his state that "practically all activities relating to the war have been conducted under the auspices of the Republican Governor. The State Council of National Defense consists entirely of Republicans, with one exception. That Council . . . has brought into its employ a large number of people, practically all of whom are Republicans. At a special session of the Legislature of New Mexico, $750,000 was appropriated [for] . . . the Council of National Defense which was not required to make any report of its expenditures to the next Legislature. I am reliably informed that this money is being used in a large way for the purpose of bolstering up Republicans and the Republican Party."[36] Inevitably such shenanigans became a burning issue in the 1918 elections, but so well entrenched were most of the state political organizations through extralegal means that very few of them could be overturned.

As numerous complaints about these reprehensible practices reached the White House, the President noted early in December that "it is becoming more and more evident that throughout the country the draft organization, the public defense organization, and the Fuel and Food Administrations are being made use of for political purposes."[37] Wisconsin gave him considerable concern in this respect. Irate Democrats there accused Republican Governor Emanuel Philipp not only of showing marked tepidity toward the war effort but of exploiting the extensive anti-war sentiment in the state to insure his re-election in 1918. With this in mind he had packed draft boards with his own henchmen and organized the Defense Council along strictly partisan lines. "Such activities," protested Senator Husting, "would not fail to have a great political effect and not to the benefit of the Democratic party." Wisconsin Democrats had their own patriotic organization, called the Loyalty League, which the senator urged Wilson to treat as the official body for combatting subversive influences. Recognition of the governor's Defense Council, explained Husting rather naïvely, "makes it very difficult, if not impossible, to build up an organization for the Democratic party."[38] Since Husting was an administration stalwart, Wilson ordered Creel's Committee on Public Information to use the Loyalty League rather than the Defense Council in all publicity and propaganda matters.[39]

Indiana set a particularly bad example. The Republicans had established control in 1916 by a narrow margin, and the young and energetic state chairman, Will H. Hays, sought to strengthen his party by any means that came to hand. After Governor James P. Goodrich named him chairman of the Defense Council, Hays blanketed the state with Republican politicians in voluntary war jobs that not only brought them prestige and profit but also put them in close and constant touch with the mass of voters.[40] Key positions on the Council went to prominent party members, including a millionaire coal operator as head of its coal production committee. Angry Democrats complained to Washington that Republicans manned all the draft exemption boards, while the state conscription agent was the Republican boss of the First Indiana Congressional District, one of the few remaining Democratic strongholds in the state.

Hays and his cohorts added insult to injury by refusing to allow prominent Democrats to participate in patriotic rallies, bond drives, and four-minute-man speaking activities. Conspicuous at such gatherings were the two Republican senators, Harry S. New and James E. Watson, who boasted that Wilson's name was never mentioned on these occasions. Consequently, the Indiana Democratic Editorial Association, representing 150 party newspapers, refused at its annual convention in June 1917 to endorse the Defense Council on the ground that it was nothing more than a Republican publicity machine, approval of which would only play deeper into the enemy's hands.[41] Ultimately the Defense Council had to accept a Democratic banker from Indianapolis as fuel administrator in place of the Republican millionaire named by Hays. Such limited patronage did not satisfy the disgruntled party leaders, who proceeded to bring their grievances before the November meeting of the Democratic National Committee.

The Committee, which discussed plans for the 1918 congressional campaign, asked the Postmaster General to call the President's attention to the fact that Republican governors generally were playing politics in organizing the war services of their states. Indiana had a particularly bad record because the Hays-Goodrich combination refused to consult with Democrats or bring them into war work in any way. "Such things as these," the Committee pointed out, "have aggravated the Democrats of Indiana who feel that they have been badly treated at a time when partisanship ought not to be considered."[42] The Committee urged that Hays and Goodrich should not be allowed to embarrass the national administration further by abusing their power to nominate henchmen to war posts.

Wilson responded to the Committee's appeal by instructing the Secretary of War, in the latter's capacity as chairman of the Council of National Defense, that while "we shall make no obvious partisan distinctions in our war activities . . . we shall not allow them to be made against us as in Indiana." In reply Baker pointed out the difficulty, in dealing with political people, of avoiding or preventing partisan manifestations such as those to which the President had referred. "I am afraid," he said, "the Governors in some of the States have used the Federal machinery which it has been necessary to create among them for political ends."[43] Indiana he considered a rather extreme case; otherwise the system had worked out about as well as could have been expected under the circumstances. Hays's elevation shortly thereafter to the chairmanship of the Republican National Committee brought no diminution of partisan activity in war work either among the Hoosiers or on the national front.

Location of the sixteen camp sites for the National Army provided another fecund source of partisan discord. The decision to train the drafted men in the South raised a hue and cry among Northern politicians, who could see nothing in it but pork and sectional discrimination. Senator Harding denounced as "asinine" the policy of sending soldiers to an enervating southern climate to harden them for the rigors of trench life in France. Neither the governor of Indiana nor the two senators could understand the need for training their troops across the Ohio River in Kentucky, where a camp had to be built, when Fort Benjamin Harrison, an Army post near Indianapolis, offered adequate facilities for the purpose.[44] The Chicago *Tribune* claimed that every Democratic member of the House Military Affairs Committee had obtained at least one camp site for his district. Whatever the truth of such charges, the administration was subjected to tremendous political pressure in allocating sites. The Secretary of War, foreseeing trouble from the start, warned Wilson that every congressman wanted a camp and that there would be many bitter disappointments.[45]

Apart from the political pulling and hauling, the choice of the actual camp sites in each of the six military districts into which the country was divided for Army administrative purposes depended on the general in command of the district. In case of doubt or disagreement, the final decision rested with the War Department.[46] Most of the trouble occurred in the Southeast, where the department commander happened to be Major General Leonard Wood. Still smarting under the "stinging and unmerited rebuke" of his transfer from the New York area,[47] the general now had a unique chance to square accounts. His theory that camp sites should be located along the Atlantic seaboard to facilitate the transfer of troops abroad conflicted with the views of the War Department, which wanted such sites established near important rail centers.[48] Southern universities showered him with honorary degrees, while southern cities and towns, eager to have one of these potential military gold mines located in the vicinity, vied with each other in lavishly entertaining Wood, who was prodigal in promising War Department support for their respective claims. His impish practice of publishing his camp site recommendations in the local newspapers before submitting them to Washington for approval created an extraordinary amount of confusion and hard feeling. The Secretary of War wanted to develop Fort Oglethorpe in northwestern Georgia as the principal training center for that region. When General Wood publicly recommended Memphis instead, he embroiled Baker in a bitter controversy with the potent Crump machine and its henchman, Senator Kenneth D. McKellar. The senator complained that the failure to allot Tennessee a camp, when Georgia got four, South Carolina three, and every other southern state except Florida at least one, embarrassed him at home ''where people say my friendship for the administration gets nothing for Tennessee.''[49] Although McKellar's friendship for the administration was a myth, such was not the case with Senator Duncan U. Fletcher of Florida, an old party wheelhorse. The omission of Florida greatly irritated the senator, particularly after the War Department chose Hattiesburg, Mississippi, instead of Jacksonville, which Wood had recommended, as the troop concentration center for the Gulf Coast. Fletcher made such a disturbance that Baker wearily advised the President to put a camp in every state to take the pressure off his Department.[50] Although Fletcher finally got his camp near Jacksonville, the dissension that Wood created deepened the anti-Baker animus of a number of southern senators, few of whom felt disposed to come to his support that winter when the Republicans staged their massive attack on his management of the War Department.[51]

CHAPTER IV

THE COMMITTEE ON THE CONDUCT
OF THE WAR

DURING the long hot summer of 1917 Congress remained in Washington, wrestling with the manifold problems raised by the war and fighting the President's recommendations at almost every turn. Originally the leaders had intended to conclude the session by July 1, but the inordinate amount of time consumed in political maneuvering on the floor and logrolling in the committees delayed adjournment for another three months. Because of repeated deadlocks over important legislation, it was October before the weary statesmen could return home to explain to their puzzled constituents the necessity for such protracted argument on urgent issues. The press took a critical view of the delay, comparing it unfavorably with the record of Lincoln's first war Congress, which met for a month in the summer of 1861 and in that brief time clothed the Executive with the powers to defend the Union. Nevertheless, the accomplishments of Wilson's war Congress were by no means inconsiderable. It provided nearly $20 billion in loans and taxes and enacted a number of important measures, but the political pyrotechnics set off in the process tended to obscure the net effect.

I

THE TWO major measures engrossing the attention of Congress that summer were war revenue and food control, both of which provoked bitter and prolonged controversies. The food situation was especially serious. A poor 1917 wheat crop that had yielded only 630,000,000 of the anticipated 900,000,000 bushels barely sufficed for domestic consumption, and no surplus remained for the hard-pressed Allies, who required an additional 300,000,000 bushels at least.[1] The second poor crop year in a row, it also left the country practically without reserves. Consequently, farmers with a short-crop financial bonanza in sight hoarded their wheat rather than deliver it to the mills, and grain prices soared dizzily on the exchanges. Moreover, the activity of speculators in diverting vast quantities of eggs, poultry, meat, and other perishables to cold storage sent all food prices skyrocketing and stirred a tremendous ground wave of popular discontent, especially in the cities.[2] Since the government under existing laws was powerless to cope with the situation, and since appeals to the patriotism of farmers and speculators were in vain, the administration promptly sought authority from Congress to put an end to these intolerable conditions.[3]

Although not a little alarmed by the gravity of the situation, Congress found it easier to denounce food speculators than to curb their activities by laws patently objectionable to a host of vested interests, including all the producers, processors, and distributors of the nation's groceries. Many congressmen, moreover, professed great unwillingness to discard, even temporarily, the system of free enterprise under which the country had prospered for a system of government controls, which might pervert democratic principles and lead to some sort of dictatorship in Wilson's hands. They preferred instead to divert attention from the real causes underlying the agitation over the high cost of living by shifting the blame to the Department of Agriculture or to the tentative Food Administration, established on May 20 without congressional sanction. While the press, the pulpit, and every other medium of public opinion united in condemning congressional dilatoriness, the lawmakers barricaded themselves behind the classical economists and argued for months that price control had never worked in the past and therefore could not be applied to the present emergency.[4] The administration deployed all its influence to overcome this resistance, but Wilson's party was split on the question, and the Republicans were massed against controls of any kind. In the end the President had to accept a compromise that not only proved largely unworkable but failed to give relief from high prices and profiteering.

Congressional reception of the food control bill submitted by the Department of Agriculture on April 21 had been distinctly unfriendly.[5] The House revised the measure several times to meet a variety of objections, mainly to the sweeping powers conferred upon the Executive to dictate food prices and regulate the other necessities of life. Ignoring the clamor for immediate relief, the representatives wrangled until June 23 before voting 365 to 5 to grant the President the authority to take whatever steps he might deem necessary to stimulate production, assure fair prices, and protect the public against extortion.[6] The administration had to pay a high price for such unanimity, however, in the shape of a rider effectively making the nation bone-dry for the duration of the war.[7]

The triumph of the prohibitionists threw the country into an uproar. Convivial elements roundly denounced it as an imposition on the public and a gross abuse of the war powers of the government. Urban newspapers again earnestly admonished Congress to stop playing politics with every issue that came before it and to get on instead with the essential business of winning the war. It was no time, the press asserted, to be trifling with a grave problem by yoking it to a reform unacceptable to millions of people.[8] The reform was also unacceptable to the President, who had interceded vainly with ''dry'' leaders not to complicate the food bill with restrictions on the use of grain in the manufacture of alcohol. Rather than seek recommitment and court certain defeat, Wilson preferred to exert pressure on the Senate to strike out the rider and restore all controls to the Food Administration.

The Senate gave the food bill even rougher treatment. If prohibitionist sentiment was somewhat less rabid, objections to centralized control and price-fixing were far more vehement. Moreover, relations between the Senate and the Chief Executive had deteriorated as a result of other conflicts. Senator Henry F. Hollis of New Hampshire, a progressive Democrat disillusioned by the arbitrary character of the war program, warned Wilson that the measure could not pass without a vigorous fight on his part. "There are very few Democratic Senators," he said, "who feel well enough disposed toward the Administration to take hold actively. My personal opinion is that a large part of the hostility is unnecessary and might have been avoided by showing reasonable consideration for the feelings and wishes of the Democratic Senators. Some of it might be removed even now, but it is too late to put the bill through by an appeal to the friendliness of the Senators.'"[9]

Matters were too urgent to permit the smoothing of ruffled senatorial feathers. Instead the President carried the fight to the public with vigorous appeals concerning the urgency, fairness, and necessity of the measure. He also set up a Food Administration on an unofficial basis without awaiting legislative approval, an action that further annoyed many of the senators.[10] His appointment of Herbert Hoover as temporary Food Administrator stirred a frenzy of apprehension in statesmen like Reed of Missouri, who declaimed violently against him as a tyrant, a despot, a dictator, a czar, and a George III endowed with such power as no human being should ever receive.

Resistance of farm organizations to price-fixing made senators from wheat and cotton states particularly hostile to the legislation.[11] The chairman of the Committee on Agriculture, Gore of Oklahoma, washed his hands of the matter entirely and left the management of the bill to another committee member, Chamberlain of Oregon. In the free-for-all that followed, the House measure (the Lever bill) served as a working basis for a possible agreement. After the Senate pruned the "bone-dry" feature, to the relief of millions of citizens, a movement developed to put every commodity of any importance to the war effort under government control.[12] In a frenzy of horse-trading, western senators yielded on the control of grain prices in return for the inclusion of farm machinery, binder twine, and other items essential to farming operations. Southern senators likewise agreed to permit the regulation of cotton if northern senators had no objection to fixing prices on manufactured articles. For a while, price control appeared about to become universal in scope, but a reaction set in that quickly altered the whole character of the bill.

The stampede in the other direction nearly wrecked the President's program. Southern senators, frightened by the outcry from Dixie against the proposal to regulate cotton, hurriedly backed away from the scheme. A host of other interests, hitherto favorable to the principle if applied to everything, joined the cotton representatives, and the Senate beat a hasty retreat.[13] Senators Gore and McKellar seized the occasion to put forward substitute proposals which extracted all the teeth from the original bill by preventing the government from checking on wasteful or extortionate practices.[14] These maneuvers forced Wilson to redouble his efforts to rally public support to secure effective safeguards. Without much enthusiasm for the idea, the Senate finally yielded to presidential pressure and popular clamor to the extent of reviving controls on wheat and coal, the two commodities on which profiteering was most harmful and public discontent most vocal. On July 21 a compromise bill emerged after every parliamentary trick to defeat it had been exhausted.[15] Nevertheless, before the measure went to conference, where another long deadlock ensued, the President's enemies managed to insert two provisions which were highly objectionable to him.

One of the unacceptable features provided for an administrative board of three to carry out the act. While reflecting the Senate's ingrained distrust of augmenting the executive power, it was for the most part a rebuke to Wilson's choice of Herbert Hoover as Food Administrator. An astonishing amount of hostility had developed against Hoover for his part in supporting the President and pushing the bill. Moreover, he had no political following and thus presented an easy target for senators nursing a grudge against the administration. As these were numerous and the Food Administrator had few defenders, the multiple executive feature had carried overwhelmingly, 60 to 23. Far worse than this, however, from Wilson's point of view, the Senate had resurrected the resolution for a Joint Committee on the Conduct of the War, and with a few minor changes, had tacked this ''instrumentality'' onto the food bill in the form of a rider.[16]

II

THIS MANEUVER, inspired by Senator Weeks, came as no surprise; but the White House could do nothing about it in view of the general feeling of senatorial hostility promoted by Lodge, Hollis, and the other obstructionists.[17] Heretofore the opposition to the idea of government regulation had been sectional rather than partisan. Western wheat and southern cotton interests had aligned themselves against northern manufacturing interests, who were suspected of wanting raw material prices controlled in order to inflate the profit on finished goods. Because of the disaffection in the Democratic ranks, the Republicans had no trouble in finding a disgruntled western Democrat, Robert L. Owen of Oklahoma, to sponsor the proposal as a spurious nonpartisan gesture. The War Department's refusal to put an Army camp in Oklahoma, "despite my loyalty to the President," had put the senator in a sour mood and made him unreceptive to a protest from Wilson that he could not run the war successfully if he was to be placed under the same sort of "daily espionage" as Lincoln.[18] Fourteen Democrats, including the usual anti-Wilson clique of Gore, Hardwick, Hitchcock, Shields, Reed and Vardaman, went along with the Oklahoman in joining 38 Republicans to put this "instrumentality" over the top by a 53 to 31 vote, the opposition to it being solidly Democratic.

The Weeks resolution had popped out like the skeleton in the closet during the course of a heated debate in the Senate on July 17 concerning the corruption and extravagance alleged to exist in the letting of war contracts.[19] The affairs of the Shipping Board in particular had fallen into sad disarray despite the vast funds placed at its disposal. A spectacular quarrel between the Board's chairman, William Denman, and his rival, Major General George W. Goethals of the Emergency Fleet Corporation, over the relative merits of wooden ships versus steel ships in the desperate race against the German submarine had brought shipbuilding operations practically to a standstill.[20] With little work accomplished and much money squandered, the situation had become a public scandal and senatorial tempers incandescent before Wilson finally broke the impasse on July 24 by forcing both men to resign.[21] To his exasperated critics the time seemed propitious for Congress to assert its prerogatives and take over the management of the war effort before all was lost.

Senator Hale of Maine had urged the adoption of the Weeks resolution as a necessary check on the flagrant abuses about which the President refused to do anything. His colleagues Borah of Idaho, William S. Kenyon of Iowa, and Charles E. Townsend of Michigan all agreed with him that something of the sort was absolutely necessary to watch executive expenditures and prevent further graft and boodling by private industry at the government's expense. Weeks, in introducing the resolution, explained that every European belligerent employed a similar device to keep track of war expenditures. It was an "insult," he said, to think, as the press was asserting, that he bore any partisan malice toward the President, and he warmly defended the motives of Thaddeus Stevens and the Civil War radical Republicans who had thrust a similar instrumentality upon President Lincoln. From the Democratic side no one challenged these statements or moved to defend the administration, and the Weeks-Owen rider became part of the food control bill on July 21 without further debate.[22]

Newspapers of both parties denounced the maneuver as a cheap partisan trick inspired solely by personal or political antagonism to the President.[23] These aspersions sparked an angry reaction on Capitol Hill, whence Senator Lodge complained that the administration through its influence with the press had succeeded in getting all the newspapers from one end of the country to the other to pour torrents of abuse on Congress.[24] Nevertheless, before debating the merits of the Wade-Chandler committee at length, both sides engaged in considerable historical research. Lodge, the Senate authority on all matters historical, maintained that this group had never harassed Lincoln in the conduct of the war. Weeks asserted that an examination of the Great Emancipator's correspondence revealed that he had never written anything critical about the Committee. On the Democratic side, Josiah O. Wolcott of Delaware quoted from Gideon

Welles's *Diary* to prove that the activities of Wade and his radical friends had been far from helpful to the Union cause, but Weeks dismissed Welles as a "common scold" and a creature of Stanton. Williams of Mississippi explained that Lincoln had not objected to the Committee because he was "a long suffering, patient man . . . of great intellectual humility," qualities which, the senator implied, were not abundantly present in the current occupant of the White House, who would stand for no nonsense on this score.

In the meantime the President had acted promptly to head off the obnoxious rider in the House. In a letter to Asbury F. Lever of South Carolina, the manager of the food control bill, he pointed out that the Weeks proposal was completely foreign to its subject. He particularly stressed the "ominous precedent" of the Civil War committee which, he said, had been a "cause of constant distressing harassment and rendered Mr. Lincoln's task all but impossible." Although willing to grant that the Senate's motives were patriotic rather than partisan, Wilson could not agree that such a method of cooperation was practicable in view of the "abundant and existing means" already at the disposal of Congress for checking on government expenditures.[25] The Democratic leadership responded readily to his objections with a special rule shutting off debate and directing the House conferees to disagree to all Senate amendments. Minority Leader Mann's refusal to grant the unanimous consent necessary to send the bill to conference threw the measure back on the floor and precipitated a sharp fight. Party ranks held firm, however, and the special rule was sustained by a 169 to 101 vote, with the opposition coming entirely from the Republican side. The invidious newspaper comment about their loyalty and patriotism frightened Mann and his followers into quickly abandoning further obstructive tactics.

The food control bill bogged down in conference while speculators, in anticipation of ultimate regulation, gambled wildly on the exchanges and the commodity price structure deteriorated rapidly. Agreement was soon reached on every matter but the Committee on the Conduct of the War. The Senate conferees divided 4 to 3 in favor of retaining this instrumentality when

Gore of Oklahoma sided with the Republican minority, which consisted of Carroll S. Page of Vermont, William S. Kenyon of Iowa, and Warren of Wyoming, against his Democratic colleagues Chamberlain of Oregon, Hoke Smith of Georgia, and Ellison D. Smith of South Carolina. On August 2 Senator Warren came once again to the administration's rescue, as he had on the occasion of the Roosevelt amendment, by switching his vote. The fact that Wilson had appointed his son-in-law, General Pershing, commander of the Expeditionary Force, may have had something to do with it. In any case, Warren's action helped quiet the storm of public indignation at the Senate's cavalier attitude toward the vicious profiteering that was daily pushing the cost of living higher, and gave Wilson another hard-won victory over his congressional foes.

Although the House immediately adopted the conference report with only scattered opposition, the Senate exploded with wrath. The chagrined radicals devoted another week to denouncing the principle of government control and deploring the fate of the Committee on the Conduct of the War. The historical side of the matter was thrashed out in great detail, with the irate Republicans stubbornly maintaining that the Civil War committee had saved the Union despite what Wilson might think to the contrary.[26] After a final blast at Wilson and Hoover for their usurpation of power, the Senate passed the bill on August 8 by a vote of 66 to 7. Two days later the President signed what was one of the most important as well as controversial measures adopted during the war. Neither the political nor the economic consequences of the Lever act were clearly understood or foreseen. Certainly no one anticipated the crucial bearing that the price-fixing feature was to have on the outcome of the 1918 congressional elections.

As for the Committee on the Conduct of the War, it was scotched but not killed. Senator Weeks immediately announced his intention to attach it as a rider to everything that came before that session of Congress.[27] His first opportunity occurred in connection with the $11.5 billion war bond and certificate bill, which granted additional credit to the Allies and authorized the issuance of war savings stamps. Wilson, alerted to this fresh attempt upon his prerogatives, appealed to House Democratic leaders for help. "I am counting on you," he wrote, "to outmaneuver these gentlemen [the Republicans] who are doing their best to get their hand on the steering apparatus of the Government."[28] When the Speaker responded by ruling three hostile amendments out of order, the Republicans taunted Wilson with fearing to permit open debate on the question.[29] Joseph W. Fordney of Michigan arraigned the President for having insulted the memory of Zachariah Chandler, a radical Civil War senator from Fordney's state. Lincoln, said Fordney, had done more to hasten the day of victory by taking Congress into his confidence than Wilson, who refused to trust Congress and kept all affairs in his own hands. John J. Fitzgerald of New York closed the angry debate by reminding the House of the number of committees already at the disposal of Congress to check upon the executive expenditures of the government.

A final attempt to revive the resolution came in connection with the deficiency appropriation bill, the last measure considered at that session. By this time, however, the Senators were eager to adjourn after a grueling summer in the Washington heat, and the move received little support. Weeks thereupon dropped the matter with a warning that early in the next session a "determined fight" would be made to adopt his plan. Congress then adjourned on October 6, not to reconvene until early in December, when the fight was renewed along somewhat different lines and in connection with developments that were to give Wilson one of the stiffest congressional battles of his career.

III

IN THE closing weeks of the first session, after disposing of the food control bill, Congress grappled with the problem of financing the vast military preparations of the government. The rapidly mounting expenses of the war staggered congressmen unaccustomed to thinking in billions. The controversy that developed over the method of paying for the war soon became as acrimonious as the heated exchanges accompanying the enactment of conscription, the espionage act, and the food control bill. Wilson and McAdoo favored a pay-as-you-go plan, with heavy taxes on incomes and war profits and with as little as possible of the burden relegated to posterity in the form of bond issues.[30] This policy had strong support in the House, where the "conscription of wealth" idea was very popular among members from the rural South and West. It was anathema, however, to northern Republicans, on whose section the brunt of such a scheme would fall. The urban press, irrespective of party, denounced as rank socialism all talk of conscripting incomes in the same manner that men were drafted for the Army, and urged Congress to adhere to a sound and sober distribution of imposts.

Prominent financiers like J. P. Morgan and Henry L. Higginson begged the Treasury Department to ignore all radical suggestions for taxing the rich. The imposition of luxury taxes and stamp taxes, in Morgan's opinion, was the ideal way of raising the necessary money, since heavier income taxes penalized thrift and discouraged investment.[31] Higginson wanted corporations exempted from higher levies "since they must be encouraged to do all the business they can." The Senate Finance Committee gave a sympathetic hearing to the hordes of businessmen who flocked to Washington to plead for smaller taxes and to protest the notion of making their generation pay the entire cost of the war.[32] In the House, however, the so-called insurgents under the leadership of Kitchin of North Carolina firmly controlled the Ways and Means Committee, which proceeded to fashion a bill that relied primarily on business taxes and exempted the farming community from practically every form of federal levy.

On May 24 the House passed the $1.8 billion tax bill by a vote of 329 to 76, with the opposition solidly Republican because of the bill's alleged sectional character. Southern Democrats had beaten off all Republican attempts to amend the measure, including a proposed $2.50 per bale consumption tax on cotton, which failed under a threat of reprisals against western farm commodities. A last-ditch effort to defeat the bill on Minority Leader Mann's motion to recommit also lost, 246 to 161, with western Republicans again deserting to the enemy.[33] Not even the insurgents pretended that it was a good bill or a fair one, but they argued that time was of the essence and no quicker way existed of obtaining the desired revenue.

The drastic increases in income taxes, surtaxes, and war profits taxes, which provided two-thirds of the total amount, stunned the business community. Senator Lodge promised his agitated Boston banking friends that the Finance Committee, of which he was a member, would never approve such a "monstrosity" but would distribute the tax burden more in accord with their views.[34] Despite McAdoo's warning that any reduction or distribution would be a "grave error" leading to "financial chaos," the Finance Committee lopped $200 million off the House figure, to the dismay of the Treasury but to the obvious gratification of upper-bracket taxpayers.[35]

Because the food control bill had legislative priority, the Senate sidetracked the war revenue measure until late August. By that time war expenditures had far outstripped anything foreseen by the Treasury, which now had to ask Congress for $5 billion more than the amount requested in May. The unhappy business community scored McAdoo for bad guesswork and begged Congress to raise the additional money by loans.[36] On this point, however, the administration remained adamant, with Wilson still firmly of the opinion that paying a substantial share of the war costs out of current revenue placed no undue strain on the economic structure. In view of the exorbitant profits flowing from government contracts, the President held that business leaders had no legitimate ground for complaint.

A small group of progressive senators, including Borah, George W. Norris, Hiram Johnson, and La Follette, went considerably beyond the administration's position in this respect. The progressives demanded a drastic increase in the war profits tax in order to strip the "blood money" from the munitions makers and other profiteers engaged in "plundering the public." The professional patriots of that type, said Borah, clamored the loudest for bond issues, long-term loans, and low taxes.[37] He proposed therefore to levy an 80 per cent tax on all war profits, a figure corresponding to the impost in effect in England, which had started with a 50 per cent war profits levy in 1914 and gradually increased to the higher level.

The panic-stricken banking and business community denounced Borah and his friends as Bolsheviks intent upon wrecking the financial structure of the country. The Treasury Department also objected because of the bad effect which too drastic taxation would have on the money market in financing future government loans. McAdoo believed that the graduated profits levy, averaging 31 per cent, in the Senate bill would bring in sufficient revenue without unduly straining the national economy. The progressives rejected all such arguments, however, and when the administration bill emerged from committee, thirty-four senators met in Borah's office to pledge support to the 80 per cent levy. Under a withering press attack condemning their "conscription of wealth" appeal as the most dangerous kind of demagoguery, the "champions of the people" dwindled to about half this number. Nevertheless, Borah and a handful of followers fought stoutly for nearly a month to prevent the well-to-do from diverting a larger share of the war costs to posterity.

Leading off in defense of big business, Senator Harding almost wept over the plight of captains of industry suffering in their morale from the unfair attack on American enterprise. Their sacrifices he considered only slightly less noble than those of the soldiers on the field of battle.[38] His colleagues Lodge and Smoot warned that excessive taxes would make the war unpopular with businessmen threatened with confiscation of their earnings while patriotically engaged in extending their facilities to meet government demands. The progressives, however, insisted on pooling all excess earnings, after due allowance for manufacturing costs and reasonable profits, to pay the increased expenses of the government due to the war effort.

In a Labor Day speech in New York, Colonel Roosevelt heartened the progressives and shocked his conservative friends by coming out strongly in favor of Senator Johnson's 80 per cent levy. The Colonel maintained that a similar rate prevailed in England and had apparently done the British economy no harm. Senators Lodge and Frank B. Kellogg immediately reproached him for taking a stand inimical to American business and helpful only to the enemies of the republic, such as La Follette and his followers. The deliberate purpose of these men, said Lodge, was to pillage wealth, which they regarded as a crime, and to break down business in order to break down the war.[39] In the end the great majority followed Lodge by decisively defeating the Johnson amendment, 62 to 17, and rejecting two others which called for 70 and 60 per cent levies, respectively. The Senate then passed the revenue act, 69 to 4, on September 10 after listening to an angry outburst from Senator Borah, who charged Congress with holding property and wealth more sacred in the war than flesh and blood.[40] Nearly another month elapsed before agreement could be reached in conference, and the measure became law on October 3.

Beyond enhancing the political prospects of a few western statesmen like Hiram Johnson and Borah, who had taken a rugged stand against predatory eastern monied interests,[41] the revenue act satisfied nobody and stirred up an immense amount of class and sectional animosity. Farmers as well as factory workers remained unconvinced that Congress had accomplished anything toward checking the flagrant profiteering at the public expense. The business community resented being made the scapegoat for this state of affairs and compelled to shoulder the entire tax burden because Congress, in its zeal to please the cotton growers, had shied away from consumption taxes of any sort.[42] Consequently, the urban press never ceased to denounce the act as unfair, unworkable, and a hardship upon city people suffering from greatly inflated prices for food and other commodities.[43]

CHAPTER V

THE GATHERING STORM

I

THE FALL and early winter of 1917–18 were the darkest days of the war as Allied morale sank to new low levels under the hammer blows of repeated military reverses. The war-weary Allied peoples, appalled at the prospect of further hardships and sacrifices, seemed nearly at the end of their strength. In Russia, where the Bolsheviks were gaining the upper hand, the situation was desperate; and it was serious enough in France and Italy, where the insidious poison of treachery had penetrated high government circles and further sapped the will to resist. In England the body politic remained immune to the German virus, but popular dissatisfaction with the conduct of the war was intense, and public patience with official ineptitude had worn thin. At home, worried Americans watched with ill-concealed dismay the steady decline in Allied fortunes and the ominous rise of German strength on the western front.[1] In some quarters the dubious outlook stimulated resistance to active participation in the conflict and strengthened the demand for an immediate peace. For the most part, though, the threat of Allied dissolution brought a clear realization that the successful outcome of the war now depended upon the speed with which an American army could be gotten into the field to face the German hordes.

Theoretically it should have been possible for the United States, with its wealth of material resources and technical skills plus the benefit of three years of Allied war experience, to set up an efficiently functioning organization that would produce maximum results in the shortest possible time. Actually, almost the opposite appeared to be the case. The American war effort progressed at what seemed to many people an incredibly leisurely pace, amid a welter of graft, confusion, waste, and extravagance which dismayed citizens impatient of delay and fearful of its consequences for the precarious European situation. The time consumed and the mistakes perpetrated in providing the armed forces with equipment and supplies, in mobilizing industrial and manpower resources, and in coordinating the vast but inchoate productive energies of the nation seemed utterly at variance with the boasted American competence in overcoming obstacles of a practical nature. Both Congress and the administration incurred bitter reproaches for the delays and failures incidental to the war program, but Congress hastily divested itself of all responsibility by shifting the blame to the Executive. The resultant turmoil kept the public in suspense through the winter, which was one of the coldest on record and added greatly to the general discontent.

The appalling slaughter at Passchendaele that fall shook American confidence in the soundness of Allied strategy and provoked a political crisis in England. Prime Minister Lloyd George's startling denunciation of the military stupidity that had sacrificed the flower of British manhood in senseless attacks on impregnable German positions made grim reading for Americans about to be thrown into further offensives of that sort. In Washington, the authorities hastily minimized press accounts of heavy British casualties and vigorously denied reports that the American Army lacked the artillery to blast a way through the German defenses.[2] In England, Lloyd George's plan to coordinate the hitherto haphazard military operations on the western front by subordinating the British Army to a Supreme War Council under a French general created an uproar that almost brought down his government. His would be the third Allied Cabinet in less than three weeks to fall on the issue of competency in the national war effort, and this did not include the unfortunate Kerensky regime then fleeing the victorious Bolsheviks in burning Petrograd, where dissatisfaction with the war effort had reached another kind of climax.

On November 19 Lloyd George managed to rout a hostile coalition bent on overthrowing him on the Supreme War Council issue. The part played in this bitter controversy by the sen-

sational Northcliffe press in exposing red tape in the War Office
and forcing several bureaucratic bumblers out of key Cabinet
position aroused envy in American journalistic circles chafing
under the censorship and suspicious of the candidness of the
authorities in Washington.[3] On the other hand, the administration looked upon Northcliffe's journalistic methods with a jaun-
diced eye, and when the famous editor appeared in Washington
that summer at the head of the British War Mission, Wilson had
as little to do with him as possible.[4] Northcliffe's slashing style
of attack appealed to Roosevelt and his friends, however, and to
all those who felt that the American war effort would benefit
from a similar approach.

Inspired perhaps by the Northcliffe example, Roosevelt that
fall embarked upon a one-man crusade to expose Wilson's shortcomings in the conduct of the war. The spectacle of the Rough
Rider stumping the country in Cassandra-like fashion, predict-
ing total collapse and ignominious defeat unless more intelligent
direction prevailed at the head of affairs, made good newspaper
copy, but it also made many people apprehensive that the effect
on public morale might not be quite what Roosevelt so fondly
anticipated.[5] In White House circles "Teddy's ravings" were
considered little short of seditious. McAdoo denounced his "utter
hypocrisy and lack of patriotism in trying to make the rest of
the world believe that America is as feeble and as weak as he
represents her."[6] Hatred of Wilson, however, blinded the Rough
Rider to all remonstrances, and nothing could divert him from
the congenial task of unmasking his rival's pretensions.[7]

Republican newspapers, without fully endorsing the Colonel's
opinions, welcomed them as an indication that Wilson had not
succeeded completely in his efforts to muzzle the press. The New
York *World*, on the other hand, angrily dubbed Roosevelt, Northcliffe, and their collaborators "War Naggers" and stoutly maintained that American war preparations had been "magnificent"
despite blunders incidental to unfamiliar efforts on such a vast
scale.[8] Nevertheless, in view of the wall of silence surrounding
all official activities, many Democratic organs could not suppress
an uneasy feeling that although Roosevelt might be exaggerating,
all was not well with the war effort.

Allied spirits soared momentarily late in November when 378 British tanks cracked the Hindenburg line at Cambrai for substantial gains. The rejoicing quickly subsided, however, as a German counterattack immediately recaptured most of the lost ground, a disaster which seemed to confirm Lloyd George's poor opinion of the caliber of British military leadership. Hard on the heels of this setback came the celebrated Lansdowne letter appealing to the belligerents to save civilization by making an immediate peace, on the basis of no retaliation or reparations for German war damage, and conveying a disagreeable impression of British unwillingness to hold out much longer. Such views, coming from a distinguished elder statesman who had held many high government posts, shocked official Washington and raised an angry dither in the press over the extent to which the British peer reflected the peace sentiments of Wilson himself. Some Republicans even attributed Lansdowne's shocking performance to the malign influence of Colonel House, then in London on another mysterious mission for the President. Lodge, Roosevelt and Major General Leonard Wood all solemnly reached this conclusion while breakfasting together at the New York home of Roosevelt's brother-in-law on December 9.[9]

II

THE SIXTY-FIFTH CONGRESS assembled on December 4 for its historic second session in an atmosphere made tense by anxiety, suspicion and taut nerves. In view of the depressing circumstances at home and abroad, the lawmakers approached the critical tasks ahead of them in no amiable frame of mind. The apparent snail's pace of vital war preparations troubled Republicans and Democrats alike, and they fumed over the official policy of withholding information on all such matters. From the remarks of the statesmen arriving in Washington, the indications pointed to another stormy session, but just how tumultuous it was to become, no one at the time had any inkling.

Republican leaders faced the dilemma that any criticism of the government would incur the odium of appearing to hamper the war effort. The fate of the Democratic party after the Civil

War was still vivid in their memory, and they were aware that any attack would be imputed to partisan motives, whatever its apologists might say to the contrary. The danger also existed that an exposure of military weakness would render aid and comfort to the enemy, or at least discourage the already badly depressed Allies.

Hence it behooved the Republicans to proceed cautiously lest their opportunism backfire and do the party incalculable harm. As Senator Lodge stated the situation to a Boston friend: "We cannot beat the Kaiser by standing silently by Wilson. Sooner or later the exposure must come and just when to start it is the problem now confronting us."[10]

Several Republican senators, as well as Colonel Roosevelt, had already made a start by touring the Army cantonments in search of enough first-hand evidence of mismanagement to warrant an investigation and possible impeachment of the Secretary of War.[11] Roosevelt's friend, Major General Leonard Wood, as a camp commander, was especially well-situated to furnish the Republican cabal with authentic figures on shortages in the War Department program.[12] The results of these researches were placed at the disposal of the Military Affairs Committee, the Democratic majority of which put no obstacles in the way of their exploitation by the minority. It was a curious situation, strongly reminiscent of the Civil War, with hardly a senator on this powerful committee on good terms with the Chief Executive or eager to support his policies. Although the high-strung Wilson enjoyed greater success than the humbler, and perhaps wiser, Lincoln in repelling assaults on his prerogatives, the resulting conflict proved equally disastrous to presidential plans for the future.

As Congress convened, Wilson was well aware of the hostile atmosphere and the likelihood of trouble ahead. He showed no inclination, however, to conciliate his critics. His message on the State of the Union constituted, instead, a ringing challenge to all those who disagreed with him. He calmly took cognizance of the unsatisfactory state of the war in Europe, alluded to the pacifism and defeatism rife in the Allied countries, and bitingly referred to the mounting clamor at home of the "noisily thought-

less and troublesome,'' whose gloomy prognostications were filling people's hearts with doubts about the ultimate outcome. All
this he brushed aside as of no consequence in view of the noble
objectives to which the nation was consecrated.[13] Drowning out
the carpings of critics and the fears of men of little faith, said
Wilson, were the voices of humanity, which were demanding a
just and righteous accounting from the enemy who in the end
would be compelled to yield. Wilson's firm expression of faith in
the sanctity of the Allied cause, his confidence in the adequacy
of the measures being taken to crush the foe, and his assumption
of the inevitability of defeat for the Central Powers despite their
recent military successes had a heartening effect upon public
morale. Nevertheless, his sarcastic allusion to the ''noisily
thoughtless and troublesome'' fitted Roosevelt and his collaborators so well that the address did nothing to lessen the growing
tension between the parties.

On December 11 the Senate moved to the attack by ordering
a ''drastic inquiry'' into the administration's war work.[14] His
colleagues, said Lodge, were all ready to take up an exposure of
Wilson's methods. James W. Wadsworth, Jr. of New York had
gotten the Military Affairs Committee to approve a thorough investigation of the machine-gun situation. Weeks of Massachusetts
was assembling evidence on the deplorable conditions in the
Quartermaster Corps. Lodge himself planned to direct the inquiry into the coal and food shortages in order to show the ''utter
mischief'' Wilson was doing with his price-fixing schemes.[15]
Harding of Ohio would look into the affairs of the Shipping
Board, which after ten months of effort and the expenditure of
half a billion dollars had yet to launch a ship.

Although Harding heatedly denied that his investigation was
motivated by partisan considerations, the sponsorship of these
various inquiries and the manner in which they were conducted
soon brought such disclaimers into question. The Republican
press justified them on the ground that it was necessary to put
punch into the war effort and new methods into the executive
agencies. Democratic journals, although willing to admit that
beneficial results might follow if the Senate committees acted
with impartiality and in good faith, viewed the inquisitions with

more reserve. The New York *World* called for the overhaul of Congress, which had handled war legislation in a slovenly fashion, as part of any scheme of reorganization designed to improve governmental efficiency.[16]

III

BY THE MIDDLE of December five major investigations were under way. The Senate Committee on Manufactures, headed by Reed of Missouri, ably assisted by Vardaman, Smoot, and Lodge — all inveterate foes of Wilson and of governmental regulation of commodities — had the Food Administration under hot attack. The Committee set out to demonstrate that the Hoover organization, by interfering with the law of supply and demand and by conniving with private interests to raise prices, had created a situation inimical to the public welfare. Senator Reed's furious browbeating of Food Administration witnesses who disagreed with him, particularly his highhanded refusal to let Food Administrator Hoover testify or even put in the record a statement giving his own side of the argument, turned the hearing into a one-man sideshow that quickly forfeited public sympathy. Senate Republicans, feeling that Reed's tactics were not too helpful, hastened to direct the inquiry into a more rewarding field — the coal shortage, which was threatening the comfort of American homes, the health of the people, and the ability of industry to keep producing at high levels.[17]

With the advent of cold weather, the fuel situation became acute as the public began to feel the pinch of diminishing supplies. Panicky state and municipal officials seized coal trains en route through their jurisdictions and distributed the coal in defiance of the Fuel Administration's orders. Finally the coal ceased to move altogether as the worst winter in years settled over the land. Suffering was intense among the urban poor, and the police with difficulty kept mobs from raiding the coal piles of industrial concerns. As orphanages, asylums, and prisons ran out of fuel, helpless inmates suffered from frostbite or froze to death. Even the well-to-do did not escape the general discomfort. Senator Lodge's chilly Boston friends complained bitterly about governmental inefficiency that kept their coal bins empty and their teeth chattering.[18]

Public wrath quickly focused on the Fuel Administration for not having anticipated the emergency. To charges of incompetence, favoritism, and downright dereliction of duty, the harassed agency replied by throwing the blame on the railroads. This the carriers promptly refuted by pointing to the priorities imposed upon them for the movement of freight from war plants, an arrangement that tied up loaded coal trains on sidings for weeks while stocks accumulated at the pitheads for want of empty cars.[19] Interesting as this controversy was, it provided no solution to the immediate problem, although by calling attention to the serious lack of coordination at top levels of the government, it furnished Congress with another cause for complaint.

The Republicans traced most of the trouble to the Fuel Administrator appointed by Wilson. Harry A. Garfield was a fellow college president and old personal friend whose progressive outlook paralleled Wilson's but whose qualifications for running a major war agency were less evident. Critics asserted that he was without political experience and lacked administrative capacity beyond that required to manage a small New England college.[20] His loyalty to Wilson, more than any other factor, had brought Garfield to Washington, at least in the opinion of Roosevelt, who detested him and considered his appointment another instance of Wilson's penchant for putting unfit people into key positions for personal or political reasons.[21]

Over the Christmas holidays Congress patriotically omitted the usual seasonal recess and pushed zealously ahead with its inquisitorial activities. The weather, on the other hand, relaxed its rigors somewhat, and a thaw opened traffic lanes sufficiently for a little coal to be moved from the mines to the northern cities most severely pinched by the fuel famine. Then on December 28 the worst blizzard in forty-one years swept the entire area east of the Rocky Mountains.[22] It was followed by a prolonged wave of sub-zero temperature that froze everything outdoors into a glacier-like solidity, completely paralyzing traffic by land and water and aggravating conditions that were already bad.[23] In the meantime, public attention was diverted somewhat from the miseries of a frigid existence by the pyrotechnical display accompanying the investigation of that citadel of red tape and bureaucratic obfuscation — the War Department.

IV

OF ALL the bottlenecks that had developed in the country's hasty preparations for war, the most serious was the shortage of arms and ammunition. Recruits in the camps had to drill with broomsticks while budding artillerymen learned their art on wooden cannons. Such makeshifts greatly excited Colonel Roosevelt and his congressional allies, who cherished the notion that a public airing of the dismal facts would blast the Secretary of War out of the Cabinet and wreck Wilson's political prospects. Consequently, the first witness called by the Military Affairs Committee in its sweeping probe of the War Department was Major General William Crozier, chief of the Ordnance Bureau. It was before a hostile audience, which had condemned him in advance, that Crozier appeared on December 12. The press felt that he lacked aggressiveness and administrative ability in failing to get an adequate performance out of his organization. The Lodge-Roosevelt faction considered him "worthless" and ascribed his retention in office to Wilson's dislike of Major General Wood, whose poor opinion of Ordnance was shared by many Army officers, including General Pershing.[24]

Crozier, however, had the veteran bureaucrat's ability to put up a tight defense of his organization, which led the New York *Times* to complain on December 20 that the "most exasperating aspect of his testimony was his evasion of responsibility." The Committee, therefore, could extract little from him that was helpful to the case against the administration. He frankly admitted that no unusual ordnance preparations, nothing other than the routine peacetime program, had been undertaken until June, three months after the start of the war. The blame for this situation he placed firmly on Congress, which had appropriated no funds for war purposes until March, and on American manufacturers, who either refused to accept contracts until they were in possession of the money needed to expand their plants or else demanded prices which the War Department considered excessive. Furthermore, production in government arsenals had been hampered by labor troubles which were traceable to congressional penuriousness in refusing to raise the wages of skilled workers to meet the lure of private firms with huge Allied contracts. Crozier contended that the arms program envisaged by his senatorial critics would have required three years of preparation by the government and private industry.

Since it was not part of the Committee's strategy to inculpate Congress, there was no point in pushing this line of inquiry too far. The machine-gun shortage promised more sensational developments, and to this Crozier's critics turned with gusto. Confusion and delay in machine-gun production had resulted from the War Department's inability to decide between two competing types, the Lewis and the Browning. The British used the former, which had also been in use in the American Army to a limited extent until May 1917, when political pressure had apparently forced the adoption of the latter. After a short competitive trial, Ordnance officials claimed that the Lewis gun jammed and could not use American-made ammunition, whereupon the weapon was dropped in favor of the new and relatively untried Browning, although no contracts for it were let until some months later. Consequently, the Army had few machine-guns of any sort and little prospect of obtaining an adequate number before the next spring.[25]

Sensing something peculiar at the bottom of this situation, the Committee gave the partisans of the Lewis gun, including the inventor and the president of the arms company owning the patents to the weapon, a free hand in attacking Crozier, who vigorously denied any personal animus in the matter. Nevertheless, technical considerations went largely by the board as his critics sought to prove that he had rejected the Lewis gun solely because General Wood favored its adoption.[26] All told, the evidence seemed to indicate that the Army, left to develop an automatic weapon without political interference, would not have been as acutely short as was the case. Since Roosevelt's friend, General Wood, appeared at least equally involved with Crozier, the investigation failed to do any particular harm to Wilson and

Baker beyond demonstrating the obvious fact that the Ordnance Bureau, like much else in the government, stood badly in need of reorganization and modernization.

Further deficiencies in the armament program came to light when a group of Republican congressmen who had just returned from a visit to American troop installations in France gave the Committee the benefit of their experiences. Thanks to the censorship, the public knew almost nothing about the War Department's overseas operations until enlightened by the damaging observations of these witnesses as to what they had seen and heard at the front. Representative George H. Tinkham of Massachusetts had found far fewer troops in France than the public had been led to believe; moreover, the lack of supplies and equipment was exerting a ''most demoralizing effect upon all preparations and efforts'' over there.[27] Clarence B. Miller of Minnesota averred that General Pershing suffered great embarrassment from the acute shortage of guns and ammunition for his units.[28] The gloomy observation of Porter H. Dale of Vermont that the situation in France was ''going anything but right'' appeared a gross understatement beside the sensational testimony of McCormick of Illinois. McCormick, a Roosevelt collaborator who aspired to a Senate seat in 1918, staggered the Committee with the news that total defeat within a few weeks appeared inevitable because the Allies could no longer supply American forces from their dwindling armament stocks. French and British generals at the front, he said, had told him that without the immediate acquisition of twenty-five thousand cannon from American sources, the war was as good as lost.[29]

McCormick's testimony made the situation look grim indeed, since no facilities existed in the United States for production on the scale demanded by his informants. The General Staff had been reluctant to send American troops abroad without their full complement of weapons but had yielded to Allied arguments that any arms deficiencies could be supplied from European arsenals until American manufacturers could meet their quotas.[30] The arrangement had seemed a reasonable one despite a good deal of Republican grumbling about the humiliation of being unable to supply the Expeditionary Force from home resources. Now, if

McCormick was to be believed, the worst fears of Wilson's critics seemed about to be realized.

Others in the congressional party friendly to the President flatly contradicted these disquieting statements. Nevertheless, they were widely reported and revived the Republican demand for a Coalition Cabinet with a separate Department for Munitions.[31] Since Wilson adamantly opposed such a scheme and remained unmoved by Republican tales of the miracles wrought in France and England by the separation of military and supply functions, the Senate investigation moved forward to a head-on collision with the Executive. Before that occurred, other painful revelations were forthcoming, which further embittered the already heated feelings between the two parties.

v

THE CANTONMENTS housing the National Army had been hastily thrown together that summer by contractors interested primarily in quick profits. Barracks and hospitals lacked heating arrangements; sanitary and plumbing facilities were often inadequate; and a number of camps occupied sites that were difficult to drain.[32] Sickness soon became prevalent among the horde of recruits that poured into the camps after September 1. All lacked adequate medical supplies, heavy clothing, blankets, and other equipment. As long as the mild weather prevailed, the discomforts could be endured, but with the onset of winter complaints began to multiply. Worried parents passed them on to their congressmen, and Colonel Roosevelt in particular reacted strongly to such stories. In order to allay the growing uneasiness caused by reports of extensive suffering, the Secretary of War toured the southern camps in November. On his return he issued a statement denying the presence of epidemics and declaring the health of the troops excellent.[33] Shortly thereafter, the surgeon general of the Army reported that health conditions in all the cantonments were "most satisfactory." The Medical Corps, he said, stood ready to safeguard the health of the soldiers and return them home at the end of the war "stimulated and strengthened in body and mind."[34]

Unfortunately for the realization of this happy ending, the cantonments were hard hit late that fall by the coldest weather on record. As sub-zero temperatures blanketed the entire South, water systems froze, sewage disposal units ceased to function, hospital facilities broke down, and the incidence of disease increased at an alarming rate. Deaths from pneumonia and meningitis multiplied rapidly in overcrowded quarters.[35] From every Army post came reports of men without blankets or overcoats, hospitals taxed beyond capacity and without heat or water, death lists mounting daily from contagious diseases, and morale approaching the verge of panic. State authorities begged Congress and the War Department to do something to mitigate the plight of their local boys.[36] Newspapers investigating several of the camps revealed a dark picture of suffering and distress, which excited editors ascribed to official incompetence, shortsightedness, and neglect.[37] For a while it appeared that the country was about to witness a repetition of the deplorable experiences of the Spanish-American War, only on a much vaster scale.

The Army camp situation came as a boon to the Military Affairs Committee, struggling manfully to build up a case against the administration. The public took little interest in the technical or political ramifications of the machine-gun controversy, but reaction to unnecessary suffering among the nation's heroes would be swift and strong. The Committee therefore dismissed General Crozier with a stern word of warning and on December 19 called upon Surgeon General William C. Gorgas to explain why the Army had permitted the cantonments to get into such dreadful shape. Gorgas did not deny that conditions were far from satisfactory or that there was much sickness from lack of proper clothing and poor sanitary facilities, but he emphatically cleared the Medical Corps of all responsibility for a situation over which it had no control.[38] If the plumbing was inadequate, if heating and water systems failed to function, and if the hospitals were terribly overcrowded as a result, the fault lay with the government, which had permitted contractors to install fixtures on a cost-plus basis with no guarantee of the results. Since the Committee flinched from challenging the medical profession and had bigger game in view than a few dishonest contractors, it quickly dismissed the surgeon general in favor of witnesses whose testimony might prove more satisfactory.

The grilling of the quartermaster general, Major General Henry A. Sharpe, revealed the existence of a disheartening amount of red tape and inefficiency in the bureau concerned with clothing the troops. Sharpe admitted that the Army had been extraordinarily slow in placing orders with manufacturers and in estimating future needs, so that scarcely a camp, especially in the South, had its proper quota of blankets, overcoats, and heavy clothing. His organization had also allowed materiel to accumulate in the depots while men froze in the camps. In extenuation of this sorry state of affairs, Sharpe pleaded that the cold weather had betrayed him and that the textile mills had been unable to adjust quickly enough to wartime requirements. Nevertheless, he was harshly criticized for failing to foresee the emergency and for not acting energetically to combat it.[39]

Late in December the Committee added a touch of melodrama to the proceedings by summoning the commanders of the camps reporting the greatest incidence of disease and suffering. The War Department was insisting that while a certain amount of seasonal contagious disease was to be expected in the crowded cantonments, the death rate was not abnormal; nor were conditions as alarming as depicted in the press or in hysterical letters from parents to their congressmen. The testimony of Major Generals William Wright, Edwin Greble, and John T. O'Ryan — commanding officers respectively of Camps Bowie, Sevier, and Wadsworth — qualified the Department's version in several respects. The generals attributed the sickness in their commands to lack of winter clothing and the great loss of life to inadequate hospital facilities.[40] No one in Washington had anticipated the severe outbreaks of measles, scarlet fever, meningitis, and diphtheria. The mortality rate had begun to drop with the arrival of warm clothing in mid-December. The Committee derived particular satisfaction from General Greble's statement that despite several written protests since September calling the War Department's attention to the dangers inherent in the lack of proper facilities, his communications had gone unanswered.[41]

These revelations made a profound stir in the press and produced a despondency bordering on panic in administration circles. Democratic as well as Republican newspapers blasted the War Department for the shocking state of the camps and inveighed bitterly against a system that sacrificed human lives to bureaucratic incompetence.[42] The President's secretary feared that no matter how the Democrats might try to explain it, the generals' testimony was making a very bad impression on the country. Particularly harmful was Greble's account of the high death rate at Camp Sevier, where several thousand men were crowded into a hospital built to accommodate eight hundred. Tumulty, worried lest the Committee make a "very radical report" on the basis of such evidence, urged Wilson to take "some action of a radical character" at once to head off this disastrous contingency.[43] The administration could do little at this juncture, however, except to sit tight, hope for the best, and let the storm blow itself out.

Republican leaders, jubilant at the way in which Baker was being convicted out of the mouths of his subordinates, decided to strike while the situation was hot. On December 21, Senator Boies Penrose informed the New York *Times* of his party's plans to use the investigation to start an early campaign for control of the next Congress. The issues, he said, were present in great numbers — the appalling state of affairs in the War Department, the bungling incompetence of Baker and his subordinates, the frightful conditions in the army camps, the failure to supply the troops in France with weapons, and the utter collapse of the government's efforts to regulate food, fuel, and transportation in the public interest. Moreover, politics of the worst sort had appeared in the conduct of the war, with Democrats named to all key posts regardless of their fitness, while Republicans were either ignored or relegated to minor jobs. His party intended, declared the Pennsylvania senator, to demand an accounting and carry the fight to the people in 1918 in order to save the nation from defeat in Europe and disaster at home.

The Penrose announcement aggravated the Democratic jitters and produced hurried consultations in high quarters. Frank I. Cobb of the New York *World* undertook to approach Chairman Willcox of the Republican National Committee, known to be one of the few Republican leaders not in sympathy with Old Guard plan to attack the President on the war issue. Willcox suggested that the best way to silence criticism of the Penrose variety was for Wilson to take a few prominent Republicans into his administration. It would enable loyal Republicans like Root, former President Taft, Hughes, and himself to thwart the schemes of the Lodge-Penrose-Roosevelt faction to reorganize the party preparatory to staging a grand assault on Wilson in 1918.[44] Cobb conveyed these views to the White House with the recommendation that it work more closely with the Willcox group. He wanted the President in particular to realize that the charge of partisanship in appointments to important war jobs, although a ''fake issue,'' was dangerous in the hands of men like Roosevelt, whose ''capacity for injury is very great.''[45]

Wilson deferred to Cobb's advice to the extent of appointing Willcox to the Railway Compensation Board, a quasi-judicial post of no great importance.[46] The gesture accomplished nothing, however, in the way of securing the beneficial results anticipated by the President's advisers. Instead of strengthening Willcox's hold upon the national chairmanship, it only accelerated his departure. A mere figurehead since the defeat of Hughes, his days as party chairman were already numbered. In a few weeks the Old Guard was to replace him with a henchman who had no qualms whatsoever about overthrowing Wilson and his cohorts by any means that came to hand.

The Democratic National Committee, hastily summoned to estimate the damage done to the cause, expressed great confidence in the party's ability to weather the storm. Nevertheless, it proceeded to warn the President that ''the Republican organization may become so partisan that it will be necessary to abandon a soft-glove policy, but if the opposition does pursue such a course, it will invite attack and we cannot be blamed for meeting it on its chosen ground.''[47]

If Wilson had ever for a moment considered pursuing a soft-glove policy, it was merely to conceal the iron fist within. The implacable nature of the political opposition, as demonstrated over the first months of the war, and the determination of his foes to encompass his total destruction made any other course seem futile if not suicidal. There was nothing of the martyr and too much of the old Presbyterian *gaudium certaminis* in his make-up for that. Except for one awe-inspiring outburst against Senator Chamberlain, he ignored his critics and rejected offers from friendly editors, like Arthur Brisbane of the Washington *Times*, to stage a counterattack against public nuisances like Colonel Roosevelt.[48] His tactics were to shift as the elections approached, but for the nonce his silence served to increase the rage and frustration of his enemies, to whom he gave additional offense at that time by taking over the railroads of the country and appointing his son-in-law McAdoo to run them.[49] Occasionally, to placate his worried advisers, who feared an unfavorable public reaction to charges of partisanship, the President might appoint some inoffensive Republican like Willcox to a minor war post, but he had no faith in the efficacy of such a practice. On the contrary, he stood grimly ready to meet his adversaries on their chosen ground with whatever weapons they might elect.

CHAPTER VI

"TANTRUMS ON THE HILL"

I

CONTRASTING SHARPLY with the gelidity of the holiday season was the hot air generated by the blistering attack on the War Department. Inflammatory headlines screamed such gruesome news as GENERALS TELL HOW RED TAPE FILLED GRAVES, while editors animadverted at length upon the evils of bureaucracy, demanded a drastic shake-up in the antiquated mechanism of the government, and called for the replacement of Baker and his subordinates with business executives who could get results.[1] Even the organs of orthodox Democratic opinion joined in the hue and cry for the ousting of Baker, Sharpe, Crozier, and the rest in the interests of winning the war. The Committee on Public Information strove manfully to drown out the chorus of criticism by issuing inspired effusions in defense of the Army's cantonment program. One such panegyric, which stated that "within ninety days after the driving of the first nail [June 15], the selected men entered the new homes that did not fail in a single comfort or convenience" and asserted that "no greater or more expert care was ever given than has been given to our soldiers and sailors," the President prudently suppressed as not consorting wholly with the facts brought to light by the investigation.[2]

The danger inherent in the situation impelled the administration to take a few hasty steps to improve conditions and allay criticism. A reorganization of top War Department personnel on December 20 relieved several of the officers under congressional fire and "promoted" them to a Supreme War Council, which was to act as an advisory body to the Secretary of War. The administration also recalled Major General George W.

Goethals from retirement to replace Sharpe as head of the Quartermaster Corps. Despite his removal under a cloud a few months earlier from the Emergency Fleet Corporation because of the impasse in the shipbuilding program, Goethals still commanded great public respect as the builder of the Panama Canal, and his appointment was beyond partisan cavil.

Gratifying as these changes were, they did not satisfy the Republican press, which sneered at the fluttering in administration quarters and charged Wilson with running to cover with a series of half measures designed to minimize the results of the investigation.[3] Baker's critics wanted him replaced by Elihu Root on the ground that while the Secretary of War might be satisfactory to the President, his party, and the South, he had lost the confidence of the rest of the country.[4] They contrasted Root's great service under President Roosevelt in creating a modern General Staff system with Baker's pacifist preference for leaving power in the hands of the bureau chiefs because it was a less militaristic type of organization. Republicans derided Baker's new War Council as a ''pacifist's substitute for a real General Staff'' and asserted that no genuine reform of Army methods could be achieved that did not elevate the military aspects of the profession over the civilian. Excited citizens, inspired by the clamor in the press, wrote their congressmen deploring the President's stubborn refusal to call upon the best talent of the country to help clean up the shocking mess in the War Department.[5]

When Congress reconvened on January 3, 1918, it faced a session of great political if not legislative significance. There was very little new legislation of importance on the calendar, most of the vital war measures having been enacted at the previous session. Much of this work, however, had been done in such a slipshod fashion that it had generated a host of problems needing immediate attention and adjustment. The entire business community was clamoring for clarification and revision of the war tax bill, the obscure and contradictory provisions of which required interpretation by a corps of Treasury experts. The confusion and uncertainty generated by the price control situation had stimulated a public demand for a uniform extension of the principle to all commodities in short supply. A modification of the draft law was necessary in order to obtain enough men to fill the ranks of the Army in view of the high exemption rate under the original law. Then there were other matters stemming from the shipbuilding program, the airplane program, the mobilization of manpower for industrial and agricultural purposes, and the need to coordinate the means of production and transportation to better effect than had been done in the first few feverish months of the war. On the way in which Congress handled these problems, its members would be judged to a large extent in the elections that fall.

II

NO OTHER PROBLEM at the moment gripped the public interest with the force of the battle over the War Department, and the country anxiously awaited the outcome. Over the New Year, Wilson's congressional enemies had contrived two measures to force the issue with him. One, presented by McKellar of Tennessee, called for a reorganization of the Council of National Defense in order to correct the slipshod methods of awarding war contracts and to end the favoritism shown to firms with representatives on the civilian advisory committees. The other, sponsored by Chamberlain in the Senate and William P. Borland in the House, proposed to create a new Cabinet post which would take over all the procurement functions of the War and Navy Departments for the duration of the war and one year afterwards. The Secretary of Munitions would displace Baker and Daniels from all but the purely military aspects of their duties.[6] Had Congress been able to think of some way short of impeachment, it would have cheerfully eliminated both men entirely from the picture.

Theoretically, the unification of the supply functions of all the armed forces in a single agency had much to recommend it in view of the great amount of waste and duplication of effort to date. The idea found considerable support in administration circles anxious to avoid further trouble with the Senate. Colonel House felt that the President could "easily reorganize that part

of the Government concerned with the conduct of the war" and
deplored Wilson's obstinacy about administrative affairs.[7] Convinced that the replacement of Baker had become imperative,
House discussed the matter with several administration leaders,
including Vance McCormick.[8] No one presumed, however, to
press these views upon the President, who did not need the
urging of other advisers to stand firm against what Tumulty
called "the tantrums on the Hill." Through his secretary Wilson curtly informed the newspaper correspondents that he regarded the matter "as nothing more nor less than a renewal of
the perpetual effort of the Republicans to force representation
in the administration."[9]

Business circles warmly approved the Chamberlain plan as
a praiseworthy attempt to bring order out of chaos in the war
agencies.[10] In Republican eyes, the fact that its sponsor was a
prominent Democratic senator attested to its non-partisan character and would smooth the way for the President to appoint
a man like Roosevelt to the new Cabinet post, thus injecting the
energy and vigor hitherto lacking in the war preparations. Most
newspapers, however, were willing to settle for a less controversial figure and urged the appointment of a prominent industrial-
ist like Daniel Willard or Edward R. Stettinius, in whose ability
to get things done the country was said to have great confidence.
The Democratic press, which was almost as unrestrained in its
criticism of Baker, agreed that changes in the War Department
were necessary but felt that expanding the Cabinet would not
necessarily improve the efficiency of operations. The journalistic
consensus on the chances of the Chamberlain bill indicated
passage in the Senate by about the same margin as accorded
the Roosevelt amendment and the Weeks resolution.[11]

Wilson, faced with the gravest challenge yet to his control
of the war effort, had to move swiftly to avert the impending
catastrophe. In view of the bad impression made by the Army
cantonment scandals, public opinion might not rally as readily
behind him as in previous clashes with Congress. On the evening
of January 10, Wilson summoned the two principal Democratic
supporters of the reorganization measure, Senators Chamberlain
and Hitchcock, to the White House and tried to persuade them

to drop the scheme. Not only would it seriously dislocate the activities of the Navy Department, he said, but it would also accomplish nothing substantial with respect to the War Department. As for the French and British experience with separate munitions ministries, of which the newspapers made so much, Wilson assured his visitors that he had "intimate information" from abroad indicating that these agencies had not fulfilled the expectations of their advocates. In conclusion the President warned that the Senate plan not only would disappoint the country in its results but would embarrass the "processes of coordination" on which he had spent a good deal of time and pains and which were rapidly yielding results.[12]

Chamberlain and Hitchcock left the White House that evening quite unimpressed by the President's arguments. Neither senator had ever been an admirer of Wilson, but only Hitchcock had actively identified himself with the anti-administration faction of the party. Vain, opinionated, and aloof in manner, the Nebraskan was a man of considerable inherited wealth and culture, who prided himself on a scholarly and well-groomed appearance rather unusual in a prairie statesman of that string-tie and baggy-pants era. European education and travel had given Hitchcock a warm attachment for the German way of life, so much so that during the neutrality controversy he had used his newspaper, the Omaha *World-Herald,* to support the Central Powers and oppose preparedness. As one of the "willful eleven," his filibuster of the armed-ship bill had incurred the wrath of Wilson, while his pacifism and Germanophilia made him anathema to the patriots. In turn, the senator had no particular reason to like the administration, which had consistently supported his bitter enemy, William Jennings Bryan, in the perennial struggle for control of the Democratic party in Nebraska.[13] Consequently, the government reorganization scheme again found him in the forefront of the disturbers of Democratic unity, and Wilson disliked him thoroughly.[14]

Chamberlain's split with the administration came on entirely antithetical grounds. In the earlier battles over the war program he had rendered Wilson good service, but on preparedness matters he stood much closer to Roosevelt, whose views on compul-

sory military training he had championed for some years. In
general appearance the short, stocky senator, with his pince-nez
and his straggly white moustache, somewhat resembled the
Rough Rider; and in pugnacity he was not far behind, as events
were soon to show. In matters of grand strategy he much preferred the Lloyd George-Roosevelt concept of turning the German flank through the Balkans to the General Staff plan of
throwing American troops in repeated bloody assaults against
the hitherto impregnable German western front.[15] The summary
rejection of these views by the Secretary of War on the advice
of the chief of staff greatly irritated Chamberlain, already
skeptical of the professional competence of both men. Anxiety
over the unfavorable course of the war and suspicion of War
Department mismanagement were aggravated by ill health,
which was to hospitalize him a few weeks later.[16] All this put
the chairman of the Military Affairs Committee in an unamiable
mood and made him receptive to Republican suggestions for
sweeping changes at the top, regardless of the opposition of the
President or the disapproval of his party.

The climax of the Senate investigation came with the three-
day grilling of the Secretary of War by the Chamberlain committee on January 10-12. A gifted platform speaker much admired for his rhetorical skill, the diminutive Baker proved a
very able witness in his own and the administration's cause.
Smoking big cigars and entirely at ease in the presence of his
hostile inquisitors, the Secretary refused to be flustered by the
volley of charges and accusations which continually interrupted
his testimony.[17] His nimbleness in parrying the sharpest thrusts
of such formidable cross-examiners as Weeks, Wadsworth,
Hitchcock, and Chamberlain nonplused his enemies and impressed the country at large. Abandoning the evasive tactics
which had hitherto characterized his Department's public relations, the Secretary presented a barrage of facts and figures to
show the satisfactory state of the Army's preparations. Although
frankly admitting that there had been inevitable blunders and
delays, Baker stoutly denied that these mistakes had any appreciable bearing on the Army's fitness for field operations in
France. The Committee listened skeptically to his glowing ac-

count of the way in which the Army had been raised from a handful of regulars to an effective fighting force of 1,500,000 men. Even harder to believe were his figures showing that the death rate from disease was lower among the soldiers than among civilians. Particularly galling to the Republican members were his frequent references for comparative purposes to the Spanish-American War, when the death rate in the camps had been 20 per thousand men, compared to 7.5 per thousand in the 1917 cantonments.[18]

Unable to get the Secretary of War to attach any significance to the evidence collected by the Military Affairs Committee, the senators switched their attack to the administration's refusal to accept a Munitions Department. They accused Wilson of underhanded tactics in thwarting the will of the people by putting pressure on the Democratic members of the House Military Affairs Committee to prevent the Chamberlain-Borland bill from reaching the floor. Baker held to the opinion, however, that a Secretary of Munitions would be nothing less than a War Minister in view of the powers Congress wanted to confer upon him. To his argument that the creation of a War Council had accomplished all the objectives sought by Congress, the Republicans retorted that merely kicking a few superannuated bureau chiefs upstairs did not solve the problem, which required an entirely different approach.[19]

Throughout the ordeal the Secretary's unruffled composure and courteous but rather offhand manner irritated his enemies, who charged him with assuming an air of cocky complacency that was entirely out of place in view of the gravity of the occasion. Republican newspapers, although grudgingly conceding that Baker was too quick-witted for many of the senators, who had not thought things out very clearly, disliked the "lawyer-like adroitness" with which he bolstered up a dubious case.[20] Senator Weeks accused him of trying to lull the country into a feeling of false security with misleading statements about the War Department's achievements and reforms.[21] The Committee itself, at the conclusion of Baker's testimony, voiced the opinion that the Secretary of War had put it and the country off with a series of flashy but unreliable figures and paper reforms which should deceive no one. Hence the Senate had to continue the investigation until the whole truth stood starkly revealed.[22]

The Democratic press accepted Baker's data and accorded full, if belated, praise to his achievements.[23] The anti-Baker animus of the Committee it ascribed to the Republican desire to secure a bigger share in the direction of the war by foisting a coalition Cabinet upon the President. Republican newspapers, on the other hand, went to great lengths to discredit Baker's testimony in the eyes of the public. One of the party's journalistic pundits, William Hard, in a widely circulated article entitled "Why the Blame is Baker's," refuted in detail the facts and figures cited by the Secretary with material derived chiefly from his contacts with Lodge and Roosevelt. Former President William H. Taft, in his syndicated column in the Philadelphia *Public Ledger,* informed his readers that they had not been told the truth. Taft had warm praise for the sincere patriotism of the Committee members, but as for Baker, "it is not unjust to the Secretary to say that, as given, his evidence did not contribute greatly to the edification of either the committee or the public."[24]

III

AT MIDNIGHT on January 16–17 the President's secretary was tumbled out of his warm bed and informed of an order from the Fuel Administration closing down all factories east of the Mississippi River for a week, except for a few munitions plants, after which all non-essential industry was to go on a five-day week until March 25.[25] No official explanation accompanied this astonishing edict, and Tumulty rightly feared for the consequences upon public morale, already shaken by other developments. The purpose, as the Fuel Administration belatedly made clear, was to break the coal blockade at eastern seaports, where hundreds of ships were immobilized by empty bunkers. In New York alone, eighteen British liners loaded with war material and in need of thirty thousand tons of coal were unable to depart, while eighty American or other vessels were in a similar plight.[26] Beset by demands to do something about the situation, the harried Fuel Administration had decided to give priority to coal shipments from the mines to the ports in order to clear them of their accumulated freight.

The order fell like a thunderbolt into the midst of the controversy over governmental efficiency, and the reaction was violently unfavorable. "Bedlam broke loose," observed Colonel House. "I have never seen such a storm of protest."[27] Angry businessmen flooded Washington with protests against Garfield's "edict of idleness." Labor also objected on the ground that few factories intended to pay their workers during the enforced layoff, and the loss in wages attributable to the administration's alleged blunder would be considerable. The New York *World* added Garfield to the list of officials whom Wilson should get rid of in the interests of greater war efficiency. His order, the *World* maintained, was a confession of failure, the first American defeat of the war, and Garfield's usefulness to the nation was over, however much the President might still trust in him.[28] Other papers were equally bitter, and all agreed that a schoolboy would have shown better judgment than to close down industry when only more work could win the war.[29]

Appeals to reverse the Garfield edict poured in upon Congress, where few Democrats could be found to say anything in defense of the Fuel Administrator. Senator Hitchcock offered a resolution asking the President to delay enforcement of the order for five days in order to give the Senate time to investigate the matter. After a day of angry debate, devoted mostly to a denunciation of Wilson and his advisers, the resolution was adopted 50 to 19, with the Republicans lining up 28 to 3 and the Democrats divided 22 to 16 in its favor. A similar effort in the House failed when an Indiana Democrat refused the unanimous consent required for its consideration. Wilson ignored the Senate's request and sent instead a letter explaining the nature of the crisis and giving his reasons for approving Garfield's action. The Senate did not respond graciously to Wilson's flouting of its investigative services, but there was little it could do beyond animadvert upon the President's inability to get the best out of his people in an emergency.

Fortunately, the combined efforts of the Railroad and Fuel Administrations quickly effected an improvement in the situation.[30] Within a week nearly a million tons of ocean shipping had been bunkered and the vessels sent on their way to Europe.[31] Better cooperation from the weather made it possible to unblock terminals and clear railroad sidings, so that coal also began to move into the cities, where something like normal conditions of warmth and comfort were gradually restored. Business and industry did not take kindly to "heatless Mondays" and the five-day week, however, and the "Garfield blunder" caused much grumbling. Colonel House thought it would increase the clamor for changing the organization of the government. "Men of every shade of opinion," he noted, "condemn the organization as it now exists. The President and Secretary Baker seem to be the only ones who think the organization is as it should be."[32]

House's fears appeared well-founded when, two days after the issuance of the Garfield order, the Military Affairs Committee reported favorably on another Chamberlain bill. The plan had undergone considerable revision since the announcement with regard to the earlier measure. The new bill provided for the establishment of a War Cabinet or Council of "three distinguished citizens of demonstrated ability" to function independently of the regular Cabinet but directly under the President, with almost unlimited jurisdiction over plans and policies, to insure the most vigorous prosecution of the war. It was to supervise, coordinate, direct and control the activities of all executive departments, officials, and agencies and to settle all disputes arising among them.[33] The Munitions Director now became a subordinate along with the ordinary Cabinet members, since such an official in a Democratic Cabinet completely amenable to a strong-willed President would have great difficulty in serving the purposes the Senate Committee had in mind. The proposal was retained, apparently, as a possible bargaining point with the White House, since Wilson could hardly be expected to buy the other idea under any circumstances.

There was remarkably little press opposition to this new "instrumentality," which relegated the heads of the War and Navy Departments to watching over military operations alone, thus shelving Baker and Daniels and effectively taking personal direction of the war effort out of the President's hands. Republican newspapers hailed the Chamberlain bill as the only means of cutting the Gordian knot of bureaucratic red tape in which the administration had got itself entangled. Even the independent, pro-Wilson New York *Times* declared it essential for the United States to profit from the mistakes of the Allies and, like them, set up a super-government for the duration of the war.[34] The Boston *Evening Transcript* assured its readers that the bill did not infringe on the war powers of the President but represented "an honest, straightforward and sincere effort on the part of senators who have forgotten their political affiliations in the fervor of their patriotism."[35]

To Wilson the bill represented disaster. It went far beyond anything discussed earlier with Hitchcock and Chamberlain, and he rallied his forces for a last-ditch fight. Summoning several loyal administration senators to the White House, he urged them to exert every effort to defeat the scheme. All took a gloomy view of the situation, however, because of the number of disgruntled Democrats willing for one reason or another to cooperate with the Republicans in embarrassing the Executive. Prospects in the House brightened somewhat after Chairman Hubert Dent of the Military Affairs Committee publicly announced that he did not favor a War Cabinet because greater concentration of power could be obtained within existing agencies.[36] Speaker Champ Clark told Wilson privately that he was "dead against the Chamberlain bills" and would render any service to defeat them. In thanking the Speaker for his cooperation, which was not always forthcoming in an emergency, the President remarked, "It is astonishing to me what partisanship and the spirit of criticism is capable of at a time when what we need above all things is coöperation and helpfulness."[37]

Had the President been willing to sacrifice his unpopular Secretary of War to the clamor of his critics, or had Senator Chamberlain been less stubbornly insistent that Baker must go, the country would have been spared the painful spectacle that followed the appearance of the War Cabinet bill in the Senate on January 19. Both men were native southerners with strong wills and quick tempers, whose head-on collision produced a display of verbal fireworks almost without parallel in the political annals of the republic. Seldom has an American statesman made a more devastating attack upon his government under such critical circumstances; certainly no President since Andrew Johnson has so forcefully castigated an opponent in reply. This heated, if not intemperate, exchange of views startled the public, delighted the enemies of the administration, and dismayed the friends of Democratic unity, already seriously concerned for the fate of the party in the forthcoming congressional elections.[38]

CHAPTER VII

THE BADGERING OF BAKER

I

CHAMBERLAIN's New York speech before a joint meeting of two super-patriotic groups, the National Security League and the American Defense Society, on January 19 created a sensation, the reverberations of which echoed right down to election day. Headlines across the country blazoned his charges that the war effort had broken down completely, that the War Department had failed utterly in the greatest crisis in the nation's history, and that only "heroic measures" could retrieve the desperate situation facing the Allied cause as a result of egregious blundering by American officials. Chamberlain insisted that he spoke not as a Democrat but as an American citizen, motivated by the same patriotic concern as Roosevelt, Root, and all other loyal Republicans concerned solely with the speedy defeat of Germany and the restoration of a durable world peace. The "heroic measures" to which he referred were his proposals for a Munitions Director and a War Cabinet. Both, he hastened to emphasize, were not administration measures but American measures, approved and endorsed by Republicans and Democrats alike.[1]

The reaction to the speech was prompt and violent. Republican newspapers highlighted the senator's remarks as eminently wise, patriotic, timely, and necessary under the circumstances; but the Democratic press angrily read him out of the party. Frank Cobb in the New York *World* assailed Chamberlain for slandering the administration before a partisan audience composed of professional patriots and war profiteers, and reminded him that the blundering and confusion in Congress were tenfold those in any other branch of the government.[2] Arthur Brisbane, who took up the editorial cudgels for Wilson in the Washington

Times, ascribed the Chamberlain scheme to Republican resentment at Wilson's refusal to take prominent Wall Street bankers into partnership with the government so that the rich might more easily escape paying for the war. Privately Brisbane promised the President to continue to enlighten the public about the true character of Republican patriotism, in which the dollar sign predominated above all other considerations.[3] Although this might be good long-range policy around which to rally the dejected party, Wilson at the moment was too angry to consider anything but a forthright, blistering reply to his senatorial critic.

While Wilson grimly pondered his riposte, Colonel Roosevelt plunged headlong into the fray. His dramatic appearance in Washington at that crucial moment gave the impression, which he did nothing to dispel, that he had come to take command of the anti-administration forces in the final showdown. The conviction that the Senate revelations had at last shaken the public out of its torpor and thrown his adversaries into confusion had put the Rough Rider in fine fettle. Hurrying off to the Capitol to confer with congressional supporters of the War Cabinet bill, he exuberantly informed one of the interviewing reporters that he was "going after the man in the White House."[4] Success in this undertaking would put him close to the helm of government for the rest of the war and compensate to some extent for the frustration of his military ambitions.[5] Over the next three days he continued to confer with Republican leaders at the home of the Longworths.[6]

Chamberlain's speech and Roosevelt's arrival set off a tremendous explosion on Capitol Hill.[7] Stone of Missouri held the Senate spellbound with a blistering, three-hour attack on Republican efforts to sabotage the administration's war program. He pilloried Roosevelt as a knave and a traitor, engaged with his party in a nasty plot to turn the alleged blunders of the President into political capital for the coming campaign. Stone's outburst stirred a spate of angry recrimination from the Republican side, whence Lodge vigorously defended the purity of Roosevelt's motives and extolled Republican loyalty to the war effort. Senator Penrose maintained that the war had not automatically suspended the right to criticize the administration, and he ridiculed the Democratic assumption of a "divine appointment" upon Wilson's head to lead the nation to victory. The debate concluded with William F. Kirby of Arkansas, a pacifist by principle, pouring oil on the troubled waters and getting the Senate back to the business of the day.

II

STONE's diatribe paled beside Wilson's pungent epistolary reply that same day to Senator Chamberlain's strictures. Pointedly ignoring Roosevelt, the President proceeded to demolish the senator's case with a cold ferocity that startled friend and foe alike. Without actually calling the senator a liar, Wilson skirted the edge of protocol by accusing him of an "astonishing and absolutely unjustifiable distortion of the truth" and attributing his "absurd statements" of conditions in the War Department to "total ignorance." The Senate investigation Wilson contemptuously dismissed as a waste of everybody's time, particularly the time of government officials called from important duties to testify about their departments. Nothing helpful, he said, could come out of activities that merely contributed to confusion and misunderstanding. As for Chamberlain's reorganization proposals, they were totally unnecessary inasmuch as the administration had already taken effective measures to consolidate the various wartime functions of the government. The President closed his philippic with a ringing tribute to his Secretary of War, an able and loyal public servant without whose services the country and the administration would have been much the poorer.[8]

It was good, strong fighting talk and made a deep impression. Parts of the epistle to Chamberlain were disingenuous; it was questionable how far or quickly the War Department could have been shaken out of its normal lethargy but for the exposure of its archaic methods and the ensuing controversy over the matter. If Wilson's critics had overstated their case, the President had gone further in the opposite direction than the facts warranted. Nevertheless, Wilson's sweeping denial of grave blunders, his aggressive denunciation of congressional tactics, and his vigorous endorsement of Baker sounded convincing to the average citizen, who was not well enough informed to draw his own conclusions and unless blinded by partisanship was still inclined to give the President the benefit of the doubt. If some of the premises were weak, the spirit and timing of the letter were extraordinarily effective, as even the Republican press admitted. Though critical of Wilson for losing his temper and flaring up in anger against honest and sincere efforts to win the war, the anti-administration organs glumly admitted that the war would be fought out willy-nilly along Democratic lines — to what conclusion no one could anticipate.[9]

The next evening a somewhat chastened group gathered at a dinner given by the Longworths for their distinguished relative and guest. Assembled were most of the leading lights of the radical, or anti-administration, wing of the party, including Simeon D. Fess of Ohio, Lenroot of Wisconsin, Frederick Gillett of Massachusetts, and McCormick of Illinois from the House. Among the senators were Wadsworth and William M. Calder of New York, Weeks and Lodge of Massachusetts, Frank B. Brandegee of Connecticut, Hiram W. Johnson of California, and other stalwarts in the fight against Wilson. Their patience, observed one of the guests, ''is well nigh coming to an end with a policy that the administration has continued so long, of utter exclusiveness, secrecy, and intolerance of congressional participation or anything else. The truth is that President Wilson has had his own way so long about everything that he is intolerant of anybody's else opinion on anything, as witness his performance with Chamberlain.''[10]

Not everyone present, however, thought it good politics to challenge Wilson on the results of the Senate investigation alone. Several wanted to defer the major attack until after the war, when nobody's motives would be open to question.[11] The Rough Rider swept all such considerations brusquely aside as the counsel of timidity. He vehemently urged the need for ''constructive criticism,'' to which no patriot interested in a speedy victory could take exception. To default the 1918 elections, he said, would give the Democrats such power and prestige as to destroy

Republican prospects for years to come. Although the majority concurred, all but the most optimistic realized that so far the radical proposals had attracted disappointingly little public support, without which there was no coming to grips with the foe in the White House.

Caution, therefore, was the keynote of the Republican House caucus held the next day to consider the Chamberlain proposals. Although the caucus endorsed the bill to create a Munitions Director with Cabinet rank by a 75 to 19 vote, less than half the party membership was present, and no action was taken on the War Cabinet measure. The Roosevelt, or radical, faction also failed to prevent the re-election of the isolationist Frank P. Woods of Iowa as chairman of the congressional campaign committee. The radicals angrily contended that Woods's poor voting record on preparedness legislation would preclude any kind of offensive against Wilson that fall on the war issues. The caucus ignored these objections, however, and adjourned after adopting a mild resolution to the effect that while no partisanship was involved in the war, it was the solemn duty of the party to suggest remedies for the bad conditions prevalent in the war effort.[12]

Another setback to radical hopes was Senator Borah's refusal to attend the Senate caucus that week to discuss the War Cabinet bill. Instead, he angered and dismayed the Roosevelt faction by making speeches in New York and Baltimore in defense of the President's constitutional position.[13] Senator Warren of Wyoming, the ranking Republican on the Military Affairs Committee, also disapproved of the aggressive attitude of his colleagues, which he attributed to the machinations of Wood and Roosevelt, and he kept the White House informed on developments within his Committee.[14] These defections made it less certain that sufficient votes could be mustered behind the Chamberlain proposals in view of the reluctance of a few other Republican senators, like LeBaron Colt and Knute Nelson, to agree that a change in the form of government was the proper solution to the problem.[15]

Nevertheless, the controversy raged on, with neither side prepared to yield. When the Senate convened on January 24, after a three-day recess to allow tempers to cool, Chamberlain delivered a stirring rebuttal of the President's animadversions upon his intelligence and veracity. A packed gallery cheered his assertion that he would resign from office before consenting to become a rubber stamp and refrain from all criticism of the conduct of the war. To a rehash of his previous charges, the senator added a new touch by holding Baker directly responsible for camp deaths from disease and exposure. Amid tears and sobs from the onlookers, Chamberlain read into the record letters from heartbroken parents recounting the sufferings of their boys from want of proper clothing and medical attention.[16]

The party leadership, feeling it profitless to continue the controversy on a personal level, deputed Senator Kirby to make a ten-minute general denial on behalf of Baker and the War Department. The Democratic press, however, considered Chamberlain's account of camp deaths the worst kind of demagoguery and held his conduct to be as reckless and unscrupulous as that of his ally Colonel Roosevelt.[17] Nevertheless, the gravity of Chamberlain's latest indictment impelled Baker to appear before the Senate Committee on January 28 to answer his accuser. In a carefully prepared statement the Secretary reviewed the accomplishments of his Department in stamping out vice and intemperance in the camp areas, cited health statistics to prove that soldiers were better off than civilians, and scored his Republican critics by pointing out that the camp sites located in the unhealthiest spots and subject to the greatest controversy had been chosen by Major General Leonard Wood.[18]

In the meantime Colonel Roosevelt, before returning to Oyster Bay, paid his respects to Senator Stone in a speech at the National Press Club on January 24. After recalling the senator's former pro-German sympathies and violent opposition to the war, Roosevelt defended the Chamberlain proposals, extolled the courage of the men who dared to tell the truth about the administration, and castigated the ''college professor'' in the White House for trying to fight the war single-handed with a few incompetent favorites.[19] While his remarks received the usual oracular treatment in the Republican press, Democratic newspapers angrily counseled the Rough Rider not to start his 1920 presidential campaign in Washington, where his criticism of the administration only added to the general turmoil and confusion in Congress, which was in danger of running completely amok from political pressure and excitement.[20]

III

THE WAR of words in Washington might have gone on indefinitely, to the further detriment of public confidence in the government, had not the administration made a few conciliatory gestures toward meeting the objections of its critics. On January 14 the procurement functions of the War Department were reorganized: the five purchasing divisions were coordinated into a single unit and placed under a capable staff officer. At the same time, the purchasing agencies of the Army, the Navy, the Shipping Board, and the various Allied missions were ordered to clear through the Council of National Defense in order to eliminate competition and duplication.[21] The appointment on January 25 of Edward R. Stettinius as surveyor general of all Army purchases mollified the advocates of a consolidated Army supply program administered by a centralized authority. Publicly the appointment was hailed as the administration's answer to the demand for a Director of Munitions, except that the position did not carry Cabinet rank. Otherwise, the New York banker fitted all the Republican specifications for a wartime executive of national reputation, wide business experience, and impressive connections in financial and industrial circles. Nevertheless, skeptics doubted that Wilson would confer much actual authority upon a Morgan partner. The Republicans contemptuously dismissed the new post as a sham to mislead the public about the intent of Wilson and Baker to retain their personal control over all phases of the war effort.[22]

These developments only partially dispelled the gloom in Democratic circles. Colonel House, among others, continued to be greatly depressed by what he considered an unjustifiable optimism on the part of Wilson and Baker that all was going well. At a White House luncheon on January 27 he noted with disapproval the good mood of the President, who appeared quite unworried by the attack on his management of the war.[23] Even a visit from Stettinius to explain the improvements in the War

Department failed to shake House's distrust of Baker. The Secretary, he felt, deceived himself by looking on criticism of his activities as a "trumped up affair by the republicans to make capital in the next congressional campaign" and remained blind to the fact that everyone had lost confidence in him.[24] The administration, however, was not as insensitive to the threat as House feared. On the political front it proceeded to develop a counterstroke calculated to reassure its friends, put its critics on the defensive, and take the pressure off the harried executive departments of the government.

This took the form of a bill giving the President authority to reorganize the government by shifting or consolidating or abolishing at his discretion the functions of the various agencies.[25] On February 1, Wilson summoned a group of Democratic senators to the White House to explain the plan and urge its substitution in place of the Chamberlain scheme. Several of his callers objected to the wide power Wilson wished to confer upon himself and doubted that his request for authority to create or abolish agencies or merge them without specific reference to Congress in each instance would be acceptable to that body. Finally, with some reluctance, Overman of North Carolina consented to sponsor the measure, which was called up for consideration on February 7.

The Republican senatorial caucus agreed to oppose the bill unconditionally as a demand upon Congress to abdicate its powers. Smoot of Utah declared the scheme would make Wilson a king in everything but name, while the party press denounced it as savoring of presidential arrogance and disdain for the constitutional system. The opposition managed to bottle it up in the Judiciary Committee for several weeks until Senator Borah and two other Republicans voted with just enough Democrats to report it out. For this service Borah was warmly thanked by both Overman and the President,[26] but the Senate Minority Leader, Gallinger of New Hampshire, bitterly reproached his colleagues Nelson of Minnesota and Colt of Rhode Island for making possible the ultimate passage of the measure in somewhat amended form. "We have a mighty poor Republican outfit at present in the Senate," the old man grumbled, "and it disheartens me when I stop to think of it.''[27] Wilson employed the act only sparingly to effect a few minor changes, but it achieved its original purpose of dividing the attention of his enemies.

Undaunted by administration efforts to sidetrack the War Cabinet bill, its sponsors continued to force the issue, if only to keep the controversy alive. On February 4 Senator Hitchcock opened a ten-day debate on the measure with a furious diatribe against Wilson and Baker. The President, he said, kept court like a king surrounded by a little group of favorites who withheld vital information from him. Baker, on the other hand, shamelessly misled the public with a display of absurd optimism concerning the number of troops the Army could get to France to meet the anticipated spring offensive of the Germans.[28] Hitchcock's most telling thrust was the accusation, widely repeated at the time, that the Secretary of War could not think correctly in terms of ships and men but only abstractly, in terms of principles and theories; hence no reliance could be placed upon any facts or figures he might produce.[29] Baker in his previous appearance on January 28 had shown the Committee confidential War Department figures on the amount of shipping needed and available to transport an army to France and maintain it there. The senators now challenged that report as another figment of the Secretary's imagination. In their opinion, neither the United States nor the Allies possessed enough ocean tonnage to get an army to the front in time to exert a decisive influence on the course of the war. This argument seemed particularly convincing in view of the almost complete paralysis that appeared to have overtaken the government's shipbuilding program and the Navy's efforts to cope with the devastating German submarine campaign in the North Atlantic.

The administration could not ignore the depressing effect of all this upon public morale. The Democratic press might call Hitchcock a Copperhead and read him out of the party, but more assurance was needed of the government's ability to cope with the crisis. Consequently on February 6, in his third appearance on Capitol Hill, Baker categorically refuted the charge that even with the use of Allied shipping, not enough men could reach France to meet the dreaded German drive. He was savagely heckled by Wadsworth and Weeks, ably assisted by Hitchcock and Chamberlain, who treated his troop transport figures with skepticism if not outright disbelief. A long and heated argument ensued over the number of tons of shipping required to maintain abroad an army of a million men. Baker insisted it could be done by allowing two tons per soldier, but his critics angrily claimed that at least twice that amount was needed. Nevertheless, Baker's air of confident assurance weighed heavily in favor of the War Department's estimates, while the rancorous attitude of his questioners strengthened the impression that they were talking for the record rather than from any profound knowledge of the subject. Even the New York *Times,* no admirer of Baker, called the latest hearing a waste of time, without direction and without purpose, and on February 8 suggested that "everybody get back to work."

Despite the badgering of Baker by the Military Affairs Committee and the hue and cry against him in the Republican press, it was patent that the War Cabinet issue was becoming moribund. An informal poll of the Senate late in January indicated only 27 senators in favor and 33 against the proposal, 10 Democrats having switched their support to the President after his blast at Chamberlain.[30] Unrelenting pressure from the White House had also brought into line a few unfriendly Democrats like Hoke Smith of Georgia, whose friends convinced him that the plot against Wilson was work of northern financial interests hard hit by the rising price of raw cotton and anxious to establish Republican control over the war effort in order to bring that commodity under governmental regulation.[31] Even the obstreperous Reed of Missouri opposed the measure, but on constitutional grounds and not out of affection for the President.

Especially discouraging to the Republican "plotters" was the failure of public opinion to crystallize against the administration on the strength of the evidence turned up by the Senate inquiry. On the contrary, such a volume of letters and telegrams urging Congress to stand by the President and get on with the war descended upon Capitol Hill as to give Wilson's critics pause to reconsider. The popular outcry forced Senator Lodge to admit ruefully to one of his Beacon Hill cronies, ''We should run the risk of defeating our own ends if we made the attacks on Wilson we all want to make.''[32] An astute politician, Lodge preferred to await a more opportune time to renew the struggle rather than see his party fall into the pit it had dug for its adversary.

IV

As a consequence of dwindling support and public disapprobation, the War Cabinet bill never came to a vote. The second session of the Sixty-fifth Congress had lasted two months and produced no major legislation despite ever-darkening war clouds over the European front. There were pointed suggestions in the press that a few speechless days on Capitol Hill would contribute as much to winning the war as the heatless days decreed by the Fuel Administration. Moreover, much of the zest went out of the anti-Wilson drive when a serious illness temporarily inactivated Colonel Roosevelt and hospitalized him on February 7. A similar misfortune befell Senator Chamberlain about this time. The great offensive petered out after February 15 when Senator Weeks delivered a Parthian shot at the President for injecting politics into the Senate inquiry and besmirching Republican motives. His party's sole concern, said Weeks, was to expedite the progress of war preparations, which were badly handicapped by the incompetence of a pacifist Secretary of War.[33] Congress thereupon turned reluctantly from its inquisitorial activities to the task of disposing of the accumulated business on the calendar.

Failure of their plans to encompass the destruction of Wilson and Baker was a bitter disappointment to the Republican backers of the inquiry. Senator Lodge considered it ''pretty sickening'' inasmuch as the Military Affairs Committee had given the public ''enough information to defeat a dozen Administrations.''[34] The senator blamed the lukewarm public reaction on the press, which he accused of remaining silent from fear of being branded pro-German for daring to criticize the administration. This was sheer nonsense, of course, since the press of both parties all over the country gave full coverage to the controversy.[35] If Democratic journals were less biased in presenting the evidence, very few of them expressed any confidence in Baker or rallied to his defense until Wilson had made a personal issue of the matter with Chamberlain. Lodge derived some consolation from the fact that Wilson had been driven to make a few beneficial changes in the War Department, and he was comforted by the approval of his Bay State admirers for his part in the attack on the President. Only Brooks Adams among the senator's circle of Brahmin acquaintances withheld fulsome praise. Adams returned the copy of the senator's January 21 speech defending Roosevelt's patriotism with the frosty observation that both Lodge and Roosevelt would be better employed in helping the government instead of hindering its efforts to prevail over Germany.[36]

No man was more disgruntled than Roosevelt with the way the investigation had fizzled out, leaving the impression that the administration had been vindicated. The Military Affairs Committee, he felt, had bungled matters by not handling Baker ''a little more roughly.'' As a consequence, the country was left with a general feeling that the Secretary had made a pretty good showing, whereas all he did was make golden promises regarding the future and lie about the present and omit all reference to the War Department's past failures.[37] He was convinced that ''the frightful mishandling of the machine gun situation alone ought to have meant the impeachment not merely of the Secretary of War but of the President,'' and he drew little consolation from the fact that several ''fuddled elderly fools'' of the Regular Army had been forced to vacate their swivel-chair jobs in the War Department.[38] Particularly annoying to the Colonel was the open-mouthed admiration of the British for Wilson and his achievements, which made it difficult for patriotic Americans to combat the administration's shortcomings. To an English friend he complained that American newspapers, by reprinting long excerpts from the British press extolling Wilson's wonderful work, put Roosevelt and his senatorial allies in the position before the public of not knowing what they were talking about.[39]

Nevertheless, if the investigation failed to accomplish what the radicals had hoped, it produced a number of results for which they had been clamoring. For one thing, the press censorship was considerably relaxed and better relations established thereby between the public and the War Department. Excessive secrecy about non-essentials had been responsible for much of the disagreeable impact and sensational flavor of the Senate Committee revelations. Furthermore, the reorganization of certain War Department functions made for greater expedition and smoother operation in an agency notoriously dilatory in many ways. The War Industries Board underwent a somewhat similar reorganization at this time in an effort to eliminate the violent competition among private firms for war contracts, which seriously hindered the adjustment of industrial production to wartime needs.[40] The credit for all these improvements was modestly assumed by Colonel Roosevelt. "It is my honest belief," he wrote, "that my criticisms and attacks have represented almost the sole reason why we have done anything at all, and that if I had not been here we would not have had troops on the other side and would not have even begun a shipbuilding programme — in other words, that Wilson has only been hectored into any kind of activity at all by his fear of the effect I was gradually producing."[41]

There was some danger at this stage that Roosevelt, in the intensity of his loathing for Wilson, might run the party off the rails. It was well enough for the Rough Rider, with his immense prestige and popularity to protect him, to indulge in unbridled criticism of the President, but for the rank and file to follow such a course was to invite political disaster.[42] The Senate investigation, concerned chiefly with sniffing out past blunders and indifferent to what was praiseworthy in the achievements of Baker and his subordinates, risked causing a reaction which, if allowed to get out of hand, might blast Republican prospects for years to come. Many Republicans therefore welcomed the respite afforded by the end of the investigation and Roosevelt's enforced retirement from the public arena. The wisest, or safest, course now was to consolidate whatever gains had been made at the President's expense and to continue to probe the administration's position for weak spots that did not bear so directly on the war itself as to alienate the voters. In the meantime the party faced the onerous task of putting its ramshackle political house in order. To this the Republican high command turned its attention in the weeks immediately following the abandonment of the great frontal attack on Wilson's management of the war.

CHAPTER VIII

OVERHAULING THE PARTY MACHINERY

I

AT THE MOMENT Republican fortunes were at a very low ebb. The party seemed fated to go into the 1918 elections handicapped by internal dissension and stigmatized by captious opposition to the war effort. No appreciable trend one way or the other had appeared in the 1917 elections, which were mostly contests to fill a few gubernatorial posts and congressional vacancies. Victories over Wilson-sponsored candidates in New Hampshire and Indiana had momentarily cheered the Republicans, however, and chagrined their adversaries. In both cases Wilson had ill-advisedly made the outcome a demonstration of popular confidence in his conduct of the war. Especially embarrassing had been the result in the Sixth Indiana Congressional District, an area around Fort Wayne, to the voters of which the President had addressed a letter asking them not to repudiate him by electing a Republican.[1]

Wilson's propensity for writing letters of this sort also failed to help the party win a hot gubernatorial battle in Massachusetts, although he again stressed the serious consequences to the war effort of any deviation from political allegiance to him. The President undertook this gesture solely at the insistence of Colonel House and against the advice of Tumulty. Although House "could see no harm in sending a message" to the Democratic candidate, Tumulty rightly predicted "disaster" and urged deferring such tactics to the congressional elections of the following year.[2] The impact of these rebuffs to the President was somewhat offset by the loss of Republican congressional seats in Pennsylvania and North Dakota.

The sweeping Tammany victory in New York City's mayoralty election further dampened Republican hopes in view of the strong effort put forth by the party to re-elect Mayor John Purroy Mitchel.[3] After a wildly hysterical campaign, the ''Hearst-Hylan-Hohenzollern'' combination backed by Boss Murphy routed the forces of loyalty and civic reform personified by Mitchel, although Roosevelt, Root, Hughes and other prominent Republicans had demanded his return to office as a patriotic duty. Elected initially in 1913 on a Fusion, or reform, platform with strong administration support, Mitchel had turned the White House against him by lapsing into reactionary Park Avenue Republicanism and by supporting Hughes in 1916.[4] Mindful of this — and perhaps influenced by a blunt threat from the Tammany congressional delegation to oppose the war program unless Wilson kept his hands off the mayoralty contest[5] — the Democratic high command strictly enjoined all federal officeholders in the metropolitan area not to take sides publicly or commit the President in any way to Mitchel's cause.[6]

The administration, ironically, received little credit for its forbearance in the only wartime election in which the President conspicuously refrained from taking sides. Instead, embittered patriots in both parties denounced him for putting new heart into the Kaiser and his hordes by sacrificing Mitchel to Tammany Hall. In their view, Tammany's enthusiasm for the war scarcely exceeded that of the anti-war Socialist party, which had nearly quadrupled its normal vote in the city. Nevertheless, the administration benefited to the extent that John F. Hylan's victory put Tammany in a more amiable frame of mind and somewhat improved party prospects in the state for the 1918 elections.[7] Democratic national headquarters hailed Mitchel's defeat as symptomatic of Republican weakness everywhere, and the Republicans were too depressed to issue a suitable rejoinder.[8]

On February 12, a day of charismatic significance, the dejected and discordant Republican party leaders assembled in St. Louis to choose a new national chairman. The Old Guard's determination to replace Chairman Willcox with a henchman less partial to the Wilson administration aroused little enthusiasm among large segments of the faithful. The choice of the party bosses was John T. Adams, the national committeeman from Iowa, whom the New York *Tribune,* which was not particularly noted among party journals for its liberalism, considered a ''bone-headed reactionary.''[9] He had been virtual head of the party, however, since January 1917, when the Executive Committee in secret session had stripped Willcox of all but nominal authority by electing Adams to the newly created post of vice-chairman and giving him control of party finances and publicity.[10] His closest competitor, and the man around whom the so-called progressive forces built their hopes, was the promising young national committeeman from Indiana, Will H. Hays. A shrewd and agile opportunist, Hays had shown remarkable organizational ability as state chairman in retrieving Indiana from a decade of Democratic control, but his comparative youth and recent appearance on the national scene weighed against him. With Adams apparently assured of thirty-two of the National Committee's fifty-two votes, the Iowan's elevation to the chairmanship seemed a foregone conclusion.

Hays, however, had a number of potent friends in his camp, including Colonel Roosevelt. The Rough Rider's first impulse had been to support Adams, but after the Hays faction had alerted him to Adams' isolationist record, he immediately joined the fight to keep the Iowan out of the party leadership.[11] The Colonel now considered Hays ''an extraordinarily fine fellow'' and would have appeared openly in his behalf but for the danger that any such brash interference might prejudice the Hoosier's already slim chances. Instead he wrote to John T. King, the national committeeman from Connecticut and ''my particular and confidential friend,'' enjoining King to do all within his power for Hays ''on an occasion which I believe to be of very grave import to the future of the Republican party and therefore of the nation.''[12] He asked King to show the letter to as many other committeemen as he and Hays might consider helpful to the cause.

Senator Borah also brought his considerable influence to bear on Hays's behalf. Borah had stumped Indiana for Hays in 1914, when the latter at the age of thirty-four had waged his first campaign as state chairman. Although it turned out to be a losing battle, the political talents displayed by the young Hoosier impressed the senator, who felt that they could be usefully employed on the national front in place of the usual haphazard reliance on party oratory and fustian. Because the crisis in Washington over the Chamberlain reorganization scheme kept Borah from attending the St. Louis meeting, although it did not deter many of his colleagues, he sent the proxy given him by John W. Hart, the ailing Idaho national committeeman and Adams supporter, to Governor Goodrich of Indiana, who was directing the Hays campaign and desperately in need of help from any quarter.[13] The proxy came at a critical moment, and Hays was most grateful for the senator's timely support.[14]

Behind Adams was a solid block of midwestern isolationists and eastern conservatives. In ordinary circumstances he could not have been beaten, but the war fever gave the progressive minority on the Committee a unique opportunity to destroy him. The ace up the minority's collective sleeve, which it played with devastating effect, was a letter that Adams had written from Germany in the late summer of 1914 and subsequently published in his hometown newspaper, the Dubuque *Telegraph Herald*. What gave particular currency to the epistle was not his interesting account of his experiences as a tourist caught in the European war zone but the frankly pro-German bias of his offhand analysis of the causes of the conflict. Adams had justified the German invasion of France and Belgium as a legitimate defensive measure against British ambitions to crush a dangerous commercial rival. This might once have flattered midwestern prejudices, but it no longer served as a recommendation for public office.

The reading of the letter by Senator William M. Calder of New York threw the meeting into an uproar. Adams vehemently repelled the imputation of disloyalty and protested that his previous views on the war in no way compromised his patriotic devotion to his country. His chances virtually vanished, however, after Senator Penrose, whose faction held the balance of power on the Committee, demanded the election of a ''harmony candidate'' able to restore public confidence in the integrity of the party.[15] The next day eleven Penrose committeemen deserted Adams because of the letter, and Hays became chairman by the close margin of 24 votes to 21. Thus narrowly did the Republicans save themselves from disaster in 1918, since the party could not have gone before the country with a chairman as vulnerable as Adams on the loyalty issue.

Lest bitterness over this coup mar the hoped-for restoration of unity, Adams was allowed to retain the vice-chairmanship. Abolished, however, were the various conflicting advisory groups appointed from the Old Guard and progressive factions to supervise Willcox' handling of the Hughes campaign and to keep close watch on each other's operations. Thus control was returned to the hands of the chairman in a move to end factional strife and to streamline the cumbersome internal structure of the organization.

The St. Louis meeting ended in a burst of patriotic songs and flag-waving and general handshaking all around. Republican newspapers of all shades of opinion hailed the outcome and expressed unbounded confidence in Hays's ability to restore the party to its old primacy in national affairs. The fears voiced by a few that the retention of Adams would permit the Democrats to raise the loyalty issue in the campaign proved groundless. The Iowan discreetly withdrew from the national scene and nothing more was heard of him, while the Democrats, badgered to distraction by Hays's tactics, overlooked him completely in the course of the campaign. This self-effacement had its reward after Hays had entered the Harding Cabinet. With patriotic fervor then subsided into normalcy, Adams served as national chairman until the advent of Coolidge. In the meantime, the party under Hays's adroit direction won two stunning victories over Wilson, thus justifying the high hopes held out for the ''young Napoleon,'' as his admirers at St. Louis had dubbed him.

In his first statement of policy to the press, Hays pledged his party to support of the war and announced that there would be no attempt to take partisan advantage of the administration in that respect. He was careful, however, to reserve the right of ''constructive criticism'' in order to obtain the adoption of measures that would express ''efficiently'' the determination of the people to gain a speedy victory.[16] Senator Penrose, who had now become the real boss of the party, bluntly asserted, when asked for his opinion, that the country had lost all confidence in Wilson and that only a return of the Republican party to power could guarantee victory in the war and a satisfactory peace settlement. Both Hays and Penrose were in agreement, however, that their first objective was to secure control of the next Congress; and they condemned the Wilson administration as paternalistic in behavior, sectional in outlook, and incapable of meeting national issues on a broad constructive basis.

Although Hays did not oppose the attitude of his more bellicose associates who felt that an incessant hammering of the President was the key to electoral success, he preferred to divert attention whenever possible to less dangerous fields. He worked unflaggingly during the campaign to persuade the people that they could support the Republican party without imperiling the war effort or doing injustice to the President, a feat he performed with great dialectical skill and conviction.

His immediate task, however, was to allay any hard feelings left by his own election and to pour balm into the still festering wounds of the Hughes campaign. As a start toward assimilating all the factions, Hays came East for conferences with such antithetical party prima donnas as Senators Reed Smoot and Hiram Johnson, ex-Presidents Taft and Roosevelt, and former candidate Hughes. He spent little time in the New York headquarters but traveled incessantly to explore political sentiment in the various states.[17] His genial presence, soothing personality, and flexible views, as well as his unbounded optimism, boosted the morale of many a dispirited or pessimistic local leader.[18] In a remarkably short time and over an extraordinarily wide area he managed to indoctrinate them with his own confidence regarding the party's chances of prevailing against the power and popularity of the Wilson regime, an achievement of no mean significance in a campaign as hard to coordinate and direct as a congressional contest.

One large fly in the Republican ointment was the bitter dissension in the congressional campaign committee. The Roosevelt minority on the committee roundly condemned the retention as chairman of Frank P. Woods of Iowa on the ground that his isolationist record laid him open to the same objections that had cost his fellow Iowan the national chairmanship. Woods, however, enjoyed considerable esteem as a resourceful and capable politician who had raised his party's representation in the House by eighty-seven members in the last two congressional elections. The House caucus would not remove him against his will, and since he had no intention of retiring under pressure, the rift not only impaired the committee's effectiveness but embarrassed Hays in his efforts to achieve party unity.

II

THE DEMOCRATIC ORGANIZATION underwent no such upheaval as that visited upon the Republican. The National Committee stood pat, with one important exception, with the men who had pulled Wilson through in 1916. Between elections a nine-man executive committee, of which the national chairman and vice-chairman were ex officio members, managed party affairs. Chairman Vance McCormick supervised the wartime patronage but had little to do with the congressional campaign. In fact, he felt so left out of the national picture that he complained bitterly to Colonel House that Wilson took political action on the advice of others and seldom consulted him.[19] In October he sailed for Europe on government business under the impression that the Democratic cause was in no danger. Nor was the vice-chairman, Homer Cummings of Connecticut, particularly active, even after McCormick's departure. A small paid secretariat headed by two seasoned politicians, W. R. Hollister, the assistant secretary, and W. D. Jamieson, the assistant treasurer, did most of the actual work. This group maintained close liaison with McAdoo and Burleson, the chief patronage dispensers, and also with Tumulty, through whom the President kept in touch with political developments on the various fronts. Seldom delegating authority and rarely accepting advice on important matters, Wilson assumed all responsibility for party policy and strategy as the situation dictated in the course of the campaign.

Since the National Committee was so little active, the full

burden of conducting the contest in the field fell upon the chairman of the congressional campaign committee, an energetic young representative from Oklahoma named Scott Ferris. The caucus had elected Ferris to the post in March 1918 — the only important change in the party high command — to replace Frank E. Doremus, a machine politician from Detroit. Doremus' unsavory reputation as a vote trader with the local Republican organization and his poor showing in the last two congressional elections against Woods had made his retirement advisable. Ferris was much more in accord with the administration's Fair Deal philosophy and stood high in the President's regard. He also knew the western farm situation better than most of Wilson's advisers. Had the President seen fit to follow his suggestions with regard to political strategy in that area, the campaign might have had a happier outcome for both. Instead he had to accept the party platform, built exclusively around the appeal to stand by the President, the efficacy of which suffered considerably from repeated insubordination in the Democratic ranks. Nevertheless, Ferris was to wage a vigorous campaign; and had he been less handicapped by the rigidity of the party formula, it is conceivable that he might have proved a match for the astute and wily Hays.

Financially neither party was in very good shape, and both had to resort to drastic fund-raising drives. The Democratic National Committee, which had incurred a debt of $550,000 in 1916, only four fifths of which had been paid off by the beginning of the 1918 campaign, had an empty treasury. In equally straitened circumstances was the congressional campaign committee, which owed $100,000 to the National Committee and could not collect from the congressmen whom it had helped. Only thirty had contributed anything at all toward the expenses of the last election.[20] Consequently it became necessary to shake down the horde of federal officeholders throughout the land for substantial contributions. This method of filling the party war chest laid Wilson open to much criticism, especially after the Republican press published the form letter sent to postmasters and other federal functionaries indicating the sums they were to raise from their employees.[21]

The Republican organization also emerged from the 1916 campaign with badly depleted funds. The congressional campaign committee, with no assistance from the National Committee, had spent $380,000 in 108 districts and managed to defeat fifteen Democratic congressmen.[22] Now, with an empty treasury, it proceeded to "fry the fat" in a familiar but frequently frowned-upon manner. A circular letter had already been sent to various businessmen asking for contributions to keep up "a determined fight" to win the next Congress, but apparently with indifferent results, thanks to the committee's internal troubles.[23] In July it sent out another appeal to a select list of one hundred prominent bankers and industrialists, asking for individual contributions of $100,000 and giving the reasons why Congress should be restored to Republican control.[24] This communication also fell into enemy hands and received widely unfavorable publicity. Since these were time-honored methods of nourishing the sinews of party warfare, it is doubtful that many voters were affected by the revelations, although the matter probably sat less well for Wilson and his lofty professions of idealism.

All in all, the Democrats admitted to raising and spending $665,000 to elect congressmen in 1918, a sum far in excess of any spent before for such a purpose.[25] The Republicans reported collecting $676,875, or almost twice what they had spent in 1916. The total cost, including the large amounts spent in the primaries and the sums dispensed by the National Security League to elect "loyal" congressmen, most of whom turned out to be Republicans, probably came to several million dollars.[26] It was the most expensive election of that kind on record and a fair indication of the importance which both parties attached to winning control of the next Congress.

The Democrats laid the groundwork of their campaign far in advance. In June 1917 the Executive Committee met in Washington to discuss the preliminaries connected with the 1918 senatorial contests and directed party leaders throughout the country to do everything possible to promote interest in them.[27] At an October meeting it canvassed the financial situation and explored ways and means of getting out the maximum party vote in every state.[28] The session held on January 14, 1918, to estimate the impact of the Republican attack on Wilson and Baker reached the conclusion that all was not lost despite the bad impression created by the Senate revelations. If war preparations were kept to schedule, the Committee stated, American troops could stop the Germans before the Republicans could snatch control of Congress from the Democrats.[29]

Nevertheless, in the months ahead the public would need convincing that the administration, contrary to Republican charges, had competently met an unprecedented situation with a minimum of mistakes and delays. The Executive Committee, having authorized the treasurer to proceed with the raising of campaign funds, directed the publicity bureau to accelerate the quantity and improve the quality of the material furnished to the press. A surprising number of publications proved willing to use such material. They included 1,275 Democratic and independent daily newspapers, 8,506 weeklies, semi-weeklies, and tri-weeklies, 450 farm journals, 262 labor newspapers, 736 foreign-language sheets, and 193 monthly periodicals.[30] Creel's Committee on Public Information also went into high gear and churned out a stream of pamphlets alerting the voters to the perils of the Republican plot against the President. Colonel Roosevelt, who found this literature extremely obnoxious, urged the Republican publicity bureau to spare neither money nor effort to nullify the Democratic propaganda drive.[31]

An active and prolific source of anti-Wilson propaganda throughout the war, the Republican publicity bureau in Washington got out a weekly *Bulletin* edited by George H. Moses, a New Hampshire newspaper publisher of decidedly reactionary views. The *Bulletin* was responsible for the remarkably uniform character of the viciously anti-Wilson articles and editorials in that section of the press not politically affiliated with the administration.[32] The efforts of Moses and his coadjutors were ably supplemented by the syndicated pens of ex-Presidents Taft and Roosevelt. Prominent political commentators like William Hard and Mark Sullivan, both former editors of *Collier's* magazine, also lent their talents to the work of denigration, which multiplied in volume and shrillness as the election approached.

III

BEFORE PREPARATIONS for the 1918 campaign had proceeded very far, a portent of what lay ahead appeared in a special election held in Wisconsin on April 2 to choose a successor to the late Senator Paul O. Husting. Husting's death in a hunting accident on October 21, 1917, not only deprived the administration of a staunch supporter but dealt a severe blow to Democratic hopes of retaining control of the next Senate. Elected in 1914, the forty-five-year-old senator, had he lived, would have served until March 1921, thus preserving Democratic control of the Senate (by virtue of a tie) during the crucial struggle over the Versailles Treaty despite other losses at the polls in November.

Death played havoc with the membership of the Senate during the war sessions of the Sixty-fifth Congress, with fate being particularly unkind to the administration in this respect. Of the ten senators, including Husting, who died during this period, eight were Democrats, three of whom were replaced by Republicans. The attrition reduced Wilson's majority to a point where the loss of a very few seats would transfer control to the opposition. Of the ten, however, only the seats of Husting of Wisconsin and Stone of Missouri would not have been contested in 1918. It was by this margin of two that the Republicans captured the Senate and brought Wilson's post-war program to naught.

Husting's death highlighted the peculiar political situation in Wisconsin, where the two senators stood at cross purposes with respect to the war. Only a month earlier La Follette had inflamed the patriots and touched off a vociferous demand for his immediate expulsion from the Senate by informing a large gathering of pacifists in St. Paul that the United States did not have sufficiently good reasons for becoming involved in the European conflict. Husting, on the other hand, had always strongly backed the war effort, and President Wilson paid warm tribute to his courage and devotion in a cause toward which many of his constituents were lukewarm if not downright hostile. The local press, irrespective of party, expressed sincere regret and dismay at the senator's untimely demise. ''Coming at this time,'' said one Republican newspaper, ''when Wisconsin's representation in Congress is under suspicion, and the whole state is subject to injurious reflection on account of its official representatives, the death of Senator Husting is a calamity.''[33]

Democratic prospects for electing another senator were not good unless the Republicans split again as they had in 1914, when Husting won by less than a thousand votes.[34] For a while this appeared not unlikely as three strong candidates vied for the Republican nomination. James Thompson of La Crosse flew the white flag of the La Follette faction, while former Governor Francis E. McGovern, a devoted Roosevelt follower, competed with Representative Irvine L. Lenroot, a more conservative type, for the support of the regular organization. Local party leaders, anxious to avoid a disastrous three-cornered contest which would divide the ''loyal'' vote and thus throw the nomination to the La Follette man, got Roosevelt to persuade his good friend Mc-Govern to withdraw in the interests of patriotism and party harmony.[35] After McGovern had reluctantly complied, Lenroot barely emerged the victor in the March 19 primary, with 73,186 votes to 70,772 for Thompson. The size of the Thompson vote came as a shock to people concerned for Wisconsin's position with respect to the central issue of the day.

The Democratic party in Wisconsin was somewhat at a loss for good senatorial timber. Since infrequent success at the polls had not produced a body of seasoned leaders, decisions with respect to candidates were apt to be made in Washington. Such was the case in 1918, when the choice fell on Joseph E. Davies, whose acumen in backing Wilson in the 1912 pre-convention campaign against the bosses had jackknifed him into control of the moribund party organization.[36] Appointment to the Federal Trade Commission in 1914 had placed substantial patronage at his disposal and also kept him in close touch with the Democratic high command.

What complicated the Wisconsin picture and raised goose flesh on earnest patriots everywhere was the presence of a strong Socialist candidate, Victor L. Berger, running on a platform that demanded immediate withdrawal from the war.

Berger's newspaper, the Milwaukee *Leader,* had been suppressed by the federal authorities for obstructing the draft, and the candidate himself was under indictment for violation of the espionage act. Despite, or perhaps because of, these handicaps, he had polled 36,562 votes in the Socialist primary, two-thirds of which came from his Milwaukee stronghold, a hotbed of pro-German and pacifist sentiment. The fact that most of Thompson's 70,000 supporters would switch to Berger made the prospect a nightmare for the Wisconsin Loyalty League and other patriotic groups, which urged one of the ''loyal'' candidates to drop out in favor of the other. When neither Davies nor Lenroot showed any interest in the proposition, a campaign of unprecedented virulence ensued.

The contest attracted nationwide interest as the first significant test of popular sentiment toward Wilson and the war. Oddly enough, Lenroot rather than Berger became the target of journalistic disapproval. The press attacked his isolationist House record, scored his votes for the McLemore resolution and against various preparedness measures, declared his nomination a disgrace to the Republican party, and accused Republican leaders of playing fast and loose with the German vote in a shameful attempt to win. The Davies campaign, on the other hand, got off to an auspicious start amidst almost universal patriotic acclaim. In a bid for White House support, the candidate assured the President that a Democratic triumph would indicate that in the crisis Wisconsin ''stands four-square behind you.''[37] Wilson, probably recalling some earlier misadventures on this score, referred the appeal to Burleson, saying that he was at a loss to know whether merely to accept Davies' resignation from the Federal Trade Commission or to express some hope with regard to the fortunes of the election in Wisconsin.[38]

The Postmaster General quickly convinced the President of the importance of throwing the whole weight of the administration behind the effort to elect Davies. At his suggestion also, Wilson asked Vice President Thomas R. Marshall to lend his spellbinding talents to the campaign. The attention of the country would be centered upon it, said Wilson, ''because of the universal feeling against Senator La Follette.'' The President personally did not doubt the loyalty of the great body of Wisconsin citizens, but he feared that Lenroot's election would "by no means demonstrate that loyalty, because his record has been one of questionable support of the dignity and rights of the country on some test occasions."[39] At the same time Wilson replied to Davies with a statement that was to cause his party acute embarrassment and the administration endless trouble on the national political front before the campaign was over.

Taking his cue from the press attack on Lenroot's record, the President proceeded to raise in dramatic fashion the issues he deemed to be of paramount importance in determining a candidate's wartime fitness for office. After commending the patriotic impulses that had led Davies to resign his federal post, the President said: "May I also add a word of thanks to you for your steadfast loyalty and patriotism during the trying period before we were thrust into the war, while to avoid becoming involved therein every effort was being made aggressively to assert and fearlessly to maintain American rights. The McLemore Resolution, the Embargo Issue, and the Armed Neutrality Measure presented the first opportunity to apply the acid test in our country to disclose true loyalty and genuine Americanism."[40]

The "acid test" phrase at once caught the public imagination with all the force of other famous Wilsonian locutions. Many citizens deplored the unseemly interest displayed by the President in a local election, but the implied slur enraged the Republicans to a degree exceeded only by their reaction to Wilson's October 25 manifesto. The "acid test" had been employed in the 1916 campaign, but on a local basis and against Republicans and Democrats alike. For the President to make a partisan issue of it on a national scale precipitated a controversy the repercussions of which were to prove highly detrimental to his cause.

Wilson's blast, timed to coincide with the opening of the Wisconsin campaign, rocked Lenroot badly. Stunned Republican leaders, searching frantically for an issue to take the pressure off their candidate and create a diversion in his favor, quickly found one in the fortuitous troubles of the Aircraft Production Board.[41] After ten months of effort and the expenditure of

$840 million, the country still had no combat planes, a state of affairs which moved Republican senators on March 26 to launch an exposure of the administration's criminal negligence in this respect.[42] In what the New York *Times* characterized as the "bitterest debate of the war," Lodge attacked the bureaucratic confusion and delay in Washington that had sabotaged the airplane program, while New of Indiana cited facts and figures to demonstrate that of the twenty-two thousand planes the Aircraft Production Board six months before had promised for delivery, only thirty-seven would be ready for service by July 1.[43] Smoot of Utah took the familiar tack of accusing Wilson of using his high office to discredit the loyal opposition and perpetuate his personal control of the government.

Rising in defense of the administration, John Sharp Williams of Mississippi reproached his Republican colleagues for choosing the most critical day of the war (the great German drive on Paris had begun on March 21) to launch a "poison gas" attack against the government in an attempt to influence the voters of Wisconsin. He justified the President's charges against Lenroot's loyalty, characterized his Americanism as "lukewarm," and dismissed his, as well as his party's, support since April 1917 of tax bills, military appropriations, and other routine matters as of no consequence in view of the Republican failure to demonstrate either vision or statesmanship during the neutrality controversy. Williams' disparaging remarks drew heated denials from the Republican side that criticism of the airplane program had anything to do with the Wisconsin situation. Jacob H. Gallinger of New Hampshire wanted to know, since the partisan issue had been raised, why the Vice President had deserted his post as presiding officer of the Senate to embark on a stumping tour of Wisconsin on behalf of the Democratic candidate.

Wilson's interference had a bracing effect upon Lenroot's campaign. Patriotic disapproval of his candidacy began to fade, and factions hitherto hostile to him now fell in line as the struggle took on the aspects of a straight party battle. On the advice of Chairman Hays, Lenroot stopped apologizing for his "acid test" record and pitched into Wilson for playing politics with the war and for mismanaging the war effort until brought to account by the Chamberlain investigation. Wilson's choice for senator he ridiculed as a political hanger-on who had never been required to face up to the "acid test" measures by which the President set such great store.[44]

The shift in tactics threw Davies upon the defensive and forced him into indignant denials that the President was neglecting his duties to play politics or that the failure of the aviation program had needlessly exposed American troops in France to German bombers. Of considerable help to Davies at the moment was the presence in Europe of Secretary of War Baker on a tour of the front, accompanied by a large retinue of war correspondents. Their glowing accounts of American combat readiness bespoke better War Department press relations and supplied the Democratic publicity bureau with the material needed to refute Republican canards about American soldiers being compelled to face the enemy practically barehanded because of the government's neglect to furnish airplanes, heavy artillery, field kitchens, and other essential equipment. With the German hordes moving on Paris, the hour of decision was at hand in Europe, and the Democrats made the most of the situation to put Davies in the Senate.

This they might have done but for Vice President Marshall's appearance on the Wisconsin scene. His vision and judgment badly warped by the passions of the moment, he had already given voice to a number of intemperate public utterances; but his speech at Madison, Wisconsin, on March 26 was, in the opinion of one administration official, "the biggest damfool thing in history."[45] Castigating the Republican party as the principal ally of Germany, Marshall depicted Wisconsin as a hotbed of treason and an ineffable blot on the national honor which only Davies' election could mitigate. He accused Lenroot of bidding for the vote of the pro-German, the traitor, the pacifist, and the Wilson-hater. "Your state of Wisconsin," said the Vice President, "is under suspicion. Having purified the stream in the primary, you welcome the sewage vote to help you over the election."[46] Wilson's "acid test" had been bad enough, but Marshall's "sewage vote" further infuriated the Republicans, who angrily denounced both men for traducing the citizens of a state which had met its war obligations as patriotically as any other. The excitement generated by these sensational charges brought out a record vote on April 2. The result was a bitter disappointment to those who had counted on Wilson's prestige and the war issue to carry the Democratic party to victory. Although Davies polled the largest vote ever given any Democrat except Wilson, it was not enough, and Lenroot won by a plurality of 15,267.[47] The size of the Socialist, or "traitor," vote garnered by Berger, who practically quadrupled the normal vote of his party in the state, shocked public opinion. The wholesale accession of Thompson supporters inspired further denunciation of the "treachery" of La Follette, although neither he nor Thompson took any part in the campaign. The Republican press, which shortly before had found Lenroot weak and unsatisfactory, professed to see in his election complete proof of Wisconsin's loyalty and a complete vindication of the party's position on national issues. On the other hand, Davies' defeat deeply chagrined the Democrats, who considered it a repudiation of the President and all he stood for in the war. The Milwaukee *Journal,* the principal administration organ in the state, sourly observed that Lenroot's victory put two La Follettes in the Senate and made almost hopeless the task that fall of purging the nine Wisconsin congressmen equally guilty of failing to support Wilson and the war.[48]

Republican national headquarters, naturally elated over the result, boasted that the whole weight of the administration had not prevailed against its candidate. Hailed as a harbinger of Republican success in the fall, it was the first victory under the new leadership and an auspicious beginning for chairman Hays, who had remained discreetly in the background and left the initiative largely to a Republican senatorial committee. The Democratic National Committee, on the other hand, accepted Davies' defeat with very poor grace. In a post-election statement it lamely repeated Marshall's accusation that Lenroot had violated his pledge of loyalty to Wilson in the primary by shamelessly soliciting the disloyal German vote in the election. The Democratic press, however, sharply advised the high command to forget the whole thing. It was better, said the Vicksburg *Herald,* to invite Lenroot's support in the Senate, where Wilson was badly handicapped by the hostility of such Democrats as Gore, Reed, Hardwick, Vardaman, and Hitchcock, "who were more evil and disloyal than La Follette, and this fact should be taken into consideration by the National Committee before passing judgment on Lenroot."[49] Other party newspapers urged Wilson to set a statute of limitations, dating back to April 6, 1917, to his disloyalty charges; otherwise as many Democrats as Republicans would be caught in his "acid test" net.[50]

All this good advice made no impression whatsoever on either the National Committee or the White House. Once having set his political course, Wilson did not allow a temporary setback to turn him from it in the bitter struggle that lay ahead.

CHAPTER IX

"POLITICS IS ADJOURNED"

I

WITH THE ADVENT of spring the collective thoughts of Congress began to turn toward home and the primaries. In 1918 the primaries assumed more than the usual local or passing interest because of the sensational issues raised by the President in connection with the war. Agitation for the election of a "loyal" Congress had been going on for some time, but Wilson's dramatic intervention in Wisconsin and the large anti-war vote polled by the Socialists gave the movement extraordinary impetus. Various patriotic organizations now bestirred themselves to greater efforts to prevent the return of congressmen with so-called disloyal or doubtful records.[1] The voters were urged not to repeat the mistake of the Civil War, when the Lincoln administration had been weakened and the conflict prolonged by the election of many Copperheads to the Thirty-eighth Congress in 1862. Moreover, the steady barrage of criticism directed at the Sixty-fifth Congress for playing politics with the war, shirking its responsibilities in the crisis, and preferring debate to action on vital war measures had created much uneasiness among the members and stimulated sentiment for an early adjournment.

Congressional leaders on both sides had agreed not to prolong the session beyond July 1, and to adjourn earlier if possible. To its great dismay, therefore, Congress learned early in May of the War Department's pressing need for an additional $15 billion, which would leave the Treasury with insufficient funds to get through the year. "Nothing is more important," McAdoo informed the reluctant lawmakers, "than new revenue legislation at this session of Congress. . . . Unless this matter is dealt with now firmly and satisfactorily, we shall invite disaster in 1919."[2] Disaster appeared closer than that to politicians seeking re-election, and Congress erupted in a turmoil of angry objection. Uppermost in the congressional mind was the unpopularity of the old war revenue bill with all its "inequities, crudities and imperfections."[3] Business interests had never ceased to clamor for a downward revision of excess profits taxes, but now the Treasury wanted to raise an additional $8 billion in that fashion, or double what it had asked in 1917. The amount of logrolling, back-scratching, and horse-trading necessary to reach agreement on a measure of that magnitude would keep Congress in Washington for another long hot summer while it weighed the relative merits of partisan, sectional, and class appeals for tax relief.

Agitated Democratic statesmen flocked to the White House to argue that McAdoo could find sufficient funds to carry the government over the coming elections. Another Liberty Loan, in their opinion, ought to see the Treasury through the interim until Congress could safely consider the matter. Furthermore, as they were frank to admit, the members must be allowed to get home as soon as possible in view of the widespread attacks upon their alleged dereliction of duty. Not a single Democratic seat in the North, complained one member of the Ways and Means Committee, would be secure if a new tax bill were enacted at that session. Moreover, he did not know of a single Democrat who wanted to stay in Washington for the length of time it would take to frame the requisite legislation.[4]

At several White House conferences the Treasury experts insisted that "this tax problem should be grasped with a firm hand and a tax law as a war emergency measure should be enacted at the earliest possible date."[5] The congressmen present had no wish to grasp that particular nettle. They argued that the Treasury's demand for a bill by August 1 put this delicate matter much too close to the elections to educate the public and avoid a political catastrophe at the polls.[6] Democratic senators opposed to higher taxes threatened to filibuster any bill presented at that session. In the Cabinet, Postmaster General Burleson supported the congressional contention that a good revenue bill could not be framed under the partisan atmosphere that was bound to prevail. Wilson thereupon offered to defer the matter to a special session of Congress immediately after the elections if both parties would agree to enact a bill by January 1.[7] When his insubordinate followers rejected this compromise, the press roundly denounced Congress as a collection of slackers who had thrown the Treasury into a muddle by poor tax legislation in 1917 and now lacked the courage to remedy their mistakes. The nub of the matter, said the New York *Times* on May 17, was "whether the taxpayers, the Treasury, and the country are less to be considered than the convenience of Congress, which is thinking more of politics than of finance."

II

THE EMERGENCE of the airplane scandal at this time distracted the President in his efforts to compose the tax controversy. His enemies not only seized the opportunity to embark upon another noisy investigation of the War Department but in the process almost succeeded in hanging that obnoxious "instrumentality," the Committee on the Conduct of the War, around his neck. The trouble stemmed from the administration's grandiose promises in the spring of 1917 to give the country a tremendous air armada of one hundred thousand planes — a figure later cut to twenty-two thousand by the War Department — which would sweep the Germans from the skies, pulverize their formidable ground defenses, and obviate the need for further costly infantry assaults.[8] Launched amid a spectacular fanfare of publicity, the program never got off the ground. Rumors of confusion and lack of progress in the Aircraft Production Board had grown apace,[9] but nothing definite materialized until Major General Leonard Wood blew the affair wide open upon his return from a tour of inspection of American military forces abroad.[10] Wood's testimony before the Senate Military Affairs Committee on March 25 about the complete absence of American military aircraft in Europe flatly contradicted the reassuring propaganda put out by Creel's publicity bureau and the War Department with respect to the number of combat planes overseas. The General was highly pleased with the senatorial reaction to his revelations. ''I never saw a Committee more wrought up or more excited,'' he observed. ''They were gesticulating and swearing and generally shaking things up.''[11] The Republicans, delighted to have an issue at last that might take the heat off Lenroot in the Wisconsin senatorial campaign, lost no time in mounting another blitzkrieg against Wilson and Baker; and the storm of abuse and criticism spread rapidly.

On April 10 the Committee stigmatized the airplane program as a total failure. Four Democrats and five Republicans signed the majority report, while three loyal Democrats issued a minority report which excoriated the majority for misstating the situation and stoutly denied the existence, apart from a few regrettable delays, of anything fundamentally wrong with the production program.[12] Four other members, three Democrats and a Republican, did not sign either report but reserved judgment until more information became available. The sudden removal shortly thereafter of the two top aircraft officials only added to the mystery, inasmuch as the White House refused to discuss the matter and thus left the press free to indulge in the most damaging conjectures. These changes, moreover, did not satisfy the critics of the administration, least of all the Senate, which had old scores to settle with the President. On May 2 Republican senators set off another loud explosion on Capitol Hill by charging Wilson with having abetted the Aircraft Production Board in the perpetration of a gigantic confidence game at the expense of the entire country, and the Secretary of War with lying about the airplane situation and obstructing all attempts to get at the facts.[13]

To many citizens it seemed incredible that $840 million could vanish with no more to show for it than a handful of training planes and a few ground schools here and abroad. The discovery that contracts to build combat planes had in some instances gone to fly-by-night concerns with no visible equipment, plant, or money raised a hue and cry about the possibility of fraud and stimulated demands for a grand jury investigation to fix the responsibility for any criminal acts.[14] The climax came on May 2, when Gutzon Borglum, the private investigator appointed by Wilson in January to look into the affairs of the Aircraft Production Board, publicly accused high War Department officials of deliberate deception in trying to cover up the shady practices of private contractors. Wilson then had no choice but to make public his correspondence with Borglum and to direct the Department of Justice to present the facts to a grand jury.[15]

The Borglum case was one of the most curious and incredible episodes of the war. A sculptor of note, although not yet famous for carving gigantic historical portraits in the rock face of mountainsides, he was also an amateur aviation enthusiast and designer of airplanes, none of which ever got off the drawing board. Nonetheless, this interest qualified him for membership in the Aero Club of America, a group of enthusiasts and amateurs like himself who had undertaken to promote the art of flying on a national scale and to publicize the idea of air power, then almost unknown. The Aero Club maintained an active lobby in Washington for this purpose and kept a sharp eye on developments. The members soon became dissatisfied with the War Department's fumbling approach to the problems of the new air age, and Borglum, who had known the President slightly for some years, called the situation to Wilson's attention. The numerous irregularities in airplane production he attributed to the greed of the automobile industry, which had undertaken to manufacture Liberty motors with an eye more to quick profits than to the rapid assemblage of an air fleet.[16] Wilson referred the matter to Baker, a friend and admirer of the sculptor, and after some further desultory correspondence Borglum was given a free hand to conduct an investigation with all the facilities of the War Department at his disposal. No one bothered to question his qualifications, which were derived exclusively, according to his own admission, from a feeling of kinship with Leonardo da Vinci, "who knew all that was known regarding the art of flying," or took into account a cantankerous disposition which inevitably made him a storm center of anything he chose to undertake.[17]

Borglum's report to the President on January 21 largely

confirmed his original suspicions of the dishonesty of several prominent industrialists. His sensational charges pleased neither Wilson nor Baker, who suppressed the report but took no further action, apparently trusting to time to iron out the production difficulties.[18] When this method failed to improve things, the President belatedly ordered a quasi-official investigation headed by a conservative New York lawyer and Democrat, H. Snowden Marshall, whose findings bore out certain of Borglum's allegations.[19] In the ensuing shake-up, the chairman of the Aircraft Production Board, Howard E. Coffin, and the chief of the Army Signal Corps, Major General George O. Squier, were relieved of their duties. Coffin, a high-pressure automobile salesman and publicity expert, had dazzled the country with fanciful stories of an invincible air armada, created overnight from nothing, which would spare American doughboys the horrors of further bloody ground fighting. Squier, on the other hand, was an earnest bureaucrat of limited vision and with little knowledge of flying or its related problems. Both men had soon found themselves and their inadequate organization swamped by the enormity of the unfamiliar project thrust upon them.[20]

The removal of Coffin and Squier on April 18, the separation of production from direct control by the Army, and the appointment on May 3 as director of this phase of the work of John D. Ryan, the Montana copper tycoon and staunch administration Democrat, provided only a partial solution of the problem, which rapidly began to take on a political coloration. The President had also gotten rid of the irritating Borglum, or so he thought. The sculptor's repeated advice to him to dispense with the speculators using their jobs to profit from the airplane program, reflecting as it did on Wilson's judgment in staffing the operation, exasperated the President, who curtly broke off relations on April 15, saying, "I merely gave you the right to look into the matter of your own volition, and I am sure . . . the Secretary of War . . . gave you the same purpose and idea." In view of the fact that he had informed Borglum on January 2 that "the Secretary of War assures me that he will be delighted to clothe you *with full authority* to get to the bottom of every situation . . . and will direct that every facility of inquiry be placed at **your** disposal,"[21] it is not surprising that Borglum and his friends in the Aero Club should have felt themselves badly treated. Although Wilson by now had come to refer to them as a "pestiferous crowd" bent on political mischief,[22] he contemptuously shrugged off the threat with the remark that "Borglum is sure to make an ass of himself when he tries to make good."[23] How seriously mistaken he was, the President was very soon to find out.

The angry sculptor quickly found a sympathetic audience on Capitol Hill, where his revelations sparked the wild Senate outburst of May 2. The coldly furious Wilson immediately consulted a number of friendly Democratic senators, who warned him that the affair could become dangerous because of Borglum's exploitation by "certain Senators on the other side." They also felt that the Military Affairs Committee would grant a public hearing on the charges in the absence of any other evidence.[24] When the President refused Baker's request for an immediate investigation to clear the War Department of the imputations of graft and inefficiency, the alarmed Tumulty urged him not to give the appearance of wanting to obstruct efforts to get at the truth. "I am afraid from all I hear," he said, "that the aircraft situation is more serious than any of us believe."[25] The President took no action, however, until the rising clamor forced his hand. Then on May 6 he directed the Department of Justice to make a "searching inquiry" into every phase of the program, and made public the documents in the Borglum case, or such as he considered pertinent to it.[26] He also sent the Senate a letter explaining what he had done.

The Senate was in no mood to accept explanations from the White House, nor was it agreeable to the transfer of its investigative functions to another agency of the government. Senator Chamberlain immediately announced that a probe by the Military Affairs Committee would put the finger on the men responsible for the outrageous conditions in the War Department. No government official would be spared, and the whole wretched and sinister business would be exposed without the whitewashing that would result from allowing the Justice Department to monopolize the inquiry. On May 10 he brought forth a resolution authorizing his Committee, or any subcommittee thereof, "to inquire into and report to the Senate the progress of aircraft production in the United States, or into any other matters relating to the conduct of the war."[27]

III

WITH A FEW CHANGES to bring it up to date, this was the old Weeks resolution which the President had fought off on past occasions. Chamberlain's version of that "instrumentality" was the more obnoxious, however, because it provided for the employment of paid agents with free access to all government plants during the congressional summer vacation (the revenue problem not yet having spoiled this plan). Since $10,000 was needed to defray the expenses of the probe, and without which the Military Affairs Committee could not go into the broad field of all war activity, the request went to the Committee to Audit and Control the Contingent Expenses of the Senate, a five-man group composed of three Democrats and two Republicans and, like most Senate committees, dominated by the President's enemies.[28]

Wilson immediately appealed to Senator William H. Thompson of Kansas, a friendly Democrat on the Audit Committee, to defeat the resolution or at least to eliminate that part giving the Senate authority over "the conduct of the war." Thompson unfortunately had little personal influence in the Senate, which in this matter preferred to follow Chamberlain, who was in a warlike mood and determined on getting his resolution adopted without change. He had his way when McKellar of Tennessee, the chairman of the Audit Committee and another notorious enemy of the administration, joined the two Republican members, Smoot of Utah and Joseph I. France of Maryland, in reporting it out, with Thompson and the other Democratic senator, A. A. Jones of New Mexico, in the minority.

Having lost the first round in the battle, the President now sought to rally his supporters by cracking the party whip. Through Thompson he let it be known that he expected every administration senator to oppose the Chamberlain resolution, which he condemned as a dragnet war inquiry designed solely to embarrass him in the discharge of his constitutional duties.[29] Majority Leader Martin of Virginia received a stiff letter exhorting him to hold loyal administration forces in line. "Such activities," said the President, "on the part of the particular committee of the Senate as this resolution would look forward to would constitute nothing less than an attempt to take over the conduct of the war, or at least so superintend and direct and participate in the executive conduct of it as to interfere in the most serious way with the action of the constituted Executive." In conclusion he warned that "these are serious times, and it is absolutely necessary that the lines should be clearly drawn between friends and opponents."[30]

Although the lethargic Martin showed no inclination to cooperate, administration pressure obtained a toning down of the unlimited scope of the obnoxious resolution. Chamberlain, however, would not relinquish his inquisitorial grasp upon the Quartermaster's department or upon aircraft and ordnance production, which left his Committee sufficient flexibility to embarrass the administration at almost every turn.[31] This was no more acceptable to Wilson than the original version, but it was the most that could be wrung from his opponents in the way of concessions. Defeat appeared inevitable until the President's advisers prevailed upon him to employ strategy to outflank the enemy, instead of the head-on tactics with which he usually met congressional opposition.

The idea of associating Charles Evans Hughes with the airplane investigation originated in the fertile mind of Colonel House. House discussed the matter with Frank Cobb of the New York *World* and with Attorney General Gregory, both of whom approved the suggestion but felt that the President might be hard to convince.[32] In urging the proposal on Wilson, House stressed the irretrievable harm to party prospects in the coming election from another Senate inquiry carried out with a maximum amount of mudslinging. Hughes's reputation as a successful prober of public utility and insurance scandals, said House, would do much to allay popular misapprehensions about the airplane situation. Moreover, his standing among Republicans would serve to dispel the unfortunate impression that Wilson was running the war for the benefit of his own party. "If you use Taft, Root, Hughes, and other republicans as you are doing," he wrote, "people will begin to understand that there is some reason why Colonel Roosevelt is not available. I have been doing my best to bring about a chism [*sic*] between such republicans as Taft, Root, and Hughes on the one hand and such republicans as Sherman, Brandegee, Penrose and their ilk on the other, and it looks as if it might be done."[33]

The President, as anticipated, found the scheme most repugnant. He had not forgotten or forgiven Hughes's behavior during the 1916 campaign, which, in his estimation, ranked his erstwhile rival on the same level with Lodge and Roosevelt. Only a few weeks earlier, when friends had urged him to appoint Hughes to another government post as a non-partisan gesture, Wilson had testily rejected the notion of putting so untrustworthy a critic in a place where he would have so much opportunity to make mischief. "I hope with all my heart," he said, "that Charles Evans Hughes will never be connected in any way with affairs down here, he proved himself so absolutely false in the last campaign."[34]

Nevertheless, the situation had become too acute to allow old grudges to obstruct a possible solution. Since there seemed no other way of stopping the Senate from repeating its disagreeable performance of the previous winter, Wilson yielded to necessity and invited Hughes to participate in the Department of Justice investigation, under the nominal direction of the Attorney General but with the assurance of an absolutely free hand in the search for evidence.[35] The announcement on May 16 of Hughes's acceptance created a profound and, for the most part, favorable impression. Even the Chicago *Tribune* declared that the appointment met with "emphatic public approval," while the New York *Tribune*, although commenting somewhat sourly that Wilson meant to keep all investigating in his own hands and would not allow even a limited inquiry by the Senate, admitted that it was a "stroke of true genius."[36] It tied the hands of the Republicans, who could not repudiate Hughes, and forced a grudging admission from Senator Lodge that the President had done "a very astute thing." Lodge learned from a colleague, however, that Hughes had been as reluctant to accept the offer as Wilson had been to make it, and had only consented because there was no way of getting out of it.[37]

The Senate, although considerably nonplused by Wilson's action and not a little irked by Hughes's part in it, did not give up without a struggle. Senator Chamberlain angrily insisted that his intent had been misunderstood and that his resolution must pass without further change. Although the Chamberlain faction had lost ground as a result of the Hughes's appointment, the inept administration leadership in the Senate would not force a vote but sought frantically for some sort of face-saving compromise. Hughes finally solved the impasse by a letter to Chamberlain on May 23 asking the senator to drop a course of action that would only duplicate and confuse the investigation Hughes intended to conduct for the Department of Justice.[38] Somewhat mollified by this approach, Chamberlain modified his demands: the four subcommittees were to get funds for whatever investigative purposes might be deemed necessary, but with a specific disclaimer that they were to conflict with the executive branch of the government in the conduct of the war.[39]

The administration thought it best to conciliate the pestiferous Borglum by associating him with the inquiry. He paid his way by turning up 160 of the 240 witnesses examined by Hughes. The sculptor, however, found fault with Hughes's final report, which revealed widespread cheating of the government by the airplane companies but recommended only one government official for punishment for "improper relations" with them. Borglum suspected that undue influence in high quarters had been brought to bear on Hughes to suppress the most damaging evidence.[40] He was convinced, after the event, that "this miserable scandal destroyed the Democratic party."[41] It would seem rather that the Hughes appointment got the administration out of a tight corner and prevented Wilson's enemies from doing greater damage to his cause. Hughes's report was not published until October 25, the day Wilson made his celebrated appeal for a Democratic Congress, and two months after the Senate subcommittee probing into airplane production had published its report.[42] The frankly partisan bias of the Senate document, which was more in the nature of a contribution to the congressional campaign than a disinterested attempt to get at the facts, revived for a time the angry debate over the inadequacy of the nation's air force.[43] By October, however, the German military machine was on the verge of disintegration, and the issue of air power no longer greatly mattered. The political campaign had taken other directions, and both reports were largely lost to sight in the uproar of those final days.

IV

ALTHOUGH WILSON had come out on top in his latest scrimmage with the Senate over the conduct of the war, he still faced the problem of holding a refractory Congress in session until a new tax bill could be written. Democratic leaders remained sullenly hostile to the Treasury Department's arguments for additional taxes to meet mounting military costs. Few congressmen agreed with McAdoo that Democrats in doubtful districts would have a stronger case with the public if they vigorously attacked those who were making vast fortunes out of the war. "The records in the Treasury showing up the war profiteering of the past year," he said, "will be a tremendous argument in support of the bill and will justify any Democrat for staying in Washington to get new legislation. When the facts are made public . . . every man who has had the courage to stay in Washington and fight to remedy these conditions will strengthen himself with the American people and with his own constituency particularly."[44] The lawmakers feared, however, that the business community would merely pass the higher taxes along to the general public in the form of higher prices and thus create an even greater hazard for those voting for such a course. They urged the President to drop the suicidal notion and order the Treasury to get along with what funds it could raise by Liberty Loans until the end of the year.

Wilson's determination not to jeopardize the financial position of the government by catering to the nostalgic whims and the anxieties of the lawmakers had the firm support of the press. Calling attention to the fact that several million soldiers would also like to get home that summer, the press of both parties insisted that the concept of duty was as binding on Congress as on the men in the trenches. It was a point of view, however, to which Congress flatly refused to subscribe. At a White House conference on May 23, Senator Furnifold McL. Simmons bluntly asserted that to keep a quorum of members in Washington with the November elections so close would be an "impossible task."[45]

Since further conferences would change nobody's views, Wilson solved the impasse in characteristically dramatic fashion. His sudden appearance before a joint session of Congress on May 27 with a clarion call to duty thrilled the public and left his audience with no alternative but to fall in line with his wishes.[46] It was one of his most effective addresses, although remembered only for one celebrated phrase that was twisted out of context and made to signify something quite different from what the President had in mind. The message itself dealt with the need for new taxes to fall mainly on excess profits and luxuries, and with the importance to the business community and the government of the money problem, the solution of which could not be left in doubt or suffered to lag behind production. The most memorable statement was the President's cheerful assurance to the five hundred or so politicians grouped before him that "politics is adjourned" and that the 1918 elections would go to those giving the least thought to winning them.[47]

In respect to compelling the compliance of Congress with an unpalatable course of action, the address was a masterpiece; and Wilson was never in better form than when laying down the moral law or preaching the concept of duty. His facility for garnishing his thought with rhetorical flourishes sometimes led to confusion when the exact purport of his remarks came into question. His statement about the elections going to those who gave them the least thought was sheer hyperbole; few congressmen could count on obtaining spontaneous endorsement from their constituents, particularly after the recent muddying of the waters by the President's "acid test" manifesto. His sweeping assertion that "politics is adjourned" applied only to reconciling Congress to a summer session in Washington against the centrifugal pull of the primaries. It represented no desire on Wilson's part to end all preparations for the November poll. He knew that Congress stood on too weak ground to resist a skillfully worded appeal which not only placed national interests ahead of political expediency but by inference rebuked the unhelpful attitude of his party leaders. Since Wilson could not amplify the latter point without stultifying the party, the exegesis of his remarks was left to the press, and much confusion and misunderstanding arose therefrom.

Democratic newspapers seized upon the "happily phrased declaration," as some chose to call it, to prove that the President had no interest in the coming election beyond the return of loyal congressmen who had upheld him in the crisis and could be counted upon to do so in the crucial post-war period.[48] Since this would automatically eliminate most of the Republicans in the Sixty-fifth Congress, opposition journals hastened to warn their readers not to be hoodwinked by Wilsonian rhetoric into relaxing their determination to elect a Republican Congress that would prosecute the war more energetically and settle the peace more fairly than a quarrelsome Democratic Congress which seldom followed the President in any undertaking. Nevertheless, nearly everyone agreed that adjourning politics was a splendid idea, although of little practical significance, since it was like asking a politician to stop breathing. "Throw politics out of the door," said one newspaper, "and back it comes through the window."[49] If Wilson's remark was widely endorsed in the abstract, few were misled into believing that things would be materially improved thereby.

The Democratic leadership in the House bowed to Wilson's tax demands with very poor grace. The next day Majority Leader Kitchin, enraged at being outmaneuvered in his plan for an early adjournment, accused the President and the Secretary of the Treasury of conniving with a powerful publishers' lobby to keep Congress in session until the recently increased rates on second-class mail had been repealed. Wilson remained aloof from the ensuing fracas, but McAdoo angrily demanded proof or retraction.[50] Kitchin could not substantiate his charges, nor would he apologize. A very disagreeable situation developed, with Kitchin breathing fire and slaughter against the monied interests favored by McAdoo and threatening, as chairman of the Ways and Means Committee, to harry them with taxes until they had been stripped of all their ill-gotten war gains.[51] The chairman's tantrums disturbed the business community not a little, and hearings on the $8 billion revenue bill got under way in an atmosphere of resentment that augured poorly for the soundness of the proposed legislation.[52] Ultimately an arrangement was worked out whereby members took brief summer vacations while Congress remained technically in session with enough members on hand or quickly available for the necessary quorum. Thereafter a slightly better feeling prevailed all around.

With Wilson's hard-won victory over the Senate in the airplane inquiry and his coercion of the House into writing a new tax bill, open warfare between Congress and the administration slackened for a period. Attention now shifted from the nation's capital to the states, where a number of interesting primary contests had been germinating for some time and others were about to get under way. Congressmen with notorious anti-war or anti-administration records found the home folks thoroughly alerted to the facts and in many cases inclined to act upon them.[53] Wilson's intervention in many of these contests, either to eliminate men hostile to his principles or from a desire to strengthen his personal leadership, created almost as much of a stir as the elections themselves. As for politics being adjourned, about the only discernible effect of the President's statement was to limit the home appearances of many congressmen to briefer visits than usual. Few enjoyed the esteem of their constituents to the extent that they could forgo all personal activity during the campaign. Although the press applied the currently popular epithet ''slacker'' to statesmen who shirked their legislative responsibilities to mend their political fences, Capitol Hill was increasingly deserted until only a few committees remained in session after July 15.[54]

CHAPTER X

PRIMARIES AND PLATFORMS

I

THE MORE SPECTACULAR primary contests occurred in the South. Nomination in this region was tantamount to election, and the extraordinary antics of many of the participants lent a bizarre touch to the occasion. Anti-war sentiment permeated the rural areas, where local demagogues industriously fanned the deep resentment aroused by the efforts of the federal authorities to enforce compliance with wartime laws. Here and there patriotic elements had rallied to drive from office the more obnoxious of these politicians. None stood higher on the list of such expendables than Senator Thomas W. Hardwick of Georgia, whose long-winded opposition to the President and the war had brought him into nationwide disrepute. Consequently, a number of Georgians had volunteered to undertake the laudable task of removing Hardwick from the national scene.[1]

The leading contender in the patriotic derby was William J. Harris, chairman of the Federal Trade Commission, who had used the patronage at his disposal to create a faction favorable to his ambitions. His reputation as an "original Wilson man" which came from backing the President against the local party bosses in the 1912 pre-convention campaign, was expected to incline the White House in his favor, but it did not recommend him to the Bourbon element which wanted to run Governor Hugh Dorsey or one of the old guard congressmen.[2] Nor was Harris popular with conservative circles friendly to the President, especially in Atlanta, where both National Committeeman Clark Howell, owner of the *Constitution*, and Major John S. Cohen, publisher of the *Journal* and one of Hoke Smith's lieutenants, denied that he had the ability to oust Hardwick.[3] The senator's anti-Wilson views, moreover, had commended him to Colonel Roosevelt, who suggested to the Republican National Committee that "if privately our friends in Georgia can be told to help Hardwick I think it would be a good thing."[4] What with Hardwick's overwhelming attraction for the anti-war rural voters, the Federal Trade Commissioner faced formidable odds.

Wilson, who took a deep interest in Georgia affairs because of family connections there, strongly resented the obstructive attitude of both Georgia senators. Consequently, after Hardwick had announced his intention to seek renomination, Wilson asked one of his Georgia friends to tell both Howell and Cohen that he was "warmly in favor of electing Harris to the Senate."[5] Howell proved agreeable, but Cohen demurred on the ground that such an endorsement might backfire and accrue to Hardwick's advantage in the long run.[6] The President therefore took no immediate action although frequently importuned by Georgians anxious to build up public sentiment against "Herr Hardwick, the Kaiser's friend," and his potent rural following.

Another senator completely out of step with Wilson and the war was James K. Vardaman of Mississippi. A rabble rouser of incredible virtuosity, impressive even in a region noted for high-level performances in that art, Vardaman had made himself unpleasantly conspicuous by challenging the government's authority to enforce the selective service act, by encouraging his poor white followers to resist the draft, and by packing local exemption and appeal boards with his own henchmen.[7] Since the good name of the party, if nothing else, demanded his elimination, the White House lent active assistance to patriotic elements in the state opposed to his renomination. It got behind the candidacy of Representative Byron Patton Harrison, a promising young administration supporter, and helped to further his chances by diverting to him Vardaman's share of the federal patronage.[8] Harrison's popularity in Washington, however, would be of little avail in breaking the senator's powerful hold on the sandhill and canebrake dwellers back home, where touchiness about outside interference in local affairs also made a Harrison victory something of a long shot at best.

An anti-war movement of alarming proportions had developed in South Carolina, where ex-Governor Coleman L. Blease sought the Senate seat of old Ben Tillman, then nearing the end of his colorful career. Blease's invectives against Wilson delighted the back-country folk, who flocked eagerly to hear him invoke the divine wrath upon the President's head for plunging the nation into the blood bath of war. Since Tillman had already announced his intention to retire and Blease's strength lay among the same wool-hat element that had been the basis of Pitchfork Ben's extraordinary political power, the situation caused acute concern in Washington. Consequently, the White House threw its support to Representative Asbury F. Lever, a Tillman protégé and chairman of the Committee on Agriculture, whom Wilson frequently consulted on farm matters. The fact that Lever could count upon the Tillman influence was no recommendation in the ultra-conservative Charleston area, which had its own candidate in the person of a well-to-do lawyer and banker named Nathaniel B. Dial. Since the nomination would be decided in the rural districts, few doubted that the scourge of the Cleveland era could carry the state for Lever.

Lever had no sooner embarked upon his pre-primary campaign, with private assurances of presidential support, than Tillman's health, which had kept him inactive during most of the war months, took a sudden turn for the better. The old champion now threw a spanner into the works by declaring it his patriotic duty to stand once again for the Senate.[9] Lever's refusal to withdraw raised the disagreeable prospect of a split in the "loyal" vote among several candidates. It also embarrassed Wilson, who was committed to Lever but unable to repudiate Tillman because of the senator's unblemished if inactive war record. Furthermore, a good many anti-Bleasites, including Governor Richard I. Manning, continued to support Lever on the ground that Tillman, although loyal to Wilson and the war, was too old and feeble to seek another term.[10] The state Democratic convention, which met at Charleston on May 15, adopted a militantly patriotic platform but prudently refrained from endorsing or opposing any of the people running for the Senate, with the result that the primary opened in June amid the utmost confusion.

Loyalty troubles also plagued Missouri Democrats after a stroke of apoplexy removed old Gumshoe Bill Stone from the scene on April 14. Stone's passing was not widely regretted, since neither his general reputation nor his attitude toward the war had been such as to attract admiration, but the Senate vacancy he bequeathed proved most awkward to fill. After Speaker Champ Clark declined the honor, Governor Frederick D. Gardner appointed an obscure St. Louis lawyer named Xenophon P. Wilfley to serve until the November election. Wilfley's chief claim to recognition seems to have been that he and the governor played golf together at the same country club. Normally his elevation to the Senate would have raised no objections. In 1917, however, at the time of the armed-ship controversy, he had belied the martial implications of his name and compromised his standing in patriotic circles by signing an anti-war petition along with a number of local German-American businessmen. Diligent patriots at once launched a movement to prevent him from winning the Democratic nomination in the August primary.[11]

The chief promoter and exploiter of anti-Wilfley sentiment was ex-Governor Joseph W. Folk, who had long cherished senatorial ambitions. A notable reformer, whose efforts to purify the political life of Missouri had won him the nickname of "Holy Joe," Folk had unsuccessfully contested Stone's seat with that wily veteran in 1908. Afterwards he had practiced law in Washington and prospered politically under the Wilson administration as chief counsel for the Interstate Commerce Commission. The regular state Democratic organization had no use for him, but Folk expected to overcome that handicap by trading upon his excellent connections with the White House. Many of Wilson's friends, including Colonel House, admired Folk and urged the President to support him in the fight against Wilfley and the potent Reed organization.[12]

Consequently, Folk let it be known, somewhat inaccurately, that he had undertaken his campaign at the President's behest in order to purge Missouri of the imputation of disloyalty incurred by the attitude of Senators Stone and Reed toward the administration's war policies. Although Wilson detested Reed and thought well of Folk, he let Burleson and the National Committee persuade him to keep silent on the ground that it would be suicidal to repudiate the governor, both senators, living and dead, and the powerful state machine on the eve of a crucial election.[13] So bitter was the primary campaign that a victory for either faction threatened to split the party down the middle to the ultimate advantage of the Republicans, who had no trouble picking an uncontroversial candidate in the person of Selden P. Spencer, a conservative St. Louis lawyer and circuit court judge.

II

THE EASTERN SEABOARD STATES exhibited less excitement over the loyalty issue. With a few exceptions, congressmen from this region had supported Wilson's preparedness and, to a lesser extent, his neutrality policies irrespective of party. Voters in the Twenty-fourth New York Congressional District, a conservative Westchester area, refused to renominate a Republican congressman with a poor ''acid test'' record; on the other hand, an Irish district deep in the heart of Boston rejected a Democratic congressman for having gone too far in support of Wilson and his British ally. Boston Democratic leaders declined to endorse Representative Peter F. Tague of the Tenth District because he had gone against their wishes by voting for the declaration of war and for certain preparedness measures.[14] In the New York metropolitan area the major parties effected a fusion against the Socialist menace and launched a determined drive in the Twelfth District to oust Representative Meyer London, the only Socialist in the House.[15]

Across the Hudson River in New Jersey a lively contest developed over the seat left vacant by the death on January 30 of Senator William Hughes. A longtime friend and staunch supporter of the President, Hughes' loss dealt the administration a severe blow. Governor Walter E. Edge made matters worse by giving a temporary appointment to one of the most reactionary Republican bosses in the state, who was expected to keep the seat warm until the governor could run for it in the fall.[16] In an effort to undo the mischief, the Democrats staged a monster rally of all the factions on March 21 in Newark. Tumulty and Scott

Ferris stressed the need for party harmony to stop the Republican drive for the control of Congress and to send another Democrat back to the Senate. The gathering also listened with a great show of enthusiasm to a letter from the President informing his fellow Democrats that if they forgot the old party slogans, performed their duty adequately with respect to the war, and committed themselves to the disinterested service of humanity, the party had nothing to fear at the polls in November.[17]

Inspiring as the message was, it left open the question of a strong candidate to face Edge. Tumulty bestirred himself actively in the matter, although declining to seek the nomination personally. The President, keenly interested in New Jersey affairs, tried hard to persuade Judge Thomas G. Haight of the Superior Court, an old and highly esteemed friend, but Haight refused to leave the bench. In the end Wilson had to settle for a candidate sponsored by the Nugent machine and given little chance of beating Edge's smoothly functioning organization. Tumulty's last-minute effort to split the enemy's ranks by endorsing Edge's primary opponent, Representative George W. Gray, on the ground that he had supported the war program without undue carping, failed of its purpose and merely put the Republicans in a more determined mood than ever.[18]

Delaware Republicans showed signs of emerging from the stupor into which the factional quarrels of the reigning Du Pont dynasty had plunged the party for several years. Revolt against the boss rule of T. Coleman Du Pont had given the Democrats both senators and the state's single representative in Congress. Early in 1918, however, the retirement of T. Coleman in favor of another Du Pont, who reorganized the state central committee in a manner satisfactory to both regulars and independents, restored party harmony and threatened the re-election of Senator Willard Saulsbury. The vigorous efforts put forth by the administration to insure his return created no little resentment, especially the oft-repeated assertion that a campaign against Saulsbury was tantamount to a declaration in favor of the Kaiser. Such "colossal impudence" incensed the local Republican press, which warned Delaware voters not to be fooled by the same administration tactics that had failed so badly in Wisconsin.[19]

Republican hatred of Wilson reached its fullest flowering in

New England, where the limited employment of Yankee talent in the direction of the war severely galled the native aristocracy. The New England party press, taking its cue from the remarks and conduct of Lodge and Weeks, the regional oracles, kept the administration under a steady barrage of "constructive criticism."[20] Of the ten Republican senators from that area, only Colt of Rhode Island had not joined the anti-Wilson clique in the game of embarrassing the President at every opportunity. On the other hand, Democratic support of Wilson, especially among the Massachusetts Irish, was only lukewarm at best. Consequently, party prospects were not too bright, amounting at best to two or three additional congressmen from industrial areas where wartime prosperity had brought high wages and a possible feeling of gratitude toward those responsible for such blessings.

Of the two New England Democrats in the Senate, Henry F. Hollis of New Hampshire dashed his party's hopes by declining to seek another term because of his disapproval of many of Wilson's war policies. This left the state organization with no strong candidate to compete against the wealthy and popular war governor, Henry F. Keyes, the man Colonel Roosevelt heartily endorsed as the one New Hampshire must send to Washington to help in the task of stopping Wilson.[21] Rhode Island Democrats entertained some faint hopes of repeating the upset of two years before which had shaken the grip of the mill-owning Republican plutocracy upon the state. In Senator Colt, however, the Republicans had a strong candidate with an unimpeachable war record. As for Bert M. Fernald of Maine and Weeks of Massachusetts, despite their seemingly impregnable positions in traditional Republican strongholds, a few optimists among the Democrats felt that they might be swept out of the Senate for their refusal to stand by the President.

Some grounds for optimism existed in Massachusetts, where ominous cracks had begun to appear in the monolithic party façade. The popular war governor, Samuel W. McCall, persisted in pushing his candidacy for the Senate despite the efforts of Lodge and his cohorts to clear the way for the unopposed renomination of Weeks.[22] In 1912 a sensational battle for the senatorship between Weeks and McCall had deadlocked the legislature and raised demands for an official probe of charges of corruption against the victorious Weeks and the reactionary financial forces behind him. The friends of Weeks, mindful of the unpleasant repercussions of this contest, bitterly reproached the governor for reviving the old scandal and jeopardizing party unity at that critical juncture.[23] McCall angrily denied that there was anything unpatriotic about running against the senator, whom he attacked for lip service to the President and obstructionism in the war.[24] It was uphill work, however, because the Lodge-Weeks forces controlled the Republican press and the party organization. Ultimately these factors induced McCall to withdraw, but not before party hopes for a united front in the fall election had been shattered.

While the Weeks-McCall feud brightened the situation for the Massachusetts Democracy, the choice of a senatorial candidate was a very delicate matter. Ex-Mayor John F. Fitzgerald, who had pressed Lodge closely in 1916, felt himself entitled to another opportunity against a less redoubtable antagonist. Since Fitzgerald's ties with the Boston Irish made him vulnerable in 1918 to charges of pacifism and pro-Germanism, a more suitable candidate had to be found without alienating the Irish vote and splitting the party. Early in May the chairman of the state central committee conferred with Burleson and Tumulty, at which time the administration decided to back the candidacy of ex-Governor David I. Walsh.[25] A strong campaigner and good vote-getter, Walsh was an upstate Democrat not too closely identified with the emerald green of the Boston Democracy. To State Chairman Michael O'Leary fell the task of reconciling all the factions to the choice, a feat he accomplished with great skill, since Fitzgerald's subsequent withdrawal left the party united and in an optimistic frame of mind.[26]

III

BECAUSE of the hysteria worked up in the press over the loyalty issue, many congressmen found themselves caught in the political vortex set in motion by the President's "acid test" statement. This was particularly the case in the West, where isolationism flourished and local statesmen would not discard the prejudices of a lifetime. The first casualty on that score occurred in the South Dakota primaries on May 28, when Third District Republicans rejected Representative John Dillon because of his "ruinous mistake," according to the Sioux City *Journal,* of voting against the declaration of war and wrongly on several other "acid test" measures.[27] In the Iowa primaries a few days later, the same mistake was the undoing of Representative Frank P. Woods of the Tenth District, one of several Iowa congressmen accused of catering to anti-war sentiment in the state and displaying indifference toward war legislation.[28] Since Woods was chairman of the Republican congressional campaign committee and stood high in the national councils of his party, his unexpected defeat attracted widespread interest and increased the clamor of the Roosevelt crowd for his removal. A major problem in Washington that summer, an Iowa newspaper humorously observed, was how to get rid of Woods "without spilling the political beans."[29]

On the Pacific coast, Senator Chamberlain's peculiar course anent Wilson's conduct of the war had thrown Oregon Democrats into the utmost confusion. Although the administration manipulated patronage in an effort to obtain a more well-disposed senatorial candidate, the anti-Chamberlain forces could not unite on anyone in particular.[30] Consequently, in a four-cornered primary on May 17 the nomination went to Chamberlain's former campaign manager, ex-Governor Oswald West, who had a strong following among the Prohibitionists and the Nonpartisan Leaguers.[31] In an unblushing bid for White House support, the victorious West now professed to disapprove strongly of the senator's behavior, although earlier he had signed a telegram, along with most of the federal officeholders in Oregon, endorsing Chamberlain's New York remarks. The President, however, was by no means ready to forget or forgive. "I cannot do anything in his behalf," he said, "without condoning what I cannot condone on Senator Chamberlain's part."[32] Consequently, West found himself very much on his own in facing the popular Republican senator, Charles L. McNary, who had been appointed in July 1917 to the unexpired term of Senator Harry Lane, another Democratic obstructionist and one of the "little group of willful men" castigated by Wilson for filibustering the armed-ship bill. Between them, Lane and Chamberlain, although from antithetical motives, had brought their party into disrepute locally and demoralized the state organization. McNary, on the other hand, had avoided the anti-Wilson clique and otherwise fulfilled his senatorial duties unobtrusively. Consequently, his election, as well as that of all three Republican representatives, despite the vulnerability of two of them on the "acid test" issue, was practically conceded in view of the enfeebled nature of the Democratic opposition.

The lively interest manifested in the primary contests raised fears that the major campaign would be waged with such intensity as to divert public attention from the war effort. Neither party showed much interest, however, in proposals to omit contests against congressmen with satisfactory war records. President Wilson's widely publicized endorsement that June of the re-election of Republican Senators Kenyon of Iowa and Nelson of Minnesota, who had been friendly to his program, merely made his adversaries suspect a Machiavellian move to throw them off their guard.[33] West Virginia Republicans rejected a Democratic offer to return uncontested all six congressmen, four Republicans and two Democrats, because it looked too much like a maneuver to soft-pedal the bitter feeling in the coal fields over price-fixing, which militated against Democratic chances in the more important senatorial contest.[34] When the Republicans countered Wilson's non-partisan gesture in Iowa and Minnesota with a derisive promise not to run senatorial candidates in Mississippi and Arkansas, the whole proposition became farcical.

IV

AS THE PRIMARY SKIRMISHES increased in noise and frequency throughout the country, the respective high commands began to give thought to the principles upon which to take a stand. The Democrats were more or less firmly united behind the President on a win-the-war platform, but their adversaries were in somewhat of a quandary as to the best or safest method of approaching the voters. With the party divided between the radicals of the Lodge-Penrose type, who favored a forthright attack on Wilson, and the moderates such as Senator Borah,[35] who felt that the bid for popular support should rest on less dangerous premises, the impetus to an effective campaign was lacking. The advent of Hays, a Penrose man, to the national chairmanship strengthened the radicals, however, and Hays proceeded to put on a remarkable performance of stoking the fires of partisanship while keeping the blaze from getting out of hand and destroying the organization.

If the pragmatic aspects were Hays's contribution, the platform was largely the work of Roosevelt. In conferences with Republican leaders, he had labored upon it intermittently since Thanksgiving at Oyster Bay and later in Washington. Devoted mainly to a rousing attack on Democratic mismanagement of the war, the document glorified Republican support of such measures as had been taken to encompass the defeat of Germany. Although the war planks gave no trouble, Roosevelt's stubbornness about the need for higher war taxes worried his conservative friends.[36] Admonished by Lodge not to encourage such notions, which constituted a species of demagoguery better suited to Wilson and his followers, Roosevelt referred the tax question to Root. Root agreed that the course proposed by the Rough Rider involved the destruction of capital, put the government in business, and led directly to socialism, whereupon the matter was dropped.[37] Hays suggested a few platitudes about the farmer and the workingman, and these were duly incorporated to round things off.

The Maine Republican convention at Portland on March 28 gave the radicals their first opportunity to unveil their declaration of principles. With the Senate investigation still fresh in the public mind, they wanted to strike before Wilson's errors were forgotten or glossed over by his apologists. Although still a sick man and subject to dizzy spells, Roosevelt filled the role of convention keynoter with all the old-time fire and gusto. He flayed the administration for criminal negligence in its war preparations, gave the Republicans all the credit for the progress achieved to date, and assailed the President for making the war a personal rather than a national undertaking.[38] He also included price-fixing in the list of Wilson's crimes at the suggestion of Senator Lodge, who was badly worried over the government's threat to regulate the copper industry, in which his Boston friends were heavy investors. Although of little significance at the time, the issue was to assume crucial importance elsewhere and in another connection before the campaign was over. Otherwise the speech contained nothing that had not appeared previously in the Rough Rider's anti-administration screeds.

Outside of New England the convention attracted little attention beyond some criticism of Roosevelt for trying to climb back into power at an inopportune moment. Both sides went briskly forward with preparations for the coming campaign, although thrown off stride somewhat by the President's "politics is adjourned" remark.[39] The moderate Republican press, while discounting Wilson's statement as eyewash, did not wholly subscribe to Roosevelt's truculent stand. Many party newspapers urged him to harmonize his views with those of Taft, Root, and Hughes, all of whom were setting fine examples of loyal cooperation in forwarding the war effort.[40] This attitude, as well as the soothing utterances of Hays, who was still feeling his way, tended to confirm the view that the Republicans in general meant to eschew partisan violence in the campaign. By the end of May the party realized that it must either declare its intention to fight or else acquiesce in the impression that it would not follow Roosevelt in throwing down the gage of battle.[41]

The Republicans resolved this problem at their Indiana state convention, held in Indianapolis on May 29. The noisily bellicose character of the proceedings left nobody in doubt with respect to the party's attitude toward the congressional elections. The platform closely resembled the one unfurled at Portland, although toned down somewhat from the rugged phraseology that had enthralled Roosevelt's audience. For one thing, the amount of space given over to a denunciation of Germany was increased to bring it more into balance with that devoted to condemning the administration, a concession to people who considered the

Kaiser more objectionable than Wilson. Otherwise it ran the gamut of familiar Republican grievances, from Wilson's criminal neglect to prepare for war to his deplorable habit of "practicing partisan politics to the serious detriment of the country's cause."[42] Touching only lightly upon the price-fixing issue, since the party had not yet made up its mind with regard to this controversial subject, the platform dwelt at length upon the charge of southern domination of the government by calling attention "to the fact that under the present organization of the national House of Representatives the chairmanship of every important committee that formulates the measures for legislation is held by a member from one section of the country, and that under their direction and control the burdens of the government have been largely imposed upon the Northern and Western interests and sections."

If some restraint appeared in the drafting of the platform, the oratory accompanying its adoption was anything but conciliatory. The moving spirits on the floor were the Indiana senators, New and Watson, both notable scourges of the administration. New, a member of the Military Affairs Committee, reviewed in detail the horrid revelations of the Senate investigation. Watson, after a brief denunciation of German barbarity, launched into a much longer account of the atrocities perpetrated by Wilson upon the hapless American taxpayer, eloquently defended the right to criticize the President "helpfully," and declaimed bitterly at the discrimination practiced against Indiana in the awarding of war contracts. The convention closed on a high patriotic note amid solemn pledges of loyalty and much flag-waving and singing of patriotic hymns.

The noise made by Indiana Republicans attracted nation-wide attention. Democratic papers deplored the verbal brickbats thrown at Wilson. The New York *World* sneered at the "praise-worthy sentiments" professed by Hays and his collaborators and likened their platform to the one adopted by the Democratic National Convention of 1864, which talked loudly about patriotism but showed no evidence of loyalty to the government. The Republican press, on the other hand, expressed complete satisfaction with the work of the Hoosier convention and congratulated the National Committee on its determination "to conduct a congressional fight for the purpose of bringing to the supporters of the Government the best men in order that we may both win the war and solve the problems of peace."[43]

Another straw showing the way the political winds were blowing was the celebrated reconciliation between Taft and Roosevelt at a Chicago hotel on May 26. Their meeting, the first in eight years, signaled Taft's open conversion to the ranks of the belligerents. It put an end to the hopes of Colonel House and other presidential advisers of isolating "bad" Republicans like Roosevelt from "good" Republicans like Taft. Heretofore, as his party's representative on the bipartisan National War Labor Board, Taft had served as a model of cooperative Republican wartime behavior. The War Department investigation, however, had turned him sharply against the administration, and the carping note he subsequently adopted in his syndicated newspaper articles opened the way for a reconciliation. The delighted Roosevelt readily forgave him for his initial weakness in joining the "general idiot cry" on Wilson's behalf. "He has been doing admirable work," declared the Colonel, "ever since he got waked up as to Wilson's real character."[44] "Taft and I," he wrote after the Chicago meeting, "are now in absolute accord about present needs and about our failures and shortcomings and *the cause of them* during the past year."[45]

With the Republicans closing ranks and hoisting the battle flags, the Wilson administration could no longer evade the challenge even had it cared to do so. The Democratic state convention at Indianapolis on June 18 offered a timely forum to get the party position before the country and start rallying the people behind the President. The platform was largely the work of Wilson himself, who had carefully revised the draft prepared at his request early in May by Tumulty and Burleson.[46] The document opened with a ringing declaration of the party's purpose to win the war, referred to the perils confronting democracy from German militarism, and emphasized the duty incumbent upon every American voter to elect senators and representatives in complete harmony with the President and his policies.[47] The platform praised the "splendid work and achievements" of

Secretary of War Baker and denounced the "sinister and systematic propaganda of falsehood and slander by profiteers and politicians calculated to undermine the effectiveness of the Army." The Republicans were rebuked for raising the sectional issue in their platform, and Wilson's record of peacetime achievements was cited in refutation of this canard.

Convention orators tarried with the German menace overseas just long enough to whip up the patriotism of the delegates before transferring their attack to the political menace at home. The speakers lashed Hays for resigning from the Indiana Defense Council to lead the country-wide partisan attack on Wilson, ridiculed Roosevelt for displaying bad temper over the frustration of his military ambitions, and denounced New and Watson for attempting to rouse the country against the President at a time when unity of outlook was the paramount consideration. When somebody called for Wilson's renomination in 1920, the convention burst into wild applause. So great was the commotion that the New York *Times* reminded the Hoosiers that the duty of the hour was not to elect Democrats to office but to win the war.[48]

Unperturbed by this note of disapproval, the Democratic National Committee a few days later issued a statement saying that the fall elections would be contested on the issues enunciated at Indianapolis. Control of Congress, it announced, would be fought out on the issue of the conduct of the war, "drawing special reference to the leadership of Woodrow Wilson."[49] Public hoardings throughout the country now blossomed with posters bearing such slogans as "Win the War with Wilson" and "Stand by the President," and all the vigor went out of the movement to dispense with partisanship in 1918. The two great parties, said the Washington *Post*, were lining up in earnest for the biennial struggle, and "anyone who nursed the hope that this country would omit the usual congressional campaign may abandon that hope right now. Politics is not adjourned, and there is no adjournment in sight."[50]

CHAPTER XI

THE "ACID TEST"

As far as party principles and campaign issues were concerned, the public could now take its cue from the proceedings at Indianapolis. Major issues such as price-fixing and sectionalism were to come into sharper focus at a later date, but both parties had made their intentions abundantly clear. In the meantime a number of important primary contests remained to be decided, the outcome of which would have a marked effect on the November elections. The administration became involved in some of these affairs from a variety of motives, not all of them discernible then or later. Wilson's professed reluctance to intervene at the lower levels frequently yielded to his strong personal antipathies in cases where party harmony or his own leadership appeared to be at stake. The course that he elected to pursue, often against the advice of his friends, laid him open to much criticism and confused the public generally.[1]

I

The inroads of the Nonpartisan League among the farmers of the Northwest created a great commotion in 1918. Conservatives and patriots alike viewed its progress with the dread that the irresistible advance of Attila's hordes had once inspired in civilized communities. League organizers preached the gospel of agrarian discontent with missionary zeal and remarkable success, despite severe reprisals at the hands of the frightened authorities. On Capitol Hill many worried congressmen came to terms, openly or secretly, with a movement that swept their districts like a prairie fire. Certain White House circles welcomed it as heralding the end of Republican domination in rural areas, where the Democratic party had long striven with indif-

ferent results to establish a foothold. Moreover, the harsh re-
pressive measures taken by the state Defense Councils disturbed
Wilson's liberal advisers, who felt that the Republicans should
not be allowed to use the war to crush all opposition to their
local regimes. Others in Wilson's entourage, however, cautioned
the President about becoming involved with an organization
that exploited anti-war sentiment and stirred up class hatred
among the farmers. In their estimation, Arthur C. Townley and
his cohorts constituted a political hazard which the President
would do well to avoid.[2]

The reforming aspects of the League's program intrigued
Wilson, however much he might dislike its methods of convert-
ing the farmer. The League's warmest advocate in White House
circles was George Creel, the government's wartime publicity
chief and Townley's associate in the early days of the Nonpartisan movement. On November 30 Creel brought Townley
to the White House to plead the cause of the western farmers
and to defend their loyalty.[3] Encouraged by the President's
friendly reception, Townley made a bold play for administration support. Through one of the North Dakota congressmen,
John M. Baer, he offered to put his organization at Wilson's
service to clarify the government's war aims among the farmers
and to further the political fortunes of the Democratic party.
The League, he boasted, was politically strong in thirteen states,
with hundreds of organizers who could reach the farm vote as
no one else could.[4] Wilson did not reject the offer outright but
temporized by praising the League's good work among the farmers, which, he said, was of the utmost importance to the country
and to the "universal cause."[5]

The first important test of the League's vaunted political
strength came in the Minnesota primaries that spring. As a
preliminary move toward capturing the Republican primary, the
Townleyites staged a mammoth convention in St. Paul on March
18, which attracted widespread and none too favorable attention. At Creel's suggestion Tariff Commissioner William Kent
journeyed westward to explain the administration's policies to
the gathering with the idea possibly of moderating its radicalism.
Well known as one of the wealthy, doctrinaire civic reformers

of that era, Kent subsequently joined the League out of sympathy for its objectives, although far removed from it in all other respects.[6] This hasty intervention proved ill-advised. The appearance of a prominent administration official on the same platform with Townley outraged the patriots, who immediately accused Wilson of striking a disgraceful bargain with a crowd of Bolsheviks bent on losing the war and destroying the government.[7] It also fostered the impression that the Democrats were resorting to not very subtle or honorable tactics to improve their political prospects in the Northwest.

The St. Paul convention qualified its pledge of support to Wilson by denouncing the administration for failing to protect the farmer against war profiteers. The Townleyite candidate for governor was Charles A. Lindbergh, a former congressman notorious for his anti-war views, while the senatorial nomination went to James A. Peterson, a Minneapolis labor organizer momentarily free on appeal from a sentence to the federal penitentiary for obstructing the draft. For the House the League endorsed Democrats in three districts and entered candidates against Republican incumbents in four.[8]

A veritable Donnybrook of a primary campaign ensued. The Public Safety Commission broke up League rallies, while angry crowds mobbed League organizers, and the Home Guard threw many of them into jail. Creel's Committee added to the uproar by sending speakers into the state presumably under Nonpartisan auspices. Irate citizens clamored to know why the White House employed a federal agency for such nefarious purposes when an urgent need existed for the government to speak out unequivocally against disloyalty in all its forms.[9] Creel's activities also upset the two Minnesota senators, gravely concerned over the rapid spread of Nonpartisan influence in their area. Old Knute Nelson, whose worried friends were importuning him to run again for the Senate as the only way of stopping a Bolshevist take-over, had already called the attention of the Attorney General to the fact that the attitude of the League leaders was "on the whole of a disloyal flavor, unpatriotic and dangerous." Now he bluntly asked Wilson's publicity man what he was up to in Minnesota and demanded a flat statement from him denying any cooperation or affiliation with the Townleyites. This, he said, was necessary in order "to quiet the feeling that seems now to prevail in many quarters of our State."[10]

Wilson, surprised by the hubbub and annoyed by Creel's unauthorized intervention, chided his publicity man for having committed the administration in such an embarrassing fashion. "I am afraid," he wrote, "that we are getting into deep water in that part of the country . . . and I think it will be your judgment, as it is mine, that we had better pull away from [Townley and his associates]."[11] Although Creel denied that his Committee had "sponsored" speakers for the Minnesota campaign, he admitted that it had "suggested" one or two. He insisted, however, that the League was "absolutely loyal" and that the Public Safety Commission was trying to drive it into disloyalty to further reactionary political ends. Nevertheless, he agreed with Wilson about the unwisdom of breaking openly with the state authorities over the issue. In a press release he replied to Nelson along the same lines, saying that he had never officially or unofficially approved of the League, "although it has done nothing any Patriotic citizen could disapprove of." The object of his organization, he asserted, was to put everybody behind the war, but the bitterness in Minnesota had precluded his sending speakers there, although some had gone on their own responsibility.

The President's misgivings about Townley's dubious influence had been strengthened by a report from the Secretary of Agriculture. David F. Houston depicted the League as thriving on class hatred, and while conceding that the rank and file were for the most part loyal and hardworking, this was far more than the Secretary could say for the leaders.[12] Wilson thereupon informed his friend Kent, whose report on the St. Paul convention had contradicted Houston's in every respect, that he was afraid the situation there would have to be allowed to work itself out, "much as I should like to take a hand in working it out."[13]

Kent's account had bristled with indignation at the political tyranny and high-handed methods of Governor Joseph A. A.

Burnquist and the Public Safety Commission. He argued that the League's major purpose was economic, "along the lines of constructive democracy," and that its officials were not only entirely loyal but willing to acknowledge Wilson's leadership in "constructive democratic thought."[14] Although somewhat starry-eyed in his approach to a rather questionable operation, Kent was not alone in misreading the signs. Another wealthy business-man and close friend of the President, Charles R. Crane of Chicago, also assured Wilson that the Nonpartisan League was anything but Bolshevik, that its aims were reasonable and democratic and its leaders worthy of sympathetic regard.[15] Since Wilson had great respect for the opinions of men like Kent and Crane, he never felt the loathing for Townley that convulsed Roosevelt and his followers. Nevertheless, he was careful to avoid open involvement with the Gracchus of the North Dakota prairies.[16]

On June 18 Minnesota voters in large numbers turned out at the polls to repel Townley's bid for power, and conservatives throughout the country could now breathe easier. Nonetheless, the League made a remarkable showing. Against its mortal enemy Burnquist, Lindbergh rolled up 150,626 votes to 199,325 for the governor.[17] Peterson lost the senatorial contest to the veteran Knute Nelson by a much larger margin, 89,464 to 229,-923. The difference probably represented the extent of local resentment at Burnquist's dictatorial rule, with Peterson re-ceiving only the hard core of Nonpartisan strength in the state. Frightened Republican leaders had finally persuaded the old senator, then nearing eighty, to change his mind about retiring; and Nelson's popularity, especially with the large anti-war Scandinavian element, had held together a badly disorganized party.[18] The Townleyites not only failed to nominate any of their congressional candidates but lost the one Republican con-gressman whom they had endorsed. The defeat of Representa-tive Ernest Lundeen, a pro-German pacifist and isolationist from Minneapolis, a hotbed of socialism and labor unrest, gratified the patriots almost as much as the failure of Lindbergh to over-throw Burnquist.

In other state campaigns, particularly in North Dakota

where the Democratic candidate for governor protested that the alleged Wilson-Townley alliance was causing local Democrats to back League-endorsed Republican candidates in his state, the League continued to trade upon its White House connections.[19] The interview with Townley, the President's letter to Baer, Kent's appearance at St. Paul, and Creel's blunder in sending speakers to Minnesota presented the administration's enemies with enough evidence to make the allegation appear plausible. Wilson's refusal to take a clear-cut stand on the issue subjected him to charges of conniving with a subversive movement inimical to the Republican party and destructive of American principles. It fed the suspicion, widely disseminated, that the administration was playing a double game at the farmer's expense, chilled much of the former enthusiasm for the President, and contributed to the rapid deterioration of the Democratic party in the Northwest.

II

IF WILSON's enigmatic attitude toward the Nonpartisan League created a furor throughout the Northwest, his unequivocal preference for Henry Ford as senator from Michigan startled the country and caused another uproar. In the eyes of uncompromising patriots of the Roosevelt stamp, Ford was no more acceptable or worthy of public trust in the crisis than Townley. His ardent pacifism culminating in his ''peace ship'' fiasco, his opposition to any form of military preparedness, his indifference to politics, and his crass and complacent ignorance of all subjects unconnected with his automobile business sufficed, in their estimation, to disqualify him from holding office, even if the fact of his being a multimillionaire manufacturer profiting from lucrative war contracts were overlooked. His selection also raised the question of how far the President should go in dictating candidates the electorate was expected to send to the Senate. The press recalled Wilson's course in Wisconsin, and the Ford candidacy furnished a rich and varied fund of editorial material for the rest of the congressional campaign.

The architect of the Ford senatorial boom was Secretary of

the Navy Josephus Daniels, another lover of peace and an ardent admirer of the Michigan motor magnate. On business trips to Detroit, Daniels had discussed with local Democratic leaders the political situation created by the retirement of Senator William Alden Smith.[20] Ford had fallen in with their novel idea that both parties would get behind his candidacy as a patriotic duty if he were presented as a non-partisan supporter of the administration. Daniels thereupon urged the President to "draft" Ford for the Senate race because he was the party's only chance.[21] It was a slim chance at best, because no Michigan Democrat had sat in the Senate since 1857; and a number of prominent Republicans, including two former governors, were exhibiting strong senatorial yearnings. Other leading contenders were Truman H. Newberry, a Detroit businessman then on active service with the Naval Reserve, and James Couzens, Detroit police commissioner and a former Ford partner. On June 7, however, Couzens withdrew his candidacy, explaining that his financial interest in the Ford Company, which had extensive government contracts, disqualified him by act of Congress from serving in the Senate. In view of Couzens' action, the public learned with surprise from the newspapers on June 14 that the President had summoned Ford to the White House and persuaded him to run for the Senate as an administration supporter.[22]

In appealing to Ford to enter the Senate contest because "you are the only man in Michigan who can be elected and help bring about the peace you so much desire," Wilson ignored Ford's obvious shortcomings in other respects. Idealism aside, a more vulnerable candidate could hardly have been found. Every foolish thing that Ford had ever said about the flag and patriotism and kindred subjects made him a shining target for a host of partisan sharpshooters. Nevertheless, his pioneer wage and hour policies were still popular with labor, while the extravagant praise accorded his contribution to the war effort in turning out Eagle boats and Liberty motors helped to some extent to redress the patriotic balance. He was also expected to benefit from the quirks in the Michigan primary law, which permitted cross-filing in the primaries and provided that a candidate winning them all would have his name alone appear on the November ballot. Should Ford win both the Republican and Democratic primaries on August 27, the Republicans would find themselves without a candidate. Enough Democrats were expected to vote for him in the Republican primary to insure his success, and angry Republicans declared that Wilson had cooked up a brazen plot to steal the election.[23]

Few Democratic newspapers approved of Wilson's choice. The Milwaukee *Journal* said that Ford was "not our kind of American" and disqualified him on the grounds of his earlier pacifism. The Houston *Post* remarked that if Wilson intended to drive pacifists from office, as inferred from his "acid test" statement, Ford's selection was very difficult to justify other than on the ground that, as a rich man, he stood a better chance of being elected. The New York *World* felt that the President's course, far from promoting political harmony, would only stimulate partisanship and dissension.[24] Before the campaign was over, Wilson himself had serious doubts regarding the wisdom of his action.[25] But by then it was too late to undo the mischief, especially after the Democratic strategy had misfired in the August 27 primaries, when Ford lost the Republican nomination to Newberry by nearly fifty thousand votes, thanks to a scandalous expenditure of money on the victor's behalf. Colonel Roosevelt, an ardent Newberry backer, justified the extravagant outlay on the ground that patriots everywhere that year should not count the cost of upholding 100 per cent Americanism.[26]

III

ALONG WITH the announcement of the Ford endorsement on June 14, the press carried a letter from Wilson to Representative Asbury F. Lever of South Carolina, tactfully requesting him to withdraw from the Senate race. Lever thereupon retired, as gracefully as the circumstances permitted, in favor of the temporarily rejuvenated Tillman, upon whom the White House depended to rally the vote of the state against the unspeakable Blease. Wilson acted somewhat precipitately, however, inasmuch as a stroke of apoplexy put an end to Pitchfork Ben's career three weeks later. His demise dismayed the loyalist forces, since none of the other candidates could match Blease's compelling attraction for the wool-hat element. Blease, moreover, had spread further confusion in the ranks of the faithful by cannily shifting his tactics and impudently posing as a friend of the administration, which, he said, wanted him elected in order to give the President another loyal supporter in the Senate. In response to an agitated appeal from the friends of Dial to set the record straight, Wilson sent off a statement to the effect that the people of South Carolina had enough sense to know that Blease never was and never could be a friend of the administration. With this assistance Dial trounced Blease at the polls on August 27 by a margin of twenty-one thousand votes, and the local press hailed the outcome as vindicating the good name of South Carolina.[27]

The Tillman-Lever affair inclined Wilson, for a time at least, to exercise greater caution about becoming involved in such affairs. His advisers also continued to urge him to refrain from mixing indiscriminately into primary contests across the country as not conducive to party harmony. At the bottom of a communication to this effect from Tumulty, the President obligingly scrawled, "I certainly agree with you," and from time to time he did reject appeals from various quarters.[28] Nevertheless, his low boiling point, when it came to personal antipathies, led him frequently to stray from the path of non-intervention. Among the many Democratic senators thoroughly objectionable to him was John K. Shields of Tennessee.[29] A Bourbon of the old school, Shields had quarreled bitterly with the President over patronage matters and taken an obdurate anti-administration stand on legislation concerning the development of water power resources on the national domain. Singling him out as "one of the men I would dearly love to see left out of the Senate, because I don't like either his attitude or his principles," Wilson urged the defeat of Shields on the ground that "our only hope of success as leaders of the party is in confining our support to genuine out-and-out friends."[30] He was persuaded, however, to forgo an open fight against the senator, whose good "acid test" record made him impervious to the sort of tactics employed to dispose of Hardwick and Vardaman. Nevertheless, Governor Tom C. Rye waged a vigorous campaign against Shields on the ground that Wilson did not want him in the Senate. Shields, however, rather easily surmounted this obstacle in the August 1 primary, which he carried with 67,026 votes to 55,237 for the governor.[31]

If the President showed restraint in Tennessee, albeit reluctantly, his feelings got the better of his judgment in a Texas contest, with results most harmful to his cause. The Texas congressional delegation had seldom shown much enthusiasm for Wilson or his policies, and none had achieved greater notoriety in this respect than ''Big Jeff'' McLemore, whose celebrated ''acid test'' resolution called for retribution, at least in patriotic circles. The Texas legislature had unintentionally contributed to this end by redistricting the state and abolishing the office of congressman-at-large, into which a tidal wave of anti-Wilson sentiment had swept McLemore in 1916.[32] Compelled to seek re-election in a rural district not impressed by his record, he was overwhelmingly defeated in a three-cornered contest, polling but two thousand votes out of twenty-one thousand cast. The result was widely acclaimed as a fitting reward for a congressman who had counseled a policy of cowardice and surrender in the face of German aggression.[33] Had the President been content with this modest achievement, nothing further would have been thought of the matter despite the renomination of several pro-McLemore congressmen in other Texas districts. Instead, the public learned with surprise on July 25 of a telegram from Wilson to H. L. Beach, a San Antonio newspaper editor, attacking the record of Representative James L. Slayden of that district (the Fourteenth) and implying that the administration desired his defeat.[34]

Slayden, a veteran of twenty-two years' service in the House, immediately withdrew from the race upon learning of the President's displeasure and left the field to his two rivals. His ''acid test'' record of supporting the McLemore and Cooper resolutions and opposing the draft was no worse than that of many of his Democratic colleagues. For many years, however, he had served as president of the American Peace Society and taken an active part in organizations devoted to promoting a better understanding among nations. Since this was also a subject very close to Wilson's heart, his attitude toward Slayden seemed inexplicable. The party press took Wilson sharply to task for promoting the candidacy of a renowned pacifist like Henry Ford, who was not even a Democrat, and demanding the defeat of a loyal party veteran like Slayden. The local press attributed the proscription to the fact that one of Slayden's rivals for the congressional nomination happened to be a brother-in-law of Postmaster General Burleson. "It will not," said the Dallas *Morning News*, "tend to make the public lenient in judging the President's act. Mr. Slayden's faults are not more menacing to the public welfare than is the idea that the President may properly use the power of his office and his own personal prestige to proscribe a member of Congress who has incurred his displeasure or the displeasure of one of his Cabinet officers."[35] Since neither Wilson nor Burleson could very well vouchsafe an explanation,[36] this bit of political skullduggery made a bad impression. It was grist to the Republican propaganda mill and afforded the press endless opportunity for sermonizing.

In his next attempt to purge a member of the House, Wilson encountered a less accommodating individual in the person of Representative George Huddleston of the Ninth Alabama District, comprising the city of Birmingham and some of the adjacent coal country. Huddleston's "acid test" record was one of the worst, in consequence of which the patriotic citizens of Birmingham had leagued against him and, through Frank P. Glass, publisher of the Birmingham *News*, solicited Wilson's help in driving the congressman from office. An old friend of the President, Glass kept the White House posted on political developments in Alabama and also had a hand in the distribution of federal patronage in the state. Wilson at first demurred to the request on the ground that while he would like to oblige, it would be a serious mistake "if I were to do in many cases what I did in peculiar circumstances in the case of Mr. Slayden."[37]

A few days later the President changed his mind and sent

Glass a telegram saying that while the administration did not discriminate between candidates equally loyal, "I think I am justified in saying that Mr. Huddleston's record proved him in every way an opponent of the administration."[38] Armed with this *lettre de cachet,* the local press redoubled its attack. Huddleston, however, stood his ground and politely defied the President, although the Democratic state organization abandoned him and threw its support to one of his two competitors. Speaker Champ Clark and Majority Leader Claude Kitchin rushed to Huddleston's assistance, however, with letters highly laudatory of his patriotic services in Congress. Local patriots, angered by this deliberate muddling of the situation, denounced Clark and Kitchin as a pair of "super pacifists" and urged the voters to follow the President's lead. "The Republicans today," said one Birmingham newspaper, "are trying to gain control of the next Congress and are claiming that their party has been more loyal in support of Wilson than the Democrats have been. In support of this claim they point to Huddleston, to Vardaman, to Hardwick and others who have failed to uphold the President on vital issues."[39] The upshot of all this was Huddleston's renomination on August 13 by a substantial majority. The Republicans chortled over Wilson's fancied chagrin and wanted to know why he had not intervened against other Alabama congressmen with equally poor "acid test" records.

Wilson's prestige recovered somewhat following the outcome of the Mississippi primary two weeks later. The entry of a third candidate into the Senate race had threatened to divide the "loyal" voters, already somewhat befuddled by a shift in Vardaman's tactics. The senator now went about claiming that his enemies greatly exaggerated his rift with the White House and that the President really wanted him back. After a frantic appeal from the Harrison contingent to straighten matters out, Wilson sent off a letter saying that Vardaman's re-election would constitute a repudiation of himself and everything he stood for.[40] Although Vardaman raged about outside interference in a local election, even his celebrated Negro-baiting tactics were of no avail against Wilson's prompt and biting repudiation. On August 31 he ran 13,000 votes behind Harrison, whose clear majority in a total of 107,000 votes obviated the necessity for a run-off primary and assured his election in November. The result was widely acclaimed,[41] and only Hardwick of Georgia remained to be disposed of at a later date.

IV

ABOUT MIDWAY through the 1918 campaign, an already confused situation was further complicated by the extraordinary activities of the National Security League. For some months the League had been pressuring the public to return only loyal congressmen that fall and to reject all those tainted with pacifism or pro-Germanism.[42] It had noted with approval the President's "acid test" statement in connection with the Wisconsin election, but since that time it had viewed with alarm the large number of tainted congressmen winning renomination compared to the small number of rejects. In July the Executive Committee decided to take positive steps to redress the situation. At the direction of the executive secretary, Charles D. Orth, a New York hemp importer, it drew up a chart setting forth the voting records of all congressmen on measures of vital importance to wartime American interests.[43]

Wilson's "acid test" statement had envisaged only three such measures: the McLemore resolution, the Cooper amendment, and the embargo on arms to the Allies. The League dropped the embargo issue, since it had never come to a vote, and added six other measures. Four concerned the preparedness controversy in the Sixty-fourth Congress; the other two were war measures handled by the Sixty-fifth Congress. Included in the chart were: (1) the Kahn amendment of March 23, 1916, to the Hay-Chamberlain Army bill, authorizing an increase in the regular establishment to 178,000 as recommended by the General Staff; (2) the Brandegee amendment of May 18, 1916, to the same bill, providing for a Regular Army of 250,000; (3) Section 56 of the same bill, setting up a volunteer reserve army wholly under federal control and thus in effect abolishing the militia; (4) the motion of June 2, 1916, to recommit the naval appropriation bill, which, if carried, would have authorized several more battleships; (5) the declaration of war on April 6, 1917; and (6) the Kahn amendment of April 23, 1917, to the Army bill, restoring the War Department's original provision for conscription. Later on, the League issued a chart to guide voters in selecting the right senators,[44] but this never received the attention or created the uproar that greeted the appearance of the House chart.

Until the Slayden incident the League had been in a quandary as to what to include on its list. On July 27, two days after the publication of the President's telegram, the Executive Committee issued a statement saying, ''President Wilson now comes to our assistance by laying down the principle that a Congressman's entire war record shall determine his fitness, and not his present attitude.''[45] By this criterion, only forty-seven congressmen had perfect records. Of the spotless, forty-five came from eastern seaboard states, and of these only three were Democrats. At the other end of the scale — and this was the roll of infamy — seven representatives (five Democrats, one Republican, and one Socialist) had voted wrong on all eight measures; twenty-two on seven; thirty on six; and fifty-eight on five.[46] On the basis of states, only Rhode Island had a perfect record. Massachusetts came second with only 4.69 per cent of its congressional votes in error, and Connecticut third with 5 per cent. As one went South and West, the situation deteriorated rapidly. North Dakota had the worst record of all with 79.16 per cent of its votes in error, while Colorado was a close second in shame with 78.12 per cent wrong.[47]

The appearance of the chart spread consternation in the ranks of both parties. Democrats thus invidiously singled out appealed piteously to the White House for help to clear them of the charges. Republicans caught in the same predicament had no recourse but to denounce the League on the floor of the House and hint darkly about the source of its ample funds. Critics reproached the League for not mentioning the 119 war measures enacted since the country joined the Allies. Moreover, of the eight ''acid test'' measures, only two had been subject to a straight yea or nay vote, the rest being complicated parliamentary maneuvers that did not accurately reflect a congressman's final position on the matter. To all such complaints the League replied that if Congress chose to conduct its business in a manner incomprehensible to the average citizen, it alone bore the responsibility for any misunderstandings that might arise.

The chart was circulated to 1,800 newspapers that summer, and congressional casualties picked up perceptibly. Two Democratic representatives from Ohio, a pair from Colorado, and two from Missouri all met defeat at the hands of alerted patriots.[48] Republican losses occurred chiefly in Wisconsin, where the campaign of the indefatigably patriotic Milwaukee *Journal* to eradicate the stigma of La Follettism bore fruit, partially at least, in the refusal of the voters to renominate Representatives Henry A. Cooper, John M. Nelson, and William J. Cary, all political allies of Fighting Bob.[49] Cooper, who had fathered one of the "acid test" measures, had served a quarter of a century in Congress and, with Nelson, had been among the leaders of the Progressive revolt which broke the autocratic power of Speaker Joseph G. Cannon. The Old Guard element did not regret their departure, but it raised questions as to the impartiality of the League's operations and the source of its funds.[50]

The Illinois senatorial campaign of Mayor William Hale Thompson of Chicago created the greatest embarrassment for the Republican party on the "acid test" issue. The mayor's idiotic remarks and stupid conduct with respect to the war had offended decent Americans everywhere, and his crude effort to cash in on the strong pro-German sentiment in his state was widely condemned. Thompson's local popularity promised serious trouble for Representative Medill McCormick, the self-styled loyalty candidate, while the entry into the race of Representative George E. Foss threatened to split the so-called loyal vote. Foss resented the effrontery of McCormick and the Chicago *Tribune* in monopolizing the patriotic sentiment of Illinois; he also felt that his twenty-five years of service in the House, compared to McCormick's single term, entitled him to promotion to the Senate. In this crisis the friends of McCormick prevailed upon Roosevelt to take a hand. Accordingly the Rough Rider appeared at the Springfield State Fair late in August, where he seared Thompson in a fiery speech that included President Wilson as well. He also saw Foss privately and urged him to withdraw, but relations had cooled between them since 1912, when Foss stayed with the party, and the effort came to naught.[51]

As another of the tests of loyalty to the Union, the Illinois contest attracted wide attention. Whether it was Roosevelt's support, or McCormick's lavish use of money (as his rivals claimed), or Thompson's failure to roll up his expected majority in Chicago, the *Tribune* owner triumphed on September 10, polling 192,122 votes to 132,511 for Big Bill, while Foss came in a poor third with 61,640.[52] Republican national headquarters heaved a sigh of relief, since the result simplified the task of disposing of the elegant and bewhiskered Democratic incumbent, James Hamilton Lewis, who had already received the official While House benediction in a letter saying that the President counted upon him to put his "usual spirit and energy into a campaign which I am sure will assist to make the issues clear in Illinois."[53]

After the primaries were over, the congressional victims of the "acid test" returned to Washington to pour out their tales of woe before a sympathetic House. On September 11 McLemore of Texas told how he had been undone by a venal press in the pay of Wall Street, while a few days later Cooper of Wisconsin laid his defeat to the sinister machinations of the National Security League.[54] Edmund Platt of New York defended the League on the ground that while some of the parliamentary maneuvering might have been carelessly misrepresented, four of the votes were "vital," and those voting wrong should admit the fact and accept the consequences. The majority of his colleagues, irked by all the unfavorable publicity, felt otherwise. On October 4 Congress ordered a searching investigation of the League, but decided to postpone the inquiry until after the November elections.

CHAPTER XII

THE ISSUES

WILSON'S ENEMIES would have had a harder time upsetting the
Democratic apple cart in November had the administration seen
fit to follow a more consistent price-fixing policy. Failure of the
government to establish an over-all ceiling on raw materials and
manufactured goods and to adopt a uniform system of controls
generated a vast amount of public irritation, which in turn produced unfortunate political consequences. Although federal
agencies like the Food and Fuel Administrations and the War
Industries Board possessed vague powers to regulate production,
distribution, and prices within certain limited fields, price-fixing
was confined to commodities purchased by the government in
such quantities as to sharply curtail civilian supplies. Otherwise,
producers' prices received scant attention, apart from ineffectual
attempts to influence the margins set by middlemen such as
millers and meat-packers. Consequently, profiteering flourished
mightily, and the cost of living rose spectacularly amid a chorus
of angry protests from the unhappy consumers.[1]

The spectacle of certain unregulated interests enjoying wartime benefits denied to citizens with enterprises subject to official
restraints afforded additional grounds for complaint. Actually,
little economic injustice was involved since the government took
care to fix the prices of regulated commodities well above their
pre-war levels, thus assuring generous profits all around. Politically, however, the exemption of certain commodities from
government control proved to be a serious blunder. The magnitude of the economic interests concerned, as well as their peculiar
geographical location, laid the administration open to charges of
sectional favoritism at a time when it could ill afford to give
the appearance of promoting the welfare of one group over
another.

I

WHEN, on August 30, 1917, the President set a price of $2.20 a bushel for the 1917 wheat crop, his action affected the prosperity of some three million western farmers. A short crop of 630 million bushels, of which nearly half had to be exported to the Allies, left the American consumer with less than half his normal bread supply. By guaranteeing the farmer against the dizzy price fluctuations of the early war period, the authorities hoped to expand 1918 production to at least one billion bushels. Although the price set was 27 per cent above the 1916 level, and 109 per cent above the average for the previous three years, the West considered the rate far too low.[2] Wheat growers complained bitterly that the steadily rising cost of all the unregulated items, including farm wages, which went into the production of wheat cut deeply into their margin of profit. Western farmers quickly became suspicious that an unholy alliance existed between the government and predatory financial interests bent on robbing them of their rightful share of the wartime prosperity. Agrarian discontent had reached such proportions by the end of the year that the Food Administrator warned the President of the imperative need to eliminate existing inequalities by the exercise of a general price-fixing power vested either in himself or in the Federal Trade Commission.[3]

Consequently, in his annual message to Congress on December 4, Wilson requested more specific legislation to control profiteering and wider authority to fix prices on the necessities of life in order to check inflation. Congress, however, was in no mood to extend the powers of the President or anyone else in that direction. The Senate responded by killing an attempt to regulate the newsprint industry, which had the newspapers of the country in a merciless price squeeze, after Senator Harding accused Wilson of heading the nation straight for socialism with the same iniquitous price-fixing scheme that had wrecked the coal industry.[4] Congressional opposition to governmental interference with free enterprise became even more implacable following the Garfield order of January 16 closing down all industries for several days. As a result of this unfortunate development, the price-fixing legislation sponsored by the Food Administration never emerged from committee.[5] Nevertheless, the popular agitation for wider controls continued unabated, and the New York *Tribune* predicted accurately on February 22 that ''inevitably the price of wheat will become a political issue. We have injected into politics a class question. Price-fixing will become a national issue because you cannot fix one price and not all prices.''

Congress, uneasily aware of the necessity of doing something about the matter, inclined to the simple expedient of placating the farmer by raising the minimum rate for the 1918 wheat crop. The increase would coincide with the congressional campaign that fall and benefit quite a few statesmen. Under pressure from the Granges, the Farmers' Unions, and the Federal Board of Farm Organizations — which Gifford Pinchot had established in Washington for the purpose of detaching the farmer from the Democratic party — western congressmen offered a spate of amendments to the agricultural appropriation bill that set the price of wheat at three dollars or more per bushel.[6] The Senate Committee on Agriculture finally settled on $2.50 a bushel as about the limit it thought the public would stand. On February 20 this figure became the basis of the celebrated Gore amendment, which was destined to have a significant influence on the fortunes of Wilson's party that fall.

In order to head off this inflationary gesture, which his advisers warned him would add $200 million to the nation's food bill, the President on February 23 fixed the price of the 1918 crop at $2.20. He justified extending the 1917 figure on the ground that it assured the farmer a reasonable profit. A higher price, he said, would not only work hardship on the Allied and American peoples but seriously dislocate wage scales all over the country. Such considerations made no impression on the Senate, which hearkened instead to the complaints of angry farmers who had started to cut back their wheat acreage and plant their land to coarse grains — oats, rye, and barley — the prices of which were uncontrolled and rising rapidly. Although the Food Administration urged Congress to stop this trend by bringing the coarse grains under regulation, the lawmakers preferred to tinker with the price of wheat.[7] On March 21 the

Senate adopted the Gore amendment with little opposition, although the urban press denounced the move as a blatherskite attempt to bribe the farm vote at the expense of all the nations battling against German autocracy.

The House, more sensitive to such criticism, pared ten cents off the Gore amendment figure. The Senate's stubborn refusal to concur in this modest concession to the long-suffering consumer delayed passage of the appropriation bill for three months. Although western advisers like Scott Ferris urged him to accept a compromise that would alleviate the unrest in the farm belt, the President made his opposition to such inflationary legislation abundantly clear.[8] The British government also brought pressure to bear through its ambassador in Washington to resist the higher wheat price, which would require Britain to borrow an additional $100 million for food imports.[9] Consequently, after the Senate had yielded to the lower House figure early in July, Wilson promptly vetoed the bill despite frantic protests from western Democrats that this would wreck the party's prospects in the coming elections.[10]

After the House sustained the veto, the whole West seethed with angry disappointment. Many blamed the President's advisers, mostly easterners with little or no knowledge of farming conditions, for having led him astray with regard to the inflationary character of the Gore amendment. Senator Borah, among those who had tried to get Wilson to take a broader view of the matter, professed to be "utterly demoralized by the veto," which the senator felt was "hideously unjust" in view of the shameless profiteering on the part of millers and farm equipment manufacturers.[11] Senator Gore set forth his opinions on the iniquity of Wilson's action in a magazine article, "The Wheat Farmer's Dilemma," which made excellent Republican propaganda throughout the wheat belt and did his party great disservice in that region.

II

ALTHOUGH the author of the Gore amendment informed the Senate on July 15 that Wilson's veto would deliver the next

Congress into Republican hands, the agitation might have passed with a minimum of damage to the President's cause but for other factors involved in the situation. As it was, the veto proved to be the turning point in Wilson's political fortunes. What really irked the wheat farmer, who greatly exaggerated his sufferings under his price limitations, was the immunity from control enjoyed by cotton. Under wartime conditions cotton prices had zoomed to record heights, with prospects of going higher as the war continued. To the western farmer, the opportunity thus afforded the South for profiteering seemed gross favoritism on the part of an administration dominated mainly by men from that section. The activity of the congressional cotton bloc, which fought off every effort to lay a tax or fix a price on that staple, placed a lethal political weapon in the hands of Wilson's enemies.

Trouble on this score had been brewing for some time. A member of the Federal Farm Loan Board traveling through the West in the spring of 1917 found that "a studied attempt is being made to create sectional hostility at the expense of the Democrats" over southern domination of Congress and the attitude toward cotton.[12] The controversy did not assume serious proportions, however, until December, when cotton passed the 30-cent mark, a figure roughly proportional to the price fixed on wheat. When the price reached thirty-six cents that spring, the rumblings of discontent throughout the North and West broke into an angry uproar. Beyond the confines of Dixie the 400 per cent rise in the price of raw cotton represented a menace to industry and a hardship on workers.[13] The press demanded immediate action by the government to put an end to the flagrant favoritism shown the southern planter.[14] Such talk raised a correspondingly intense commotion in the South, which not only resented northern criticism but feared that the administration might yield to pressure from Yankee industrialists. Dixie newspapers insisted that the benefits from inflated cotton prices were more apparent than real and that the Yankees exaggerated the profit angle for ulterior reasons.[15]

All attempts at regulation had failed. Cotton had been included in the Lever food control act until southern interests had forced its exclusion. During consideration of the Gore amendment, western congressmen had introduced several bills to bring the staple under control. Although rejected, they had created consternation in Dixie, depressed the price, and left the cotton market in a very nervous condition. The merest rumor of price control set off a panic of short selling that frayed the tempers of the growers and their congressional champions. When cotton slumped $30 a bale on reports that spring of a comprehensive plan to stabilize the entire industry, only a War Industries Board promise to exempt raw cotton from such a scheme checked the downward plunge.[16] Angry southerners declared that no parallel existed between commodities under regulation (like coal and wheat) and cotton, which had to be left to the uninhibited operation of the law of supply and demand.

By now the President himself had come around to this point of view. In his May 27 "politics is adjourned" address calling for new tax legislation, Wilson vigorously attacked profiteering but limited his proposals for its control to the imposition of stiffer excess profits taxes. His failure to mention price-fixing as a possible remedy greatly irritated the organs of public opinion in the North. The Indianapolis *News* remarked that by not recommending legislation to regulate cotton, the administration had put itself "into a deep hole with respect to profiteering, which it pretends to deplore but has failed to raise a hand to stop."[17] The hole became deeper when Congress, in framing the new revenue act, ignored Wilson's suggestion about excess profits taxes and exempted the $1.5 billion earned by cotton growers from all levies.

Political self-preservation now compelled several Democratic congressmen from western farming areas, including William A. Ayres of Kansas and William E. Cox of Indiana, to break with their party on the issue. Cox arraigned his southern colleagues for wishing a price fixed on wheat because cotton planters wanted cheap bread, while ignoring the fact that 35-cent cotton put even the cheapest grades of calico beyond the reach of the poor in industrial areas.[18] His proposal to fix the price at fifteen cents may have been only a gesture to mollify his Indiana farming constituents, but the immediate effect was to drive down the market price and embitter the South. Cox's bill was promptly

referred to the Committee on Agriculture, where it met the fate
of all similar legislation.

Southern planters, ignoring the pleas of the Hoover organization to use part of their land for food crops, had put every available acre into cotton in anticipation of continuing high prices.
The result at the end of June was the third largest crop on
record, or about fifteen million bales, which presented growers
with the unwelcome prospect of a huge, unsalable surplus and
severely depressed the market. Panicky southern bankers and
cotton factors immediately pressed the government to take the
unmanageable crop off their hands. They suggested a United
States Cotton Corporation, similar to the one that handled the
wheat crop, which would fix the price, store all the farmer could
not sell, and advance him enough money to cover his expenses.
The general run of cotton growers, however, found the scheme
utterly objectionable. Their representatives at a great conclave
in New Orleans early in July insisted that the price could be
kept high without government interference if the farmer
marketed his crop gradually and did not sell more than 20 per
cent of his cotton in any one month, a view endorsed by most
southern newspapers.[19]

The cotton moguls, however, carried the fight to Washington,
where Governor William P. G. Harding of the Federal Reserve
Board at their behest sent the President a memorandum strongly
recommending the fixing of cotton prices.[20] Southern congressmen quickly convinced Wilson of the inutility of such a step,
whereupon he informed the governor, "frankly my mind shies
off from price fixing, but Mr. Lever [of South Carolina], who
came to see me the other day about this same situation, had a
series of suggestions to make which seemed to me wise and which
seemed likely to meet the situation."[21] How wisely or how well
Lever's suggestions met the situation remained to be seen, but
the southern press in general commended him for having turned
Wilson against the selfish scheme of a few big operators unrepre-
sentative of the South as a whole.[22]

The decision of the government not to interfere with cotton
prices, coming as it did a few days after the President's veto
of the Gore amendment, tossed the whole controversy into the

political arena. As one western newspaper pointed out, "The Iowa farmer would be satisfied with the present price of wheat if he did not know that the Georgia cotton farmer is allowed to sell his product on an unregulated market. He thinks there is politics in that situation, and he is right."[23] Thereafter, Chairman Hays saw to it that Republican party conventions in the farm-belt states adopted planks on the subject and that the issue was played up in party newspapers and at party rallies. Nebraska Republicans, meeting at Lincoln on July 30 in a convention at which the largest attendance in years was reported, said: "We condemn the Democratic administration for discrimination in its price-fixing program and particularly for its failure to fix a reasonable price for cotton when it fixed the price for wheat."[24] In the next few weeks conventions in Ohio, Kansas, Montana, Colorado, New Mexico, and Utah adopted similar declarations.[25] By the time the campaign opened, the West was aflame with the issue, although the Democratic high command in Washington remained strangely oblivious to the danger signals.[26]

III

WHEN CONGRESS reconvened late in August after a brief recess, the members quickly got down to the business of manufacturing political capital for the campaign now at hand. With a few exceptions the primaries were over,[27] and both parties squared off in earnest for the decisive contest. Republican orators attacked the administration almost daily for mismanaging the war effort, for favoring the South over the rest of the country, and for gratuitously and shamelessly interfering in various state elections, particularly in Michigan and Wisconsin. The Democratic side entered a spirited denial of such canards, extolled Wilson's competence as a war leader amid a great display of statistical evidence, and heartily impugned both the motives and the loyalty of their adversaries.[28]

The most important item of business on the calendar, and a fruitful source of partisan discord, was the manpower bill. The rapid exhaustion of the reservoir of Class I men, caused by the scandalously high exemption rate, required an extension of the draft age at both ends if the War Department wished to avoid dipping into the lower classifications to reach its original figure of two million men.[29] The great German offensive that spring had given the problem a particular urgency and inspired Major General Leonard Wood and his Republican friends to start an agitation for an army of five million men as the bare minimum necessary to bring about the defeat of Germany. Colonel Roosevelt, once more upon the warpath after rallying from his recent illness, spearheaded a noisy drive to send one hundred divisions to France instead of the thirty that the Army planned to have there by the end of the year; and Taft, Hughes, and other notables added their voices to this campaign.[30]

When Wilson ignored their clamor and declined to ask Congress for the necessary changes in the selective service law, his critics angrily attributed his indifference to the Democratic phobia about conscription, and they tried hard to force the issue with him during the debate on the Army appropriation bill in June. Senator Albert B. Fall of New Mexico offered a resolution to extend the draft to the age group between 20 and 40, while other Republican senators moved to authorize an army of five million men. Baker's rejection of these proposals raised a storm of protest, and only a promise from the Secretary on June 26 to submit a new bill within ninety days enabled the appropriation bill to pass unamended. Although the Fall amendment failed 25 to 49, with only two Democrats voting for it, many senators continued to grumble about the unnecessary delay.[31]

The administration changed its mind apparently as a result of a demand from General Pershing on June 25 for 80 divisions in France by the following April. This would require the drafting of 300,000 men per month, or about three times the current rate. Congress, however, was hardly prepared for the drastic bill which the War Department submitted in August. The recommendation for a minimum age limit of eighteen far exceeded that proposed by Senator Fall and rasped congressional nerves always most sensitive in this respect. To the astonishment and anger of the press, which had been beating the drums for a bigger draft army, the unruly House Military Affairs Committee amended the act by deferring the call-up of those under 20 until the quotas of all other classes had been reviewed and exhausted. Although the entire Democratic leadership supported the McKenzie amendment, the House defeated it after a strenuous fight by a vote of 167 to 120. The next day, August 25, a final effort by Democratic leaders to kill the draft bill on a motion to recommit lost 147 to 194, with the Republicans dividing 57 to 117 against the motion and the Democrats voting 88 to 74 against the administration (exclusive of five minor party members). The spectacle of Democratic leaders again in collision with the President on a vital war issue lent luster to Republican propaganda claims that their support alone had enabled the nation to win the war in the face of Democratic obstructionism. Newspapers all over the country added the vote on the manpower bill to the "acid test" measures on the League chart and advertised the stand of local congressmen on the question.[32]

As the tide of battle on the western front turned in favor of the Allies, the Republicans set up a clamor for unconditional surrender and denounced as treason any other method of ending the war. Early in September, Chairman Hays told the press that the Democrats would stop at nothing, even an inconclusive peace, to win the elections. This statement was shortly followed by a manifesto from the new chairman of the congressional campaign committee, Representative Simeon D. Fess of Ohio, declaring that nothing short of a Republican victory in November would insure the nation against a compromise or inconclusive peace.[33] It was Fess's initial appearance in the campaign after the patriots on the committee had finally forced out the old isolationist chairman, Woods of Iowa, on August 27.[34] Stung by the remarks of Hays and Fess, the White House immediately fired off telegrams to both men demanding a public apology for their brazen attempt to undermine the President's war aims, "which are those of all nations," through vulgar innuendoes that would dilute those aims with doubt.[35]

The appearance of this correspondence set off a tremendous hubbub. Although the signature on the White House telegrams was Tumulty's, the phraseology was unmistakably Wilson's. The Republican press waxed vitriolic over the President's assumption of infallibility and claim to immunity from suggestion or criticism. Pro-administration newspapers like the New York *Times* regretted the megalomania which had put the inhabitants of the White House into a state of mind wherein anyone opposed to the Democratic party was guilty of a species of moral turpitude. The *Times* did not consider the ''natural hankering'' of the Republicans for victory in the elections valid grounds for treason. Moreover, it considered Hays correct in attacking the ''peace without victory'' attitude that seemed to permeate administration circles in Washington, particularly a ''certain socialist coterie'' close to the White House and anxious to end the war on any terms.[36] Wilson's adversaries, delighted by this extraordinary display of sensitivity on the peace issue, struck repeatedly and savagely at this chink in his armor in the weeks remaining before the election.[37]

IV

IN THE EASTERN STATES, Wilson's party counted strongly on carrying the industrial centers, where the war boom had brought high wages. The rising cost of living, which largely absorbed the increased earnings of the workers, handicapped the administration to some extent inasmuch as the government had failed to control the manufacturers and retailers responsible for gouging the public. On the other hand, high prices constituted a serious hazard for the Republican party, the party of big business, which had spawned most of the profiteers and championed their interests, particularly in the cities, against higher income taxes and war profits taxes and against price controls and higher wages. This sort of propaganda had little appeal for the mass of voters, who presumably sympathized with the ''soak the rich'' program of Democratic congressional leaders and remained deaf to strident Republican fulminations against such class legislation. The crass indifference of his party to the interests of the toiler alarmed Senator Borah. ''The Republican party,'' he said, ''through the action of some of its leaders has handed the labor vote of this country practically en masse to the President.

By dealing with them not in a cooperative spirit but in a spirit of criticism we have practically landed 80 or 85 per cent of them in the Democratic party.''[38]

As things turned out, Borah was unduly pessimistic. Organized labor, like other pressure groups, tended to distribute its political favors on a personal rather than on a party basis. Congressmen who had incurred the ire of workers' organizations were attacked irrespective of party affiliation. Consequently, little reliance could be placed on the statements of labor leaders like Gompers or on the action of groups like the Ohio State Federation of Labor, which at its Columbus convention on October 15 endorsed the state Democratic ticket and praised Wilson for his brave fight on behalf of industrial freedom.[39] The American Federation of Labor, moreover, had constructed an ''acid test'' chart of its own, listing fourteen measures affecting the interests of the workingman on which Congress had taken some action. The Federation had warned Wilson that it would not support Democrats with bad records in this respect. Consequently, the labor people entered a candidate in the Louisville, Kentucky, district against Representative J. Swagar Sherley, who had opposed nine of the Federation's fourteen measures and supported only two. Since Sherley was chairman of the Appropriations Committee and an important Democratic leader loyal to the President, the administration tried hard to save him.[40] After much persuasion on Wilson's part, the labor man withdrew from the race, but it did not help Sherley, who lost both the labor vote and the election on November 5.[41]

The railroad vote was an important factor in many sparsely settled western states. The numerous benefits accruing to the railroad workers from government operation of the carriers seemed to assure the Democratic party the great bulk of this vote. The prospect seriously disturbed the Republicans, who sourly viewed this vast federal undertaking, especially a $300 million wage raise in the spring, as a cynical plot to keep Wilson and McAdoo in office indefinitely. Again their apprehensions proved groundless, for, as one disillusioned Democrat glumly remarked after the November disaster, ''railroad men didn't vote as they should.''[42] Strong labor support in the Spokane area, an important railway center, failed to materialize as expected on behalf of Representative Clarence C. Dill of the Fifth Washington District. The fact that Dill stood high on the National Security League's list of undersirable congressmen may have had something to do with it, but in the opinion of many qualified local observers, the strong feeling in the state over the sectional issue ruled out the possibility of electing any Democratic congressman that year, regardless of his "acid test" record.[43]

V

THE ONLY other prominent issues that year were prohibition and woman suffrage. Each had a host of fanatical followers unimpressed by the argument that such problems were better left to an era of peace. The war merely whetted their zeal for a quick decision. The prohibitionists stressed the urgent need to conserve foodstuffs wasted in manufacturing alcohol for convivial and unpatriotic purposes, while the suffragettes insisted that the role played by women in war work entitled them to the rights of citizenship. Of the two amendments, the Eighteenth was already before the country. Fourteen states had adopted it by late summer and one — Louisiana — had rejected it. Several state legislatures would be chosen that fall on the issue of ratifying the amendment, and the temperance people had a number of state administrations under attack for jockeying on the question.[44]

Wilson disliked the prohibitionist tactics of using the war to dry up the country in advance of ratification. In 1917 he had blocked an attempt to affix a "bone-dry" rider to the food control act, but the temperance people had bounced back with the Randall amendment, which they tacked on to the 1918 agricultural appropriation bill. This piece of legislation, adopted early in September, spread gloom through convivial circles and upset Postmaster General Burleson, who urged Wilson to veto it on the ground that it would severely damage Democratic prospects in several eastern states.[45] Since Wilson had already vetoed the same bill because of the Gore amendment, he was loath to disarrange the services of the Department of Agriculture a second time, and he reluctantly allowed it to become law.

The result, while not helpful to the Democrats in the areas indicated by Burleson, brought great joy to the rural districts, where the politicians of both parties vied frantically for the favor of the Anti-Saloon League.[46] This widely feared organization had made a patriotic issue out of the Teutonic nomenclature of much American beer and had accused the brewers of a vast plot financed by German money to subvert the government. Opposition to the Eighteenth Amendment was equated with allegiance to the Kaiser, and a massive campaign of slander and intimidation launched against the advocates of individual liberty.[47] Prohibitionist tactics and propaganda produced bizarre results in some of the state elections but had negligible consequences for the congressional contests, since both parties displayed great dexterity in straddling the issue.

Far more damaging to the Democratic cause was the party's attitude toward woman suffrage. The Nineteenth Amendment, approved by the House in January after Wilson had come out strongly in its favor, had bogged down in the Senate Committee on Privileges and Elections for want of a two-thirds majority to bring it onto the floor. Many southern senators, who did not like the idea of enfranchising Negroes, would not agree with Wilson that the role of women in war work entitled them to the vote. Several influential party newspapers, including the New York *World* and the Baltimore *Sun,* broke with him on the old-fashioned notion that woman's place was still in the home. Although the President wrote to a number of anti-suffrage senators urging them at least to allow the amendment to come to a vote, none paid him any heed.[48] The situation became embarrassing for him late in August, when the Republican senatorial caucus endorsed the amendment and thus absolved the party from further responsibility for the Senate's inaction.[49]

The prolonged impasse infuriated the suffragette leaders. With feminine illogic they held the President to blame despite all his efforts on their behalf.[50] With her militant followers again picketing the White House, Miss Alice Paul, chairwoman of the

National Woman's Party, blasted him for failing to hold his
forces in line and shrilly announced that all Democratic candidates for Congress would "walk the plank" unless the party
rallied behind the amendment. The head of the less militant
National American Woman Suffrage Association, Carrie Chapman Catt, also threatened an intensive campaign against all
senators, particularly in the West, whom she considered lukewarm or hostile to the cause.[51] Consequently, a number of administration stalwarts — including Charles B. Henderson of
Nevada, Thomas J. Walsh of Montana, John F. Shafroth of
Colorado, and William H. Thompson of Kansas — found their
re-election jeopardized not by their own views on the question
but by the refusal of their Bourbon colleagues to heed the
President's appeals.[52]

Toward the end of September the White House finally prevailed upon the Senate to bring the amendment to a vote. At
McAdoo's urging, Wilson reluctantly consented to address that
body on September 30, although he had scant hope of persuading
it to listen to reason. His misgivings proved correct when the
amendment failed of adoption the next day by two votes. In
addition to ten Republican standpatters, twenty-one Democrats
refused to be shaken out of their lifelong prejudices. The defeat
shocked and dismayed the progressive element in the party.[53]
"We tried hard," said Senator Walsh of Montana, "to put
across the suffrage amendment resolution, not alone because of
its intrinsic merits, and the plain justice of the cause, but in
the belief that its success would materially aid us in keeping
control of the Senate, much imperilled as I think."[54]

This stunning rebuff to Wilson deprived the Democratic
campaign plea — to stand by the President by electing Democrats to office — of whatever cogency or merit it might once have
had. When the New Jersey state Democratic convention rejected
a woman suffrage plank on the same day as the vote in the
Senate, the Newark *Evening News* remarked: "It will not be
overlooked that while the President was pleading at Washington
for the adoption of the suffrage amendment, a Democratic convention in his home state declined to include suffrage in its

principles.''[55] The issue was not overlooked in many states, particularly in the more progressive West, and contributed not a little to the nugatory effect of Wilson's more celebrated appeal to the voters three weeks later.

CHAPTER XIII

THE CAMPAIGN

I

THE FOURTH Liberty Loan drive somewhat retarded the opening of the congressional campaign insofar as the personal participation of the candidates was concerned.[1] During the drive, which began on September 18 and ran for the next three weeks, both parties more or less agreed to minimize their overt partisan activities and devote their collective energies to raising money for the war.[2] This informal truce proved difficult to maintain inasmuch as party orators, unable to resist their natural impulses, frequently interlarded patriotic appeals to buy bonds with appeals of a less disinterested sort. Democratic workers utilized Liberty Loan rallies to hand out circulars bearing the admonition: "Don't spoil all now by letting the election go against the government. Vote with President Wilson for the Democratic ticket and hasten the end of the war." Colonel Roosevelt roundly condemned McAdoo for hitting below the belt, and rebuked the President for permitting such unsportsmanlike tactics.[3]

The terrible plague of Spanish influenza also proved a serious handicap. The disease reached the United States that summer from Europe, where it had been prevalent for some time, through the medium of people arriving at ports along the Atlantic coast. The indifference of the health authorities to the potential danger had aroused uneasiness in the press, particularly in New York. Mayor Hylan's health commissioner, stung by what he considered politically inspired press attacks upon his professional competence, replied on August 17 in the name of his Department that "we have not felt and do not feel any anxiety about what people call Spanish influenza, and we considered it so unimportant that it did not seem necessary to make a public discussion of the situation.''[4]

This classic bit of medical opinion notwithstanding, the disease spread with frightful rapidity within the next two months, killing nearly half a million Americans and striking down millions more before running its course in the late fall. The epidemic had a dampening effect upon the campaign, since many communities closed schools, theaters, and other public meeting places and prohibited gatherings for any purpose of more than two or three people at a time. Like the Liberty Loan truce, this prohibition was only imperfectly observed. In many states it did not materially affect the activity of candidates, although there were fewer torchlight parades and other typically American mass demonstrations than usual. However, this did not matter so much in 1918, for, as one historian of the American political scene has pointed out, there had been a steady decline in the appeal of the old campaign techniques since 1896 and a vast increase in the distribution of printed material aimed at a more sophisticated electorate.[5] Stimulated in part by the ban on public gatherings, the volume of campaign literature reached phenomenal proportions in 1918 in nearly every state.

Despite these various obstacles and interruptions, party warfare did not flag perceptibly. The opening gun had sounded on September 9, when that unreliable political weathervane, the state of Maine, held elections as customary in advance of the rest of the country. To the dismay of the Democrats, who complained that the Downeasters had shown themselves ''more partisan than patriotic,'' the Republicans made a clean sweep by electing a governor, a United States senator and all four House representatives. Although the vote was about 10 per cent under the record-breaking 1916 total, the Republicans increased their pluralities in every contest.[6] The victors naturally viewed the result as a happy augury and virtuously asserted that they had done no campaigning out of deference to the President's statement that ''politics is adjourned.'' They noted with particular satisfaction the failure of the improper Democratic attempt to frighten the voters into believing that a Republican triumph would prolong the war and mean months of further bloodshed and suffering.

II

THE MOST SENSATIONAL contest in the East that fall occurred in Massachusetts. Of all the Republican senators up for re-election, none was more objectionable to Wilson than John W. Weeks.[7] In appearance the short, stout, heavy-jowled, totally bald senator resembled a Homer Davenport cartoon of a typical Republican plutocrat. Saluted in the press as the "master organizer" of the anti-Wilson resistance in the Sixty-fifth Congress, Weeks had harassed the President with the Committee on the Conduct of the War, led the assault on Baker and the War Department, fought the food control act, resisted the war revenue proposals of the Treasury Department, and advocated such unpalatable measures as the Gore amendment and the Roosevelt division.[8] Driven by his presidential ambitions and wrapping his reckless opportunism in a cloak of patriotic fustian, he staked everything on one bold gamble. When his stand on a war measure happened to coincide with the President's, he was frequently and noisily at odds on matters of detail. It was on this right to indulge freely in "constructive criticism" that he based his claim to re-election. "Politics," said Weeks in the keynote speech of his campaign, "as it affects the prosecution of the war should be adjourned, but politics which will result in the election of a Republican Congress cannot do otherwise than bring about a speedy victory and a return to normal conditions."[9] The return to normalcy, however, was to light the way of a less conspicuous but shrewder colleague to the White House.

Because Massachusetts felt neglected in the distribution of wartime favors, considerable feeling against the administration had developed in many localities.[10] Consequently, Weeks's anti-Wilson campaign might have enjoyed stronger support but for the ruthless manner in which the Republican machine had forced the popular war governor, Samuel W. McCall, to drop out of the primary because patriotism demanded Weeks's return to the Senate. The rank and file remained apathetic, and even Weeks's campaign manager could work up little enthusiasm. "I didn't want the job for a cent," he confessed, "but was told I was needed."[11] Liberal and independent elements rallied behind a rather peculiar third-party movement organized by the eccentric stockmarket gambler and Wall Street speculator Thomas W. Lawson, of *Frenzied Finance* fame. Hatred of the State Street crowd backing Weeks had impelled Lawson to enter the fray ostensibly to avenge the injustice done McCall. Proper Bostonians ignored him, but he flooded the state with pamphlets denouncing the corrupt interests that had sent Weeks to the Senate in 1912 and were endeavoring to do so again.[12] Lawson's political knight-errantry was expected to benefit the Democrats by siphoning off fringe elements among the Republicans who could not bring themselves to vote for a Democratic candidate.

Senator Lodge, seriously alarmed by the extent of anti-Weeks sentiment in the Bay State, sought to enlist the stimulating services of Colonel Roosevelt in the cause.[13] The Rough Rider, however, had little affection for Weeks, who had once led the standpat opposition in the House to the reform program of the Roosevelt administration. Ignoring the invitation, he sent instead a somewhat belated message endorsing the entire Republican ticket. The communication was warmly laudatory of Calvin Coolidge, the gubernatorial candidate, whom the Colonel rather surprisingly hailed as a "high-minded public servant . . . a man who has the forward look and who is anxious to secure genuine social and industrial justice." Weeks he referred to casually as a senator who would "stand for the right kind of peace as he has stood for the right kind of war." The disappointed Lodge had to call upon ex-Senator Albert J. Beveridge to stump the state in an effort to hold the wavering liberals in line, but the Indiana Progressive lacked the dynamic attraction of the greatest Bull Moose of them all.

No punches were pulled in the senatorial campaign as the Republicans pitched into Walsh for being a draft dodger (he was under forty), a pacifist, and an opponent of preparedness who had played the German game by inflaming anti-British sentiment among the Irish voters.[14] His election, they declared, would give Wilson another rubber-stamp senator and perpetuate the rule of the South to the detriment of New England industries. Weeks in turn was attacked for his indifference to the public welfare in voting for the Gore amendment, which would have added millions of dollars to the food bill of Massachusetts citizens, and for his persistent opposition to the President in the conduct of the war. To this the senator replied that he had merely done his duty in speeding up its prosecution, and he stressed his anti-Wilson program of post-war congressional reconstruction as the most important issue facing the American people.

Elsewhere in the East there were only half a dozen senatorial contests, four in New England and one each in Delaware and New Jersey. The death of Senator Jacob H. Gallinger on August 17 had raised Democratic hopes that New Hampshire voters might split their preference and return a Democrat along with the urbane and handsome Governor Keyes, whose election to Hollis' seat was practically conceded. For Gallinger's seat the Democrats nominated an affable businessman, John B. Jameson, whose wartime service as chairman of the New Hampshire Public Safety Commission had given him considerable patronage and publicity. The Republicans put forward the Concord newspaper publisher George H. Moses, whose antipathy for Wilson precipitated a hard-hitting battle almost as rancorous as the Bay State senatorial contest. His anti-labor, anti-woman suffrage, and antediluvian views in general irked the progressive element, while the Democrats reproached him for having spent the war directing the viciously anti-administration campaign of the Republican publicity bureau in Washington. His services as Taft's minister to Greece enabled Moses to pose on the hustings as an expert in European diplomacy to the great amusement of his adversaries, who claimed that the experience had merely gone to his head and made him so far forgetful of his redblooded American antecedents as to sport a monocle and kiss the ladies' hands. From the suspicion of such high-falutin' conduct the former President had to clear his quondam diplomat in a speech at Portsmouth a few days before the election.[15]

Both Republican candidates, Moses and Keyes, ran on a platform glorifying their party's war record and denouncing southern obstructionism in Congress which, they asserted, had impeded the conduct of the war and now threatened the post-war prosperity of the nation. In Rhode Island, on the other hand, where the wealthy Senator Colt was under attack for his devotion to the trusts, the senator contrasted his loyal support of the President with the spotty record of Wilson's followers in this respect, and concentrated on demonstrating the unfitness for public office of his opponent in particular and of Democrats generally.

Wilson's personal interest in the outcome of the New Jersey senatorial contest led him to write the Democratic candidate, George M. La Monte, as the campaign neared its climax, that ''I particularly crave the support of New Jersey whose people I deem it an honor to have served and whose interests I have so long had at heart.''[16] Unfortunately for the President's cravings in this respect, the party machinery was again in the hands of the bosses, including his old enemy James Nugent. The Democratic lovefeast at Trenton earlier in the year had not abated Nugent's hostility to reformers in general or to Wilson in particular. Consequently, the machine, which was primarily interested in keeping the saloons open, had secured the nomination of its own man, La Monte, over three other Democrats who ran as unqualified supporters of the President's policies. In the campaign the Democrats raised the issue of extensive draft deferments for Governor Edge's friends and political supporters and roundly denounced his scuttling of the public utilities commission at the behest of corrupt corporate interests. Edge, for the most part, refrained from intemperate attacks on Wilson and emphasized his businesslike conduct of state affairs, a virtue he claimed would qualify him to cope with post-war national problems.[17]

In the last stages of the campaign the worried Democratic state organization scrambled somewhat incontinently aboard the Wilson bandwagon. On October 21 it issued a ukase calling upon the voters to back up President Wilson, ''America's ambassador in the service of humanity,'' and demanding that the peace be settled along the lines of the Fourteen Points. The next day Wilson responded with his appeal for La Monte's election, an exchange of pleasantries made possible by a hasty trip to Washington of a group of anxious leaders, sans Nugent, who laid before the President the desperate plight of the cause in New Jersey. Since La Monte had bragged earlier that he would never put himself under obligation to Wilson by appealing for White House support, the President's subsequent endorsement of him appeared neither very heartfelt nor convincing.[18]

Holy Joe Folk's mudslinging campaign offended a good many Missourians otherwise well disposed toward the administration. To one irate citizen who had written that, although a life-long Democrat, he intended to vote for Folk's opponent, Wilson demurred strongly on the ground that "though I know nothing against Judge Spencer, I hope that Missouri will send a Democrat and not a Republican to the Senate, because ever since the war began there has been a distinct effort on the part of the Republican leaders to take the direction of the war out of the hands of the Executive."[19] Folk not only waged a lively battle against his Republican opponent but conducted a running feud with the Old Guard faction of Senator Reed, whom he accused of disloyalty to the administration and the war effort. The state Council of Defense got involved in the controversy when the secretary, a Reed henchman, denounced Folk for slandering the people of Missouri in the person of their senator; the Council treasurer, a Folk partisan, unable to obtain an apology, forced the Reed man out by tying up the Council's funds until he quit. This spectacular wrangle scandalized the patriots and spurred the Old Guard determination to cut down the interloper on election day.[20]

Wilson admired Folk and would have heeded his fervent pleas for assistance but for the reluctance of the National Committee to running afoul of the state organization. Action became imperative, however, after the western trip of the congressional committee chairman late in September revealed the sad plight of the party in that region. Scott Ferris' report that Folk was waging a brilliant battle in the face of a bad situation and urgently needed help induced Wilson to send the eagerly awaited telegram of endorsement on October 3.[21] Judge Spencer, on the other hand, conducted a campaign devoid of fireworks despite

Colonel Roosevelt's efforts to get him to inject some ginger into the contest by taking an anti-Wilson line.[22] The judge confined himself to safe generalities about winning the war and making the post-war world a better place for Republicans, and wisely left the quarrelsome Democrats to spin the web of their own defeat.

III

THE CONGRESSIONAL CAMPAIGN in the East lacked much of the intensity and excitement of the political battle that raged throughout the West. Here the Republicans had focused their energies upon winning over the farmer, and the Democrats stood to lose most heavily. The danger to the party became acute late in September when the President, ignoring the clamor of the National Wheat Growers' Association and its congressional champions, flatly refused to advance the price of wheat to $2.50 a bushel.[23] Although warned by the Secretary of Agriculture that Colonel Roosevelt and Gifford Pinchot's partisan Federal Board of Farm Organizations were behind the agitation for a better deal for the wheat grower, Wilson would only promise to consider a price advance in the spring after the government had completed a proposed survey of the situation.[24] His decision threw western farm journals and most of the regional press into a turmoil of angry protest, which grew shriller when the government on September 18 clamped a sudden rail embargo on all wheat shipments. The United States Grain Corporation, unable to handle the huge crop as it was harvested, had allowed the wheat to accumulate at the grain elevators until the carriers were clogged and freight movements paralyzed over a wide area. Panic-stricken wheat farmers thereupon sold their crops to speculators at less than the fixed price in defiance of warnings from Washington that such sales were illegal and unpatriotic.[25] Eventually the situation got straightened out, but not before Wilson's critics had worked themselves into a frenzy over the injustice and stupidity of governmental interference in agricultural matters.

Henceforward the West rang with their inflammatory

charges. In Ohio and Indiana, where farmers were reported "sore" about the favoritism shown southern cotton growers at their expense, Chairman Fess advised the candidates to play the sectional issue to the limit inasmuch as wheat, wool, coal, and other commodities produced in the North were under regulation while cotton went scot-free. Pinchot's Board promoted sectional prejudice so effectively in this respect that the Indiana Democratic state committee hastily organized a counter-propaganda campaign to explain the purpose of the President's wheat-price decision and what it meant to the starving Allied peoples.[26]

To assist the hard-pressed administration forces in this region, National Chairman Vance McCormick urged James E. Scripps of Cincinnati to put his chain of five Ohio newspapers at the service of the party. Scripps, who had backed Wilson since 1912, was ready to oblige but advised the President to decide at once upon the issues because the Republican drive had already started and the fight would be very bitter. Moreover, he questioned the wisdom of attacking congressmen with sound "acid test" records like Nicholas Longworth of Cincinnati while endorsing Democratic representatives like Isaac R. Sherwood of Toledo, whose poor showing on the League chart the local press considered a disgrace to the state. Wilson quickly brushed aside such fine distinctions and urged Scripps to make the fight against all Republicans regardless of their war records. "Mr. Longworth," he replied, "has supported the administration in the way that most of the active partisan Republicans have supported it. That is to say, with the purpose of making criticism tell as adversely as possible and also, if it can be subtly enough managed, to take the direction of the war out of the hands of the administration and place it where the Republicans can control it more directly."[27] Others besides Scripps gave the President the same advice, but to all he returned the same implacable answer: the Republicans must be destroyed at any cost.

The Kansas congressional campaign, which opened early in September after a record-breaking primary vote, promised by all accounts to be one of the roughest in years. Predictions that Democratic tenderness toward cotton would send farmers en masse to the polls to vote the straight Republican ticket impelled Democratic national headquarters to flood the state with literature begging the voters not to disorganize the President's war program by electing a Congress hostile to him.[28] To avert the impending calamity, local Democrats sought to make an issue of Governor Arthur Capper's forbearance toward the Nonpartisan League, a matter of considerable irritation to patriots near and far.

Offsetting this, however, was the presence in Capper's camp of a potent trio of Wilson foes. Major General Leonard Wood, commander of all troop-training activities in that area, made a public issue of what he considered Wilson's politically inspired refusal to give him a divisional command at the front.[29] In William Allen White, the nationally renowned Kansas editor, Wood found a champion who gave his complaints sympathetic treatment and wide circulation. White also persuaded Colonel Roosevelt to overlook the governor's softness on the Nonpartisan League issue and "swallow" Capper's candidacy in the interests of Republican unity.[30] So grim did the outlook appear to Scott Ferris on his tour of the state late that summer that he appealed to the White House for help. "Kansas," he said, "has had a lot of trouble with Leonard Wood politics and a lot of trouble about wheat; and inasmuch as we are anxious to save five Democratic congressmen out there, I am wondering if the President would be willing to write a letter I could read to the [State] Fair."[31] Since Wilson at the time had a more general appeal in mind, he sent Kansans a few words praising their patriotism but avoiding political implications.

Nebraska also had a lot of trouble about wheat, and other farm commodities as well. Angry hog raisers berated the Food Administration for permitting a disastrous drop in the ratio of hog to corn prices, a matter of vital importance to local prosperity.[32] On the other hand, the Republicans had plenty of trouble with Senator Norris' "acid test" record. Roosevelt classified him with La Follette and Henry Ford and was with difficulty restrained from attacking him publicly.[33] The Progressive element backed Norris, however, and under the direction of Wilson's good friend Tariff Commissioner William Kent of Nonpartisan League fame, the liberals circulated a news sheet on the senator's behalf.[34] The spectacle of a White House intimate campaigning for the Republicans dismayed the local Democratic organization, already badly split by the Bryanite schism and confused by Senator Hitchcock's peculiar behavior anent much of the war program.[35] When the state chairman appealed to Wilson at least to disown Kent's activities if he would not openly support the party in Nebraska, the President brusquely replied that it was "entirely out of the question."[36] Finally, after the October 25 appeal had gone out, Norris' opponent received the automatic presidential endorsement extended to all Democrats laboring in adversity, but it lacked the personal warmth of Wilson's more spontaneous contributions of that nature.[37]

Agrarian discontent had not diminished appreciably in Minnesota, where the Nonpartisan League continued its radical agitation despite the setback in the June primaries. The League had carried about a quarter of the state's counties, including the home county of Senator Knute Nelson, one of whose chagrined local followers promised the senator, "We'll straighten this county out yet if we have to use a club to do it."[38] The campaign proceeded very much along these lines in many of the rural areas. The political situation was badly scrambled, with the Democrats in a more disorganized condition than their League-harassed adversaries. Wilson's endorsement of Nelson's re-election had split the party and taken much of the zest out of its will to resist. Although the regular Democratic organization deferred to the President's supposed wishes and did not put up anyone against Nelson, it ran the state chairman, Fred E. Wheaton, for governor against the embattled Burnquist apparently with the hope of picking up enough Nonpartisan votes to win.

The party's abnegation on behalf of an old Republican standpatter caused many Democrats to switch their support to William G. Calderwood, who had run against Kellogg in 1916 as a Prohibitionist and polled a large vote but who now appeared under the aegis of the National party. Denounced in conservative circles as a disloyal collection of Socialists, Nonpartisans, and pro-German pacifists, the Calderwood group waged a vigorous, liberally financed campaign. It became more of a threat late in October after the Democratic National Committee issued a statement declaring that the President needed him in the Senate to help carry out the administration's post-war policies.[39] The potent Anti-Saloon League, however, repudiated the renegade Calderwood and officially endorsed Nelson,[40] thus offsetting to some extent the appeal of the Townleyites in the rural areas where the sullen attitude of the Scandinavian voters had the Republicans badly worried.[41] Although the old senator grumbled that it was a "villainous campaign" and kept close watch on developments, his popularity as well as the disjointed nature of the opposition made his re-election almost a certainty. But that of Burnquist and one or two of the congressmen was much less so.

IV

CONDITIONS in the cattle-raising country and mining areas beyond the wheat belt were very bad that year. Drought devastated the region from Texas to Montana, bringing cattle ranchers and small farmers to the verge of ruin.[42] Congress rejected a $20 million relief appropriation and made provision instead to furnish seed to drought-stricken farmers, but this did nothing to mitigate the immediate distress. In the mining and lumbering areas, local Defense Councils dealt summarily with the acute labor unrest and rigorously repressed incendiary organizations like the I.W.W. and the miners' federations. Draft boards took strikers who refused to return to work, while the states provided concentration camps for those rejected by the Army.[43] Consequently, feeling ran high throughout the Northwest that fall and was reflected in the ferocity of the political struggle.

Farm troubles were prevalent at an early date in Idaho, where a large part of the 1917 potato crop was lost through the inability of the railroads to move it before the advent of cold weather.[44] Nonpartisan League influence had multiplied rapidly, particularly among the Mormons in the southern part of the state. An estimated twenty thousand Idaho farmers joined the

Townleyites in 1918, much to the alarm of the patriots and the dismay of conservative circles in both parties. Senator Borah, whose strength lay in the rural areas, refused to believe that twenty thousand Idaho farmers were disloyal, and he urged his party to work instead toward eliminating some of their legitimate grievances.[45] Although the Republican organization ignored his advice, it lacked the temerity to repudiate the League outright at the Republican state convention that summer. Candidates were thus left free to come to such arrangements with the Nonpartisans as expediency might dictate. Many did so, but none wore the League mantle more openly or defiantly than Borah.

Idaho enjoyed two senatorial elections that fall. Borah's Democratic colleague, Senator John G. Nugent, aspired to fill out the term to which he had been appointed on Senator Brady's death in January 1918. His opponent was Frank R. Gooding, a wealthy stockman and mine owner with a variety of other interests — including lumber, public utilities, and newspapers — throughout the state. Gooding's rigorous suppression of a miners' federation strike during his governorship some years before commended him to conservative elements eager for a crusade against the Nonpartisan League. This became easier after the League, to everyone's amazement and the distress of not a few, swept the Democratic primaries in September and nominated the entire Democratic ticket except for Borah's opponent, Frank L. Moore. As prosecuting attorney of Latah County, the scene of much labor unrest, Moore had enhanced his reputation by dealing harshly with all troublemakers. Under ordinary circumstances he would not have caused Borah much concern, but administration support made him more formidable. Inspired by their mutual hatred of the Townleyites, both Moore and Gooding waged a sensational battle against the traitors within the gates. Borah's refusal to stoop to such demagoguery irritated his conservative Republican friends and brought bitter attacks from newspapers owned by Gooding.[46] Late in the campaign, notices posted throughout the state adjured all loyal citizens not to vote for League candidates, and Borah's name headed the list.[47]

Wilson willingly came to Nugent's assistance on October 2 with a letter stating that "Idaho could not have a more loyal or trustworthy representative or the administration a more generous supporter." The missive naturally irked the Republicans but was of doubtful benefit to the Democrats inasmuch as the President had neglected to mention the Nonpartisan League. The state Democratic central committee, appalled by the threatened disintegration of the party, had begged him to set the voters right about the matter.[48] Wilson's silence appeared all the more unfortunate in view of Roosevelt's philippic a few days before at Billings, Montana, depicting the League as one of the principal enemies of the republic. Patriots hailed his remarks as eminently sound and wise in sharp contrast to Democratic subterfuge and evasion. Thus the Idaho campaign rocked along in tumultuous fashion to an unpredictable conclusion. Gooding obtained a handsome personal endorsement from the Rough Rider, but Borah emphatically rejected a similar boon when it was suggested to him by Chairman Hays.[49]

The Nonpartisan League eruption made the political struggle in Montana equally confusing and bitter. Unrest was acute in the eastern part of the state, where drought had blasted the crops and an estimated twenty-five thousand farmers faced ruin.[50] In the western part, the domain of the Anaconda Copper Mining Company, an industrial giant which ruled the state like a feudal barony and made and unmade politicians at will, the mining industry flourished under zooming wartime prices for copper. Bad conditions in the mines, however, had provoked severe labor trouble, which the state Defense Council suppressed with exemplary vigor.[51] Persecution of the miners' federation and the I.W.W. on the pretext that both were in the pay of the Kaiser had put a good many citizens in an ugly mood. The atmosphere on the eve of the election campaign was highly charged and the outcome much in doubt.

Political interest focused on the re-election campaign of Senator Thomas J. Walsh, an able lawyer and outstanding liberal. There were no Nonpartisan League strings attached to his candidacy, but the League did not openly oppose him.[52] Nevertheless, his rapid rise to national prominence during his single term in the Senate had aroused jealousy and opposition at home. Furthermore, his refusal to condone the high-handed methods employed by the governor and the state Defense Council to cope with farm and labor unrest had irked the inner circles of the party and raised doubts as to whether "the Company" would again support him,[53] although he had merited its good will by thwarting insurgent attempts in Congress to include a tax on copper in the war revenue bill. In the circumstances Walsh's worried friends appealed to John D. Ryan, a former president of the concern but now a power in administration circles as Assistant Secretary of War in charge of airplane production. Ryan obligingly agreed to get "the Company" behind the Democratic ticket and to see that it did the right thing by Walsh on election day, while Wilson sent the people of Montana a message warmly commending the senator's splendid services.[54]

The Republican party, still rent by the Progressive schism, had been infiltrated by the Nonpartisan League until it was almost unrecognizable in many areas. One faction supported Jeannette Rankin, the first woman member of Congress, for the senatorial nomination; but her tearful opposition to the declaration of war and her subsequent pacifist activities had offended the patriots, whose petty and malicious persecution made things very difficult for her during the campaign. Against Miss Rankin in the primaries the regular organization ran Oscar M. Lanstrum, widely known as a "Company man" and political wirepuller.[55] After a bitter struggle Lanstrum narrowly prevailed, 17,645 votes to 15,132, but the victor was not to have the last word. A few days later the lady entered the senatorial contest under the aegis of the National party, a catch-all for liberal sentiment outraged by wartime abuses of authority in the name of democracy. The orthodox parties decried its alleged connections with the I.W.W. and the Nonpartisan League, and accused Miss Rankin of catering to the worst elements in the community in furtherance of her ambitions.

While the split in the Republican ranks might have favored Walsh ordinarily, the sectional issue handicapped him severely. Republican tales of price-fixing inequities impelled a friendly

Fort Benton editor to write: ''This they claim has caused unprecedented prosperity in the south with a result that the young men in the south are not volunteering as are the young men of the northwest and thus this part of the country is furnishing a great many more men for the army than is the south.''[56] The senator's opponents also contrasted the vast sums spent on Army cantonments in the South with the meager outlay for such installations in the North, especially for the neglected Army post of Fort Harrison near the city of Helena.[57] To rebut charges that he had helped the Wilson administration ''send every possible source of income to the Southern States'' and had forgotten entirely that he came from the Northwest, Walsh could only flood the local newspapers with campaign literature calling attention to his unremitting efforts on behalf of higher wheat and copper prices and extolling the splendid war record of President Wilson and the Democratic Congress.

Nevada also experienced diversionary third-party movements, but none as turbulent as those in neighboring states. In a pentagonal senatorial contest Anne Martin, a famous suffragette leader of her era, represented the National Woman's party, an aggressively militant suffrage organization not to be confused with the National party of the much more radical Miss Rankin in Montana. Although renowned in suffragette annals for picketing the White House and brawling with the Washington police, Miss Martin conducted her Nevada campaign with great decorum and propriety. She canvassed the ranch vote by automobile and held rallies in the towns from the front porches of the best homes, with orchestral music and vocal selections interspersed among the political harangues.[58] Miss Martin directed her fire primarily at President Wilson for betraying American womanhood in failing to secure adoption of the Nineteenth Amendment. Local quidnuncs estimated her electoral appeal in the vicinity of three thousand votes, or about 15 per cent of the total, a threat of no small concern to her two principal rivals.[59]

Nevada was generally Democratic but by a very narrow margin. The party's major effort was the election of Senator Charles B. Henderson, who had been appointed to the seat left vacant by the death of Senator Francis G. Newlands in December

1917. The war had boomed Nevada's mining industry, which Congress had exempted from all excess profits taxes, thanks to the diligent efforts of Henderson and his colleagues on the Senate Committee on Mines. He had also helped repeal the restriction on the free coinage of silver, outlawed since 1873, which Congress replaced with a war measure establishing a ratio of 20 to 1 and paying silver producers a handsome bonus of a dollar an ounce.[60] While his constituents were expected to be duly grateful for such benefits, the prosperity was unevenly divided, and there was considerable labor trouble at the mines. The state Defense Council, however, kept a tight rein on Wobblies and Townleyites alike by stringently enforcing an order that forbade citizens to join disloyal organizations.[61] In the senatorial contest the Republicans handicapped themselves by ignoring the admonitions of the National Security League and running a candidate with a very poor "acid test" record. The unfitness of Representative Edwin E. Roberts in this respect made him an easy target for Henderson and the patriots.[62] The Republican press, stung by Henderson's charges and unable to find much to criticize in the senator's record besides his loyalty to Wilson, retaliated by circulating quantities of material derogatory to the President and attacking southern domination of the government.

v

ALTHOUGH relatively free of organized third-party discontent, Wyoming suffered severely from drought and a sharp drop in meat prices occasioned by the excessive slaughter of cattle otherwise condemned to starve on the ranges. Democratic hopes centered on unseating Senator Francis B. Warren, whose chief claim to re-election rested on his long service on the Military Affairs Committee and on the military pre-eminence of his distinguished son-in-law. The senator, moreover, had kept clear of the anti-Wilson cabal on Capitol Hill, where his vote on at least two occasions had rescued the administration from partisan deadlocks on measures objectionable to the President. Nevertheless, Wyoming Democrats called for Warren's defeat on the ground that "to Europe the election of a Republican Congress this year would mean a divided nation, and a refusal to stand by the principles President Wilson has proclaimed as the aims and purposes of our country."[63] To avert this dire contingency the Democrats put forward an old party wheelhorse in the person of ex-Governor John E. Osborne, an ardent follower of Bryan since the stirring days of '96 and the battle for free silver. Bryan had brought Osborne into the State Department in 1913 as Assistant Secretary in charge of administrative affairs, such as typing and filing, a humdrum post which, for campaign purposes, he exalted into one of great responsibility for weighty policy decisions on matters of grave international consequence. The National Committee rallied behind the ersatz statesman early in the campaign and plastered the state with posters proclaiming that "A Vote for Osborne is a Vote for Wilson and His Policies."[64]

The repudiation of Governor Julius C. Gunter's wartime administration in the primaries on September 10 had thrown Colorado politics into a turmoil. Gunter's defeat on charges that he had hoodwinked farmers into accepting less than the fixed price of wheat, allowed coal dealers to gouge the public, and interfered with draft boards on behalf of his friends compromised the entire Democratic ticket, already seriously handicapped by the loyalty issue.[65] The National Security League had two of the Democratic congressmen, Benjamin C. Hilliard and Edward Keating, under fire and wanted them defeated on patriotic grounds. To save the day Scott Ferris urged Wilson at least to endorse Keating, "tho some of his war votes are not quite up to standard." The President admired Keating's record as a progressive reformer and would cheerfully have complied had not Tumulty forcefully pointed out the folly of sending another letter that the Republicans could use "to embarrass us deeply."[66]

Senator John F. Shafroth, another Bryan henchman, also had a rather spotty "acid test" record to which public attention was directed. Moreover, Honest John's strong attachment to the President proved of little benefit to him in Colorado, which had not enjoyed the same wartime prosperity as more favored sections.[67] Disgruntled businessmen complained that Shafroth's boasted influence with the White House had not paid off in juicy war contracts or obtained the federal assistance necessary to operate the state's low grade mines profitably. Many marginal mines had had to close that spring in consequence of the Fuel Administration's refusal to advance coal prices, thus compelling thousands of miners to emigrate in search of employment. Irate citizens considered all this a sorry return for Colorado's generous efforts on behalf of the war in taxes, Liberty Bonds, and Red Cross donations.

Nonpartisan League inroads had stimulated discontent in the rural areas. The Colorado press deplored the fact that the farming communities were in ''sullen opposition to the war and the general conduct of the federal government,'' and denounced League organizers for inflaming the rustics over the price of wheat. The Republicans quickly turned this situation to their advantage by calling upon Senator Shafroth ''to explain the discriminations which have been practiced against the West by a Democratic Congress ruled by the South,'' with respect to wheat and cotton.[68] When Shafroth in rebuttal cited his efforts on behalf of higher wheat prices, the farmers were reported chilly and unreceptive; while in the cities his support of the Gore amendment was depicted as adding to the already excessive cost of living borne by urban dwellers. To oppose Shafroth the Republicans picked Lawrence C. Phipps, a former multimillionaire associate of Andrew Carnegie. Although Phipps's candidacy made for a stronger party ticket than had been the case for some years, his great wealth gave rise to a loud outcry about Republican plutocracy. A Denver newspaper editor observed of Phipps's free-spending campaign that ''the Republicans are making a fight on Shafroth that from a predatory wealth point of view I don't think has been equalled since Colorado has been a state.''[69]

Next to Weeks of Massachusetts, the outstanding Republican senator in the President's black book was Albert B. Fall of New Mexico. The administration cooperated heartily with local Democratic leaders in the task of eliminating Fall from the national picture. The Secretary of the Treasury, while on a trip to New Mexico in connection with the fourth Liberty Loan drive, approved a scheme to weaken Fall by detaching the railroad workers of the state from their customary allegiance to the Republican party. As director general of the railroads, McAdoo could exert considerable leverage in that direction. Upon his return to Washington he confidently assured the President that ''here is a chance to finish the unspeakable Fall of New Mexico.''[70] The Democratic convention at Santa Fe on September 27 cheered the assertion of Senator Andreius A. Jones, the keynote speaker, that a Republican victory would bring joy to the Kaiser. ''Should our country,'' said Jones, ''fail to return a Democratic majority in both the house and the senate, our enemies would be encouraged to prolong the war, and the potency of the President in advancing the peace terms would be lessened.''[71]

Republican orators at their Santa Fe convention on October 2 indignantly repudiated Jones's aspersions, condemned Democratic inefficiency in the conduct of the war, and hailed Fall as the champion of free speech and free enterprise. Colonel Roosevelt gladdened the gathering with a telegram saying that every decent American would consider Fall's defeat a calamity and that in everything relating to our international relations Fall had shown ''singular farsightedness and breadth of vision.'' According to one of McAdoo's informants, funds from the Republican National Committee had enabled the state organization to acquire a couple of newspapers with a state-wide circulation.[72] Although formerly independent in politics and often critical of corrupt Republican state administrations, these journals now launched a vicious anti-Wilson campaign, employing for the most part material circulated by the Republican publicity bureau in Washington on the sectional character of the Democratic leadership. The election of Fall's opponent, Representative William B. Walton, the press asserted, meant another presidential henchman ''pledged to vote for FREE WOOL and other socialistic measures under the Democratic peace program.''[73]

Pressed to help Walton with a personal endorsement, Wilson neglected to do so until October 30 and then in such a peculiar fashion as to negate the effectiveness of his action. The President's letter, oddly enough, was in reply to an inquiry addressed to him not by Walton but by W. P. Metcalfe, the Socialist senatorial candidate, who had wanted to know how Wilson felt about Fall.[74] Wilson may have thought he was addressing the Democratic nominee; in any case his reply was acidulously clear and to the point about Fall's undesirability.[75] The insult to Fall in Wilson's correspondence with a Socialist raised a fearful outcry among the Republicans everywhere. By this time, however, the congressional campaign had entered its final and most frenzied stage. The uproar that wracked the country from end to end almost eclipsed another development of at least equal significance — the impending collapse of the German Empire and the triumph of the crusade for democracy.

CHAPTER XIV

THE APPEAL

I

THE CONGRESSIONAL ELECTIONS preceded the armistice by less than a week. In the feverish period leading up to the poll, the President's attention was divided about equally between politics and the knotty problem of bringing the Germans to terms without sacrificing any part of the hard-won victory, as the Republicans loudly accused him of doing.[1] He discussed the political situation repeatedly with close advisers and conferred with a variety of important people who either came or were called to Washington to proffer their counsel and assistance.[2] Party leaders, national committeemen, and individual congressmen were in and out of the White House daily in connection with the campaign, while state chairmen from all parts of the Union sought interviews to explain the precarious shape of things in their bailiwicks or to plead with him to get the National Committee or the executive agencies to funnel more money, literature, or speakers into threatened territory. Above all else, everyone wanted a helping hand from the President himself. "You are the only one," the chairman of the congressional campaign committee advised him early in October, "who can give the candidates the final push which will put them across the line winners."[3]

For some months the matter had been very much on Wilson's mind. As early as June he had asked the faithful Tumulty to work out a "tactful effective plan" for making an appeal without arousing rancor or bitterness. Those were anxious days at the White House as the German armies drove toward Paris and the Allies braced again for a desperate stand on the Marne. The behavior of Roosevelt, who was blasting the War Department for its failure to send sufficient troops to France to stop the

German drive at the outset,[4] added to the administration's concern. The fall of Paris would make the Rough Rider's dismal vaticinations hard to answer, and White House circles were depressed and worried.

Tumulty, however, counseled delay. He foresaw difficulties with regard to an appeal because of the spurious non-partisan movement to which the President had unwisely lent himself by endorsing the election of people like Henry Ford. It was too late to repudiate this movement without embarrassment, and Tumulty favored awaiting a more opportune time after the enemy had accumulated sufficient rope to hang himself. The President could then state his attitude toward the election and expose the real purpose behind the Republican leadership. "I think," said Tumulty, "a letter along the lines of the Indiana platform which I suggested a few weeks ago would carry to the country just the impression we ought to make." The letter would be followed by Wilson's country-wide participation in the Liberty Loan campaign, when "speeches of a non-partisan character can be made."[5]

The idea of making such a trip through the West that summer appealed to Wilson.[6] Since becoming President he had never traveled that far except for a brief appearance in Omaha during the 1916 campaign. McAdoo and Burleson strongly urged the tour on the ground that the people of the West would warmly welcome his visit in the interests of the war effort as well as out of a lively curiosity to see and hear him.[7] The prospect so disturbed Republican national headquarters that it hastily prepared to send Colonel Roosevelt hot on Wilson's trail in an effort to counteract whatever good impression the President might make.[8] Such precautions proved unnecessary, however, since favorable developments on the European front that summer lessened the political pressure on the home front. The "black day" of the German Army, August 8, witnessed the rapid reversal of the entire military situation. As gratifying accounts of Allied gains filled the American press, the Democrats grew more cheerful, since the good news would blunt the edge of the attack on the administration's conduct of the war. Wilson's advisers now questioned the need for a presidential barnstorming tour of the hinterland. Tumulty and House strongly opposed the idea, the former on political grounds and the latter because of the element of personal danger involved.[9]

After weighing the various arguments, Wilson reluctantly agreed to abandon the junket. Although Colonel House assumed credit for the decision, the determining factor seems to have been the objection raised by Wilson's old friend Harry A. Garfield. The Fuel Administrator in somewhat Delphic fashion warned the President: "Should your hand be taken from the helm there is the greatest danger that reactionary forces at home will turn us back and the cause of democracy be indefinitely postponed."[10] How a few days' absence from Washington could bring about such dire results Garfield did not specify, but Wilson agreed with him that "the danger of what might take place in my absence," rather than concern for his safety, had turned him against the project. Curiously enough, the same danger did not deter him three months later from undertaking a much more extended trip to Europe against even stronger advice.

Consequently the White House issued a press statement early in September explaining that while the President "coveted the opportunity to discuss with my fellow citizens the great undertaking which has made such Liberty Loans necessary and in which our whole energy and purpose are enlisted," delicate and critical questions arising in Washington prevented him from having "the sort of direct contact with the people I am serving which would be of so much benefit and stimulus to me."[11] The political situation now had to be handled by letter. Tumulty was confident that if the President followed up his explanation canceling his western tour "by a statement outlining the reasons why you believe a Democratic Congress necessary," it would "knock our enemies into a cocked hat."[12] Tumulty had already prepared the draft of such a letter, which he had suggested to Wilson in June, wherein some distinguished Democrat was to ask for an expression of Wilson's political preferences and thus provide the opportunity for a telling blow at the Republicans. Colonel House had approved the draft as in every way admirable, and the Texan had expressed great hopes for its success.[13]

By insisting upon a written appeal, Wilson's advisers egregiously miscalculated the political situation and forced the President into an irretrievable tactical error. By contrast, Roosevelt's subsequent invasion of the West, ostensibly to promote the fourth Liberty Loan, aroused no unfavorable public reaction, although he by no means confined his remarks to the object of his trip. With respect to the Colonel's behavior, the Secretary of the Treasury observed that "many people thought he was speaking under the auspices of the Treasury, which was very unfortunate because he was making partisan speeches instead of Liberty Loan speeches. Most of his speeches were critical of the administration."[14] Wilson's appearance in the same connection would have evoked a certain amount of criticism, but nothing comparable to the storm that blew up over his October 25 appeal. It is possible that, had Wilson gone West in September 1918, he might have been spared the tragic journey undertaken just a year later on behalf of the League of Nations — a trip necessitated in great part by the disaster that overtook his cause in November 1918.

II

THE SUDDEN SHIFT for the better in the war situation nonplused the Republican high command and compelled a tactical regrouping of the forces opposed to Wilson. With the Germans at last on the run and a million American soldiers in pursuit, few voters would worry about the slowness of the Quartermaster Corps in providing the Army cantonments with blankets the previous winter. Even the more recent airplane scandal was of limited value in discrediting the administration. The weapon was too new and the public was too ignorant of its potentialities to feel more than a passing irritation that a great deal of money had been squandered — mostly by automobile manufacturers closely identified with the Republican party, as the Democrats were not slow to point out.[15] Diehards like Colonel Roosevelt might be loath to abandon the issue of War Department incompetence — indeed, he engaged in much angry repartee with people who twitted him on his myopic behavior — but the party needed firmer ground from which to press the assault on Wilson. Some of the advantage lost through the unexpected turn of fortune on the European front might be recovered by making an issue of the peace terms the President offered the enemy. To this new line of attack the party shifted hopefully late that summer.

Despite the nonsense written about the Republican plot, hatched on Roosevelt's deathbed, to defeat Wilson on the League of Nations,[16] the cornerstone upon which the Wilsonian peace rested, the decision to attack the President on this score resulted from the political exigencies of the 1918 congressional campaign. Republican hostility to Wilson's peace concepts went back to his efforts to end the war in the winter of 1916–17. At that time Republican congressional leaders denounced his jettisoning of the Monroe Doctrine, while Colonel Roosevelt roared and thundered in various publications against the ignominy of joining any such preposterous world organization as the President had suggested. Wilson's restatement of this proposition a year later (on January 8, 1918) in outlining American war aims to Congress did not change the Republican attitude, which, while somewhat more circumspect, remained no less hostile. The first opportunity to remind the country of that fact came at the Indiana Republican convention in May 1918. The keynote speaker, Senator Harry S. New, solemnly warned his party to pay special heed to the post-war issues, particularly the final settlement with Germany. ''The making of them,'' said New, referring to the peace terms, ''must not be left to the dreamers, the social uplifters, the pacifists, and the bolshevists who are now unhappily so much in evidence and who appear prominently among the President's chief advisers.''[17]

Senator Lodge opened the official Republican attack on Wilson's peace position, as embodied in the Fourteen Points, on August 23 during a debate on the manpower bill. Lodge cautioned the country that military reverses did not make the enemy less dangerous, because the Germans were prepared to launch a ''poisonous peace propaganda'' that would enable them to accomplish by negotiation what their armies had failed to achieve in the field.[18] A negotiated peace would therefore be the height of folly, since it would leave Germany practically un-harmed and in a position once again to menace mankind. His audience thrilled to the senator's impassioned declaration, ''No peace that satisfies Germany in any degree can ever satisfy us,'' and cheered his demand to crush the Hun completely before attempting any final disposition of his case. Lodge then out-lined the terms which Germany must accept after the uncon-ditional surrender of the Kaiser's armies. His ten-point program paralleled Wilson's Fourteen Points to the extent of calling for territorial revision based on ethnic considerations, but it contained no mention of freedom of the seas, reduction of armaments, or lowering of economic barriers and, of course, no reference to a League of Nations. It was a vigorous plea for restoration of the status quo, with Germany eliminated and the Allies enriched by the spoils of war.

Lodge was highly satisfied with his performance, which he felt had attracted a good deal of attention. ''It will,'' he in-formed Roosevelt, ''make good standing ground for the Re-publican party.''[19] Party newspapers hailed the speech as lay-ing down the ''irreducible minimum'' of conditions essential to peace; it would also smoke out the pacifists at home who were willing to end the war on almost any terms.[20] Democratic organs, on the other hand, chided the senator for omitting all mention of a post-war society of nations. His failure to approve the idealism for which the war was being fought did not, in their opinion, align him with the best liberal sentiment in Europe and America, which was demanding a new world order as an assurance against a repetition of the present catastrophe.[21] The Republicans were happy to accept the challenge, however, and the Boston *Evening Transcript* asserted on August 28 that if the party needed an issue for the coming campaign, it could be taken from Senator Lodge.

Three days after Lodge's opening broadside, Colonel Roose-velt wheeled into action at Springfield, Illinois, with his first salvo against Wilson's peace concepts. The Rough Rider, al-though reluctant to forgo his vendetta with the War Depart-ment, had finally yielded to the importunity of his friends and shifted his attack to safer grounds. Ex-Senator Beveridge had suggested the question of nationalism, which struck the Colonel favorably as "the keynote of our attitude . . . as you say, it may well be that this will be the issue which we shall have to force against Wilson."[22] It was the line he took, therefore, in his address to a crowd of 100,000 people at the Illinois centennial celebration on August 26. After blasting the disloyal pro-German senatorial candidacy of Chicago Mayor William Hale Thompson, Roosevelt dwelt at length on the two great needs of the moment: to speed up the war, and to prepare for the tasks facing the post-war world. The latter could be best accomplished, he reminded the crowd, if Americans took pride in their national past and future. "We are not internationalists," he shouted. "We are American nationalists. We intend to do justice to all other nations. But in the last four years the professional internationalists like the profound pacifists have played the game of brutal German autocracy. Professional internationalism stands toward patriotism exactly as free love stands toward a clean and honorable and duty-performing family life."[23] In conclusion he warned his hearers to beware of German propaganda in the peace negotiations, when the internationalists would "prance in the foreground and furnish the rhetoric," and to remember that the country's strength would rest on its Army and not on a League of Nations or any other machinery designed to do away with war.

The Austro-Hungarian peace feelers of September 15 brought the quarrel over the nature of the peace terms into sharper focus. With the Hapsburg Empire reeling on the verge of collapse and seeking a possible way out of its predicament, the end of the war appeared in sight. The American press, however, under the stimulus of the unconditional surrender agitation, vociferously demanded the rejection of the proposal. Only the New York *Times* among the major dailies held out for its acceptance, and the paper's willingness to hoist the white flag aroused a storm of indignation.[24] Since the *Times* frequently reflected the administration's point of view, the Republicans watched closely for any sign of wavering in Wilson, but the President's prompt and firm rejection of the overtures left little ground for criticism. Senator Lodge insinuated, however, that

Wilson could not be trusted to remain firm because of the socialists and Bolsheviks among his advisers who wanted a quick peace.[25]

III

CANCELLATION of his Western trip deprived the President of the opportunity to make as effective a presentation of his case as the peregrinations of Roosevelt and the speeches of Lodge in the forum of the Senate accomplished for the Republicans. White House manifestos lacked the punch of personal appearances, but only twice during the campaign did Wilson leave Washington, each time to push the fourth Liberty Loan drive in New York City, the nation's financial capital. On September 27 he opened the drive with great fanfare. "The crowds were enthusiastic," observed Colonel House, "and I have never seen a better reception."[26] Wilson eloquently defined his position with respect to the impending peace, stating that while he had no intention of making a bargain or compromise peace, a League of Nations would constitute the most essential part of the final settlement. He flatly informed territorial revisionists of the Lodge-Roosevelt school that no special interests would be recognized, only what was common to all. It was to be a peace of the peoples, not of their rulers alone, and all who sat at the peace table would have to be prepared to pay the price needed to create the only medium that could insure the sanctity of future international agreements.[27]

So favorable was the public reaction to Wilson's uncompromising statement of principles that the Republicans dared not reject it openly; instead, they confined their efforts to undermining public confidence in the President's willingness or ability to safeguard national interests in the process of creating his world organization. Among other things, they raised a great commotion over Point III of the peace terms as advocating free trade and doing away with the protective tariff, one of the pillars of American prosperity and Republican orthodoxy. Senator Weeks promptly introduced a resolution, reminiscent of his earlier "instrumentality," calling for a joint congressional committee of ten to take control of post-war economic reconstruction out of the President's hands. The publicity given this maneuver caused Senator Hitchcock to complain that the Republicans were perverting the free trade issue in "thousands of newspapers" for the purpose of gaining control of Congress. The harried Democrats immediately countered with a resolution of their own, sponsored by Senator Overman, which would retain executive control by authorizing the President to appoint a committee of five to handle post-war economic problems.[28]

The day following Wilson's New York address Colonel Roosevelt took off on a barnstorming tour of the West, ostensibly on behalf of the Liberty Loan campaign. The tour, which opened in Baltimore and carried him as far as Billings, Montana, with intermediate stops in Ohio, Kansas, Missouri, and Nebraska, had been carefully arranged beforehand with Chairman Hays. Although they decided to make his appearances as non-political as Roosevelt's volatile temperament would permit, the Rough Rider allowed himself a free hand in the matter of attacking Wilson's peace aims.[29] He was warmly received everywhere. At Kansas City, after urging his hearers to give to the war effort until it hurt, Roosevelt launched into a denunciation of profiteers, conscientious objectors, and striking workmen, and concluded with a strong warning against the quack peace remedies peddled by the administration.[30] The only safety for the United States, he declared, lay in an army of ten million men based on universal military training and not in any fanciful league to enforce peace. At Billings two days later the Rough Rider reached new forensic heights in excoriating the Nonpartisan League. This led him into a discussion of other pro-German influences at work in the country, the most dangerous of which was the propaganda on behalf of a League of Nations. Roosevelt had no objection to a more or less formal alliance among the nations fighting Germany; but it had to be an addition to, not a substitute for, the armed strength of the United States, without which any kind of a league would merely be another scrap of paper.[31]

While Roosevelt was creating prejudice throughout the West against Wilson's League of Nations, the country was electrified by the first formal peace overtures from the German government on October 5. The German note, accepting Wilson's fourteen-point peace program of January 8 and requesting an immediate armistice preparatory to the initiation of peace negotiations, put the President in a difficult position. No simple acceptance was possible in view of the inflamed political passions at home, where the Republicans were screaming for unconditional surrender and demanding that the matter be left entirely to Foch and Pershing. Rejection, on the other hand, might mean an indefinite prolongation of the bloodshed and destruction abhorrent to the President and a large segment of the American public. In reply, therefore, Wilson temporized by directing Secretary Lansing to pose a series of questions designed to establish the sincerity of German motives and the extent to which the government making the overtures represented the German people and not the discredited militarists.[32]

Despite its cautious and noncommittal wording, the Lansing note provoked a tremendous uproar in the Senate. Lodge lashed the President for presuming to discuss terms with the enemy before the Germans were beaten and Allied troops stood on German soil.[33] A number of Democratic senators, chiefly Reed of Missouri and Marcus A. Smith of Arizona, joined Poindexter of Washington in expatiating upon the dangers of a compromise or premature peace treaty. Hitchcock of Nebraska essayed a feeble defense of the President by pointing out that the Fourteen Points adequately covered all the objections voiced by the Republicans. This brought down upon the chairman of the Foreign Relations Committee such a verbal pummeling that he quickly subsided and left the floor to the President's critics.

The exchange of diplomatic notes that followed — there were four more before the end of the month — exacerbated the national political situation, whatever it accomplished toward hastening the end of the war. Wilson's note-writing propensities infuriated the Republicans, who asserted that this "war by correspondence" with the unrepentant foe jeopardized the recent Allied military advantage.[34] Various patriotic organizations, including the Connecticut Council of Defense, adopted resolutions condemning any peace negotiations except on an unconditional surrender basis. The agitation spread to Democratic newspapers like the Denver *Post*, which said that the negotiations were "universally condemned throughout the country" and called upon the President to cease his mischievous activities in that direction.[35]

In the Senate on October 10, Key Pittman of Nevada essayed an official defense of the administration's position. He pilloried Lodge for making misleading statements about the situation and assailed the Republicans for obstructionism not only in the peace negotiations but in the conduct of the war. Both charges were heatedly denied by the Massachusetts senator. The excitement mounted as one senator after another took the floor to demand revenge and retaliation instead of peace with Germany. Poindexter climaxed the debate on October 21 with an absurd resolution forbidding further peace talks until Germany had surrendered and making it unlawful for any government official to answer a German note.[36]

The Republican press backed Poindexter's maneuver with feverish editorials against the "Abyss of Internationalism" into which Wilson was leading the country with his socialist theories that would sweep away all the old American concepts and ideals. His diplomacy made it absolutely necessary, said the Denver *Rocky Mountain News* on October 21, that "there should be a curb on the Bolshevists of the Democratic party when the peace terms are framed at the council table. A Congress in obedience to the nod of the White House at such a time would be a positive danger to the country." Roosevelt appealed to the voters of New Hampshire to support the state Republican ticket because the improper negotiations undertaken by Wilson had made the country false to the Allies. "We stand not for a Democratic but an American peace," he said, and the only way to get it was to elect a Congress of true Americans like Moses, Lodge, Poindexter, and Weeks.[37]

The turmoil over the President's attempts to end the war made the Secretary of the Treasury fear for the success of the fourth Liberty Loan drive, which was not going well.[38] The Democratic National Committee hastily circulated myriad copies of Senator Pittman's October 10 speech to all the congressional districts where the unconditional surrender agitation had the party candidates in trouble.[39] The Democratic press blasted the narrow-minded partisanship shown by Lodge, rebuked Roosevelt for acting in a thoroughly unprincipled manner, and declared that the Allies were in full accord with Wilson's peace views.[40] When it became apparent after the third exchange of notes (on October 23) that the Germans were ready to accept Wilson's terms without reserve, the peace debate died down, although Roosevelt continued to urge his senatorial friends to torpedo the Fourteen Points at all costs.

IV

TOWARD THE END of September the White House began to incubate definite plans for asking the country to return a Democratic Congress that fall. At first the idea was to have Wilson handle the matter by writing a letter to a prominent Democrat giving his reasons for making such a request, but this was soon discarded in favor of a more general statement.[41] The date was also postponed from around October 1 until after the conclusion of the Liberty Loan campaign in order to avoid possible criticism. The press, quick to detect what was afoot, speculated freely on the President's probable intentions and alerted many in official Washington to the situation, including Representative Cordell Hull of Tennessee, a member of the Democratic National Committee. An unidentified Cabinet member, whom Hull questioned about the truth of these rumors, informed him that the President had drafted a "thoroughly suitable and appropriate statement."[42]

Although it was not Wilson's habit in making major decisions to take many people into his confidence, among those to whom he now turned for advice was Colonel House, who spent Sunday afternoon, September 22, at the White House discussing the political situation. Wilson told House of his "earnest desire" for a Democratic victory and spoke of making a speech or writing a letter about two weeks before the poll, asking the people to return his party to power. House at the time expressed no opinion with regard to the President's plan, an attitude which, he noted later in his diary, "always indicates to him my disapproval." When news of the appeal reached him on shipboard, he called it a "needless adventure" and a "great gamble" and asserted that "if I had been at home I should have counseled against it."[43] That he had not done so earlier he laid to his absorption with the German peace notes.

The first German note, however, did not reach Washington until October 6, two weeks after the September 22 conference, and House was not consulted with regard to it. He apparently confused his earlier visit with his trip to the Capital on October 15, just prior to his departure for Europe, when he participated in discussions of the second peace note. The only reference to politics on this occasion was Lansing's remark that in making an answer to Germany "we had to keep in mind the coming elections," a thought the Texan considered "unworthy" but otherwise apparently did not challenge. He did observe, however, that "it is difficult to do the right thing in the right way with people like Roosevelt, Lodge, Poindexter and others clamoring for the undesirable and impossible."[44] In any event the President had little reason to conclude from his adviser's attitude on either occasion that House had changed his mind or developed strong mental reservations about an appeal; only a few weeks earlier the Texan had been vocal enough in opposing Wilson's proposed western trip in favor of Tumulty's project of a letter.

Following the September 22 conference, the congressional campaign committee chairman issued a statement saying that the Democratic party sought to retain control of Congress on its record of support for the President and the war.[45] A routine campaign document intended for party orators in need of convincing statistics about the number of troops, ships, and airplanes in active service, the Ferris statement attracted little attention. Another appeal of this sort, however, threw the Republicans into a paroxysm of anger. Released soon after over the signatures of the chairman and assistant treasurer of the National Committee, it called for the election of a Democratic Congress lest the Government be divided, German resistance prolonged indefinitely, and world reorganization blocked. The Republican press castigated the President for permitting such a shameful exhibition of partisanship and exhorted him to silence McCormick and his co-workers.[46]

On October 6 the New York *World* answered the Republican complaint in a long editorial entitled "No Divided Government." It rehearsed the familiar arguments for the election of a Democratic Congress and declared that a Republican victory meant the repudiation of Wilson. The *World* held no brief for the performance of the Sixty-fifth Congress, which it considered shoddy and unstatesmanlike in the extreme; but it preferred a legislative assemblage of Democrats, however incompetent or shortsighted, to one of Republicans intent only on fighting the President at every turn and destroying his plans for the regeneration of mankind. Since Cobb and the *World* generally spoke for the administration, the editorial was assumed to have official sanction;[47] and the only voice of any importance now left unheard was that of Wilson himself.

The vicious Republican attack on his reply to the first German peace note dispelled whatever lingering doubts the President may have had about the advisability of an appeal. He quickly summoned a conference at the White House on October 10, attended by Senators Pittman and Peter G. Gerry of the senatorial campaign committee, Scott Ferris of the congressional committee, and Homer Cummings, vice-chairman of the National Committee.[48] Cummings, a Connecticut lawyer and politician, had recently taken over the nominal direction of the campaign from McCormick, who was sailing for Europe at the end of the month. Largely inactive heretofore and out of touch with the general situation, the vice-chairman was surprised by the violence of the political passions boiling in the Capital. He found Wilson thoroughly aroused and in no mood for further discussion about the wisdom of making an appeal, but interested solely in suggestions concerning the form and content of the manifesto. The President apparently did not bother to enlighten Cummings as to the reasons surrounding his decision, and the whole episode remained somewhat of a mystery to him. In later years the vice-chairman was one of the very few in the White House circle to believe that Wilson had done the right and courageous thing in the circumstances.[49]

Over the weekend Wilson marched down Fifth Avenue in New York at the head of a monster victory parade designed to spur the lagging Liberty Bond campaign. On his return (on October 14) the second German peace note awaited his attention. He found time nonetheless, amid the press of state business, to rough out a draft of an appeal. Summoning McCormick and Cummings on October 18 to discuss the matter, he startled both men by the intensity and bitterness of his feelings. Smarting under the fury of the Republican attack, he had used very blunt and unflattering language in referring to Lodge and other Republican nuisances. Splenetic in temper and petulant in tone, it was patently not one of the President's better literary efforts. When his callers tactfully pointed out the wisdom of moderating the provocative language, Wilson somewhat surprisingly agreed to prepare a new draft, although not often given to taking advice on matters of style. The next day McCormick and Cummings approved the new draft, which after a few minor changes was shown to Tumulty and to no one else, if the statements of Wilson's other counselors, made years after the event, are to be credited.

In the Cabinet circle, however, Secretary of the Interior Franklin K. Lane already had a pretty good idea of what was in the President's mind. Importuned by the National Committee to help out with the campaign, Lane had objected to writing anything of a partisan nature at that particular time until Wilson quickly put his scruples to rest. "There is surely a difference," the President pointed out, "between partisan action and the genuine and whole-hearted support of friends who have been serviceable in every way in maintaining the high purposes of our programme."[50] Wilson's own move in this direction apparently caught the rest of the Cabinet by surprise, much to the annoyance and disapproval of several of them. Attorney General Gregory complained that "none of us knew anything of the letter until it appeared . . . in the morning papers." He believed that without it "the Democrats would have carried the election easily, on the basis of Wilson's prestige and the fact that the war had been won."[51] The Secretary of the Navy also thought it had been bad politics and lost the party everything. Reading the appeal for the first time in the newspapers while on a stumping tour of New England, Daniels considered it the President's "first great mistake" and felt that the Cabinet at least should have had some warning.[52]

The appeal came as a shock to Herbert Hoover, a frequent participant in wartime Cabinet sessions. Hoover, like a great many others, attributed the disaster to Burleson, popularly considered the President's evil genius in political affairs.[53] At a Cabinet meeting shortly after the unhappy event, the Secretary of the Interior, ignoring his own earlier deviation in this respect, bitterly chided the Postmaster General for leading the President astray and bringing ruin upon the party.[54] Burleson, however, vigorously denied having had any part in the fiasco, and nimbly shifted the responsibility to the shoulders of Vance McCormick and Scott Ferris. Far from having any prior knowledge of Wilson's intentions, Burleson said, he had been in Texas at the time and in complete ignorance of what was afoot. His only advice to the President had been to make one speech during the campaign, preferably in a midwestern city, in which Wilson should ask for the return of congressmen who had stood by the administration during the war. The Postmaster General may have had in mind his unfortunate advice in the Wisconsin election; in any event, he now claimed that as everything pointed to a Democratic victory in November, the letter was both unnecessary and unwise.[55]

Vance McCormick, when queried about the episode some years afterwards, also considered the appeal Wilson's "greatest mistake." The form was wrong, he said, and the language "too bitter."[56] If so, the National Chairman had apparently lacked the courage to tell the President so to his face when he approved the final draft on October 19. Scott Ferris also professed to have been kept in the dark until he saw the appeal in the morning papers.[57] This was curious, too, in view of the chairman's previous insistence on Wilson's personal intervention in all the doubtful congressional districts. Moreover, the matter was no secret to his counterpart on the Senate congressional campaign committee, who had written on October 21, "I am now working with the President in hopes that we will get out another strong party letter. I believe it will be out in about two days."[58]

Apart from McCormick and Scott Ferris, it is possible, but not entirely likely, that the others knew nothing about the President's intentions. His failure to consult them beforehand, however, was characteristic of Wilson and should have occasioned no surprise. The Cabinet members had been equally dumbfounded and resentful at his failure to notify them concerning his Fourteen-point peace declaration on January 8.[59] Consequently, they had little reason for wanting to share responsibility for a blunder as egregious as Wilson's appeal came to appear in retrospect. Their reaction suggests the extent to which Wilson failed to establish any real rapport with the men presumably closest to him in public life.

Neither the Cabinet nor anyone else could have restrained the President at this stage. Opposition to a course upon which he had reached a firm decision only irritated Wilson without causing him to change his mind. On the evening of October 24 he retired to his study and typed out a fair copy of the final draft for the Public Printer. Meticulous as to details, he sometimes missed the broader implications of what he was doing. In this instance the fact did not escape Mrs. Wilson, who upon inquiring what was afoot and being told by her husband, remarked that she considered such an appeal undignified. The President was inclined to agree, but he had promised a lot of people to do something along that line, he said, and anyhow it was too late to reconsider.[60] With that the draft went to the Printer and a great controversy was set in motion.

The next day Burleson saw the President after a Cabinet meeting, according to his own account, and was shown a copy of the document. Apparently the Postmaster General did not discuss the matter then with Wilson but warned the worried Tumulty that it was a big mistake. It was too late, as the message had gone out over the wires, but Tumulty tried to get the President to issue another statement setting things in a clearer context.[61]

With the publication of the appeal, pandemonium broke loose. The Republican high command, anticipating something of the sort from newspaper reports or other sources, rushed its rebuttal out over the wires as soon as Wilson's message hit the street. Consequently, many newspapers were able to print both, those hostile to Wilson featuring the Republican reply on the front page and burying the incentive for it on an inside page where the casual reader might overlook it. On neither side was the argument fresh or novel. To Wilson's animadversions upon their obstructive conduct during the war and emphasis on the absolute necessity for an undivided government, his adversaries called attention to Henry Ford and other pacifists running for office with Wilson's approval, contrasted the superior Republican war record with Democratic insubordination, demanded a Republican Congress to settle post-war economic problems, and reminded the voters that in the consummation of a peace treaty the constitutional powers of the Senate equalled those of the President.

For the benefit of the public the Republican leaders staged a very convincing act. The simulated pain and astonishment, the shocked surprise, the horrified denials, the bitter reproaches, and the air of personal injury and affronted self-respect assumed for the occasion gave the impression that Wilson alone was to blame for reviving a very disagreeable subject which had been taboo by mutual consent since the beginning of the war. Otherwise, in the short interval until the election, neither side said anything that had not already been said *ad nauseam*, but now it was uttered in louder and angrier tones. The issues had been before the public for many weeks, and all that remained to be seen was the impact of all this in bringing out the voters on November 5.

CHAPTER XV

THE VERDICT

I

ON THE EVE of the election the administration held a narrow margin of 3 seats in the House and 10 in the Senate. Of the 435 House seats, the fate of only about 50 was in doubt. A few of these doubtful districts were in the East, but the great majority were in the West, where the Democrats were deeply involved in price-fixing and sectional controversies. Early in October the chairman of the congressional campaign committee had sent the President a none too optimistic memorandum on prospects for the House. Ferris listed 194 seats as "safely Democratic" and 199 seats as "safely Republican."[1] Of the remaining 42 districts he gave the Democrats the edge in 31, the Republicans in 11. In respect to the Democratic minimum it was a remarkably accurate prediction, the chairman being off only one seat in his estimate. Unhappily for him, his party lost nearly all the doubtful districts. Fifty-one House seats changed hands on November 5, of which the Republicans won 37, the Democrats 12, and the minor parties 2. In the Sixty-sixth Congress the House had 237 Republicans, 193 Democrats, and 5 minor-party representatives.[2]

As anticipated, the Republicans cut a wide swath through the western states, where the agitation over wheat and cotton had inflamed sectional animosities and pushed other issues, like the peace terms, into the background.[3] In the great farm belt stretching from the Alleghenies to the Rockies, the Democrats lost twenty-one seats; five in Ohio, four each in Indiana and Kansas, three each in Missouri and Nebraska, and one each in Illinois and Michigan. On the southern fringe of this area the Democrats lost single seats in Maryland and West Virginia and two in Kentucky, but gained one in Oklahoma for a net loss of three. In the Far West they lost two Colorado districts and one each in New Mexico and Washington, but managed to win a Nevada seat to hold their net loss to three. The administration made its best showing in the East, where it won six seats in New York (including one from the Socialists), two in New Jersey and two in Pennsylvania, but lost two in New York, three in Pennsylvania, and one each in Delaware and Rhode Island for a net gain of three. The Republican margin of victory was trimmed somewhat by the loss of seats to a Socialist in Wisconsin and a Nonpartisan Leaguer in Minnesota.

The Republicans had been far less certain of winning the Senate.[4] There were 37 contests in 35 states that year, with five special elections in addition to the regularly scheduled 32. The Republicans had already won in Maine and Wisconsin, and the geographical distribution appeared to favor them slightly in the remaining 33 states, although 11 of these were in the Deep South and therefore safely Democratic. The three border states — West Virginia, Kentucky, and Missouri — were always debatable territory, while of the remainder, five were in the East and fourteen in the West. The administration held twenty-one of these contested seats, nine of which were considered vulnerable, with those in Kansas and Illinois practically conceded beforehand to the Republicans. Not more than two or three of the Republican senators up for re-election were deemed in any serious danger. In order to prevail over Wilson the Republicans had to hold all their fourteen seats and capture at least five from their adversaries, not an easy task in view of the tremendous effort put forth by the administration on behalf of all its followers, loyal or otherwise. Consequently, the fact that the Democrats were able to retain only three of their nine doubtful seats was a shock, scarcely cushioned by the astonishing upset scored in Massachusetts at the expense of the obnoxious Weeks.

The result was not so much a repudiation of the President as a want of confidence in the Sixty-fifth Congress, whose obstructionism, irresponsibility, and quarrelsomeness in a time of great crisis had made a very poor impression on the electorate. That it thereby placed the Republicans in a position to nullify Wilson's peace program did not seriously concern the mass of voters. Offsetting Republican contentiousness was the extraordinary display of provincialism, selfishness, and insubordination on the part of the congressmen for whose return to office Wilson had made his appeal. Wilson was not blind to the faults in his congressional followers or inclined to seek excuses for what happened to them. ''Some of them got exactly what was coming to them,'' he said a few weeks after the election, ''and I haven't any bowels of compassion for them. They did not support the things they pretended to support and the country knew they didn't. . . . But in assessing the cause of our defeat we ought to be perfectly frank and admit that the country was not any more sure of us than it ought to be.''[5]

The Republicans, elated by their hard-won victory, naturally magnified their achievement, which they ascribed to Wilson's error of judgment in denigrating their attitude toward the conduct of the war. ''It was a very wonderful election,'' exulted Senator Lodge. ''The President had all the strength which comes to a man in that position in time of war. He had all the vast machinery of the Government necessitated by the war, which was used ruthlessly for the benefit of the Democratic Party. They raised wages in all directions just before the election, and yet they were beaten. The President made a direct appeal for a Democratic Congress and the feeling that beat him, which was apparent from one end of the country to the other, was that the people did not mean to have a dictatorship or an autocracy. When it came to telling them whom they should elect to Congress, they revolted.''[6] Lodge's explanation put the Republicans in the flatteringly heroic role of giant-killers, which they assiduously exploited in the coming months to Wilson's disadvantage in connection with the peace negotiations. It laid the foundation for the legend of a popular repudiation of executive leadership for an appeal which Presidents back to Lincoln's day had been in the habit of making on the eve of a congressional election. It was a myth, moreover, that conveniently masked the intense and unremitting partisan activity which triggered Wilson's action, a myth that is still given currency in many otherwise reputable accounts of that era.

II

WHILE PUBLISHED RETURNS for the House elections are incomplete, figures for the Senate contests are available, although the basis for comparison with previous senatorial elections is not particularly satisfactory. It was only the third time that a direct popular choice of senators had been held. On the first occasion (in 1914) the Progressive tide still ran strongly, and the three-party contests in many states that year do not provide a reliable index of the relative strength of the two major parties. In 1916 an exciting presidential election brought out a tremendous vote, so that a considerable falling off was to be expected in 1918. Nevertheless, some interesting conclusions can be drawn with regard to voting trends in 1918 on the basis of what happened in the two previous senatorial elections. Excluding eight southern states, where November elections were a mere formality, the total vote for senatorial candidates in the twenty-seven states where a reasonably close division existed was 6,643,000. Compared with the 8,121,000 cast in the 1914 and 1916 senatorial elections in the same states, this was about a 17 per cent drop. (On the basis of the 1914 vote in thirteen states, there is about a .5 per cent increase without taking the Progressive vote into account.) When the 1916 vote in the other seventeen states is considered, the decline is about 22 per cent. In view of such factors as the absence of men in the Army and the incidence of Spanish influenza, the vote was not much below what might have been expected in a typical off-year election. The variation from the above-mentioned causes was extremely slight, however.

The relative decline in the party vote is significant. Whereas 4,158,000 Republicans went to the polls in 1914 and 1916, only 3,494,000 voted in 1918, a 16 per cent decrease. On the other hand, 3,962,000 Democrats voted in 1914 and 1916 compared with only 3,148,000 in 1918, a decline of 21 per cent. (See SENATORIAL ELECTION CHART.)[7] Although only 5 per cent fewer Democrats than Republicans turned out on November 5, when this pattern was repeated in states where the division between the parties was usually quite close, the result was disastrous to Wilson's cause. In three states — Nevada, Ken-

SENATORIAL ELECTION CHART

STATE	1918		1916		1914		
	Republican	Democratic	Republican	Democratic	Republican	Democratic	Progressive
Colorado	107,726	104,347			98,728	102,037	(A)
Delaware	21,519	20,113	22,925	25,435			
Idaho[1]	47,947	48,467			47,486	41,246	19,446
Idaho[2]	63,587	31,018					
Illinois	479,967	426,493			390,661	373,043	203,207
Iowa	180,170	167,260			205,832	167,251	53,900
Kansas	281,931	149,300			180,283	176,929	116,755
Kentucky	178,987	184,385			144,758	176,605	18,998
Maine	64,431	54,289	79,752	69,478			
Massachusetts	188,287	204,478	267,157	234,199			
Michigan	220,108	212,517	364,657	257,954			
Minnesota	206,555	137,274	185,159 (B)	117,541			
Missouri	302,680	267,397	371,710	396,166	257,056	311,573	27,614
Montana	40,233	46,147	72,578	83,380			
Nebraska	120,086	99,690	131,059	142,282			
Nevada	8,053	12,197	10,450	12,868	8,038	8,078	(C)

SENATORIAL ELECTION CHART (*continued*)

New Hampshire[3]	37,783	32,763			42,113	36,382	
New Hampshire[4]	35,528	34,459					
New Jersey	175,209	151,454	244,715	170,019			
New Mexico	24,342	22,470	30,609	33,982			
North Carolina	93,697	143,524			87,101	121,342	
Oklahoma	72,903	94,994	73,292	119,443			(D)
Oregon	82,360	64,303			88,297	111,478	26,220
Rhode Island	42,055	37,753	39,211	47,048			
South Dakota	51,198	36,210			44,244	48,076	7,184
Tennessee	61,098	99,576	118,138	143,718			
West Virginia	115,216	97,715	144,243	138,585			
Wisconsin	163,980	148,714	251,303	135,144	133,966	134,925	9,276
Wyoming	23,979	17,528	23,528	26,234			
TOTALS	3,494,615	3,148,835	2,430,216	2,153,475	1,728,563	1,808,965	482,600

1. Gooding vs. Nugent;
2. Borah vs. Moore;
3. Keyes vs. Reed;
4. Moses vs. Jameson.

(A) 1914 Socialist Party vote 52,448;
(B) 1916 Prohibition Party vote 78,425;
(C) 1914 Socialist Party vote 5,451;
(D) 1914 Socialist Party vote 52,229.

tucky, and Idaho — where the 1918 vote exceeded the 1914 totals, Democratic candidates won the election. Elsewhere, with the exception of Massachusetts where the Republican rate of decline was three times greater than the Democratic, Wilson's party lost practically by default. Although the Republicans were able to increase their vote in only ten of the twenty-seven doubtful states, the failure of the Democrats to come near equaling their previous senatorial total in ten of those states cost them their chance of retaining control of the Senate. Many voters may have stayed at home out of annoyance at the President's appeal, but the party as a whole was much less effective than it had been in getting out the vote on election day.

States which exhibited the greatest decline in the Democratic vote suffered from the worst factional troubles. Missouri cast almost 200,000 fewer votes in the 1918 than in the 1916 senatorial contest, a decrease of 25 per cent. Of these, 130,000 were Democratic and 70,000 were Republican. Since Folk, the Democratic candidate, lost by only 35,000, this heavy defection was fatal to him. The 1918 total, however, was slightly larger than the 1914 vote for senator, when Stone polled 311,573 votes, or about 14 per cent more than Folk got, while Stone's Republican opponent received 257,056, or 14 per cent less than Spencer's 1918 total. In other words, a Republican off-year minority of 54,000 votes in 1914 was turned into a 35,000 majority in 1918, another off year — a swing of about 90,000 votes in a total of approximately 570,000. Contributing very largely to this striking result was the hostility between the Democratic state machine and the party's senatorial candidate. All Wilson's efforts on Folk's behalf proved fruitless, as did Folk's plea to stand by the President. His failure to make Senator Reed's obstructive course in this respect a convincing issue helped the party machine cut him down at the polls. Resentment against the administration's farm policies cost three rural Missouri Democrats their congressional seats, a factor which also accounted in part for the unexpectedly light vote cast for Folk in temperance areas, where his greatest strength lay.

Nebraska Democrats, weakened by factionalism and rent by schism, made a sorry showing. The Bryan faction, which included all the Prohibitionists, would not support the party's senatorial candidate, ex-Governor John H. Morehead, because of his connections with the disreputable Hitchcock-Neville-Mullen machine and the ''wet'' forces fighting the Eighteenth Amendment. Moreover, Hitchcock's anti-administration record also did the Democrats no good, despite the patriotic outcry against Senator Norris for trying to ride back into office on the strength of the pro-German pacifist sentiment in the state. In fact, the high-handed attempts of Governor Keith Neville and the patriots to stamp out this sentiment backfired and cost the party many votes. A Lincoln attorney observed that ''the autocratic action and domineering spirit of many of the state councils of defense lost the Germans and most of the non-partisan leaguers to the democratic party where they naturally belong.''[8]

The loss to Nebraska Democrats amounted to 30 per cent compared with their 1916 level, when Hitchcock had been reelected. Many conservative Republicans refused to support Norris, whose vote declined 9 per cent; but this made no difference to the outcome, which gave the senator a margin of 21,000 votes in a total of 220,000. The decisive factor was the temper of the rural population, exacerbated by governmental interference with farm prices, inflamed by the spectacle of unregulated cotton, and largely indifferent to the issues of war and peace. Consequently, all three Democratic congressmen were swept out of office by the same tidal wave of rural resentment that put Norris back in.

Oregon Democrats, badly confused by Senator Chamberlain's odd conduct during the Senate investigation, remained away from the polls in large numbers. Their senatorial candidate, ex-Governor Oswald West, a Chamberlain henchman, got no support from Washington, while the rank and file either ignored him on November 5 or voted for Senator McNary. Democratic strength fell 42 per cent from 1914, when Chamberlain owed his re-election to the Progressive split. The Republican vote, although 5 per cent under the 1914 total, was enough to give McNary a plurality of 16,000 out of 146,000 votes. Undoubtedly, many more Oregonians would have responded to Wilson's appeal had they been certain that another Democrat in the Senate was the answer to the President's problems.[9]

Democratic disunity in Colorado, abetted by the Republican uproar over sectionalism and disloyalty, brought about the defeat of Senator Shafroth and Representatives Hilliard and Keating. Hilliard weakened the ticket by running as an independent after his District nominating convention in Denver refused to swallow his "acid test" record, and thus partially nullified administration efforts on behalf of Shafroth and Keating. The senator, who lost by only 3,300 votes out of a total of 212,000, blamed his defeat on the brazen tactics of his opponent, who, he claimed, had spent $75,000 on a self-advertising campaign while head of the Colorado Red Cross.[10] Shafroth's vote fell off 2 per cent from 1914, when the Democrats elected a senator, but Phipps by fair means or foul managed to increase the Republican vote 9 per cent, or barely enough to win.

In Wyoming the Republican vote remained practically stationary, but the Democratic vote plummeted 34 per cent from 1916, when the party elected Senator John B. Kendrick. Hence Senator Warren had no trouble in obtaining a sixth term from his constituents. Rural dissatisfaction played a part in the result, as did the poor caliber of Warren's opponent, whose boasted connection with Bryan no longer had a magic attraction for the electorate.

Western governors like Capper of Kansas and Peter Norbeck of South Dakota, who had temporized with the Nonpartisan League during the war, experienced little trouble at the polls in 1918. On the other hand, state executives like Burnquist of Minnesota and Neville of Nebraska, who had taken a tough line with the Townley organization, found the going exceedingly rough. While Neville went down to defeat, Burnquist narrowly escaped a similar fate. He had polled 63 per cent of the vote in 1916, but now got only 45 per cent in a pentagonal contest; and would have lost had the Nonpartisan League seen fit to endorse the Democratic gubernatorial candidate instead of running its own man.[11] Senator Nelson, against whom the League had no particular grudge, won handily as anticipated. His total was about 10 per cent above that of Kellogg in 1916, when a Prohibitionist candidate took many votes away from the Republican ticket. Nelson's opponent, Calderwood, although handicapped by having to run as an independent without the backing of the Democratic state committee, jumped the 1916 Democratic senatorial vote 20 per cent, thanks largely to Nonpartisan League support and belated assistance from Washington. Labor unrest in the iron-mining and lakefront-shipping region around Duluth, however, cost one Republican congressman his seat. Wilson's appeal had turned "the Socialist labor crowd and the Nonpartisan League" against Representative Clarence B. Miller, according to one local Republican leader, who also accused McAdoo of having lined up the large railroad vote for Miller's opponent, a railwayman, during an official visit to Duluth a few days before the election.[12]

The resurgence of Republicanism in Kansas buried the loyal but luckless Senator Thompson under a landslide of votes for Governor Capper. Although the total was slightly less than in the three-cornered 1914 contest, the return of the Progressives to the fold swelled Capper's vote by 35 per cent, while Thompson's dipped 17 per cent. Rural discontent all but wiped out the Democratic contingent of five House members. The sole survivor, Representative William A. Ayres of the Wichita district, owed his re-election chiefly to his break with the administration over the regulation of cotton. A similar stand, however, failed to save Representative William E. Cox of the Third Indiana District, a rich farming area in the Ohio River bottom and the most solidly Democratic in the state, having sent but one Republican to Congress in the preceding forty years. Despite his well-publicized attacks on southern indifference to northern interests, the Republicans made a clean sweep of the Indiana congressional delegation by retiring Cox and three other Democrats.

In a few instances Wilson's appeal was of direct benefit to his beleaguered followers. In the close Nevada senatorial election it swung enough Republican votes to Senator Henderson to ensure his return to office, a fact which the arch-Republican Reno *Evening Gazette* admitted in an election post-mortem, after noting with satisfaction the failure of the appeal elsewhere in the country.[13] Henderson managed to poll 47 per cent of the vote; Roberts, the Republican, got 32 per cent and Martin, the suffragist, 18 per cent, while the rest went to a Socialist candidate. Since by no means all of Miss Martin's 4,063 votes would have gone to the isolationist Roberts, her diversionary influence had no effect on the outcome. The state administration remained Democratic as Governor Emmet D. Boyle defeated his Republican opponent, ex-Governor Tasker L. Oddie, by about 1,000 votes in a straight two-party contest, while Roberts trailed Oddie on the Republican ticket by 3,500 votes. (Two years later Henderson lost the senatorship to Oddie in another four-cornered contest by a margin of 1,100 votes. Since Henderson then did not come within 1,800 votes of his 1918 total, this increment most likely represented Republican support which melted away in the Harding landslide, inasmuch as Oddie failed to poll as many votes for senator in 1920 as he had for governor in 1918.)

Two other Democratic senators survived the general collapse of their party in the West, and in each contest the Nonpartisan League played a stellar if not decisive role. Although Senator Walsh polled only 41 per cent of the total Montana vote, he was elected when his two opponents split the remainder, Lanstrum getting 36 per cent and Miss Rankin 23 per cent. On the face of things, the lady's candidacy appeared to be the principal factor in Walsh's success, and Lanstrum was very bitter about her treachery to the party. Even had she not entered the race, however, Lanstrum's anti-League views would have won him very few Rankin votes, the bulk of which would have gone to Walsh, who never openly opposed the Townley organization. Walsh's friends attributed the 45 per cent decline in the Democratic vote from 1916 to the President's ill-advised appeal and to the vicious Republican agitation over sectionalism.[14] Since Lanstrum's vote also declined 45 per cent, it would appear that Miss Rankin drew her support in about equal proportions from her two opponents and that Wilson's maneuver had no bearing on the outcome.

Despite the hostility of the conservative wing of his party to his stand on the League, Senator Borah overwhelmed his hapless

Democratic opponent by a better than two-to-one majority. In the other Idaho battle, however, Senator Nugent eked out a victory over Gooding in a contest so close that the final result was not known for several weeks.[15] Like Walsh, the senator benefited from Nonpartisan League support without having openly sought it. Gooding, on the other hand, by taking the Roosevelt line that the League was a Bolshevik organization operating in the interests of the Kaiser, suffered the consequences at the polls. He ran 16,000 votes behind Borah on the Republican ticket, while Nugent was 17,000 votes ahead of his party ticket, the difference representing the hard core of Nonpartisan League strength in Idaho. Gooding polled almost exactly the same vote that had sent the reactionary Brady to the Senate in 1914, while Nugent, with Nonpartisan League assistance, upped the Democratic vote 20 per cent. When Gooding and Nugent again fought it out in 1920, the year of the Harding landslide, the Republican coasted to an easy victory.

III

KENTUCKY showed the greatest proportionate increase in its senatorial vote, about 12 per cent over 1914. It was one of the states that the Republicans had confidently expected to carry and almost did, falling short by only 5,400 votes out of a total of 363,000. The Democrats, disorganized by the demise of the popular Ollie M. James shortly after the August primaries, had to replace him on the senatorial ballot with Governor Augustus O. Stanley, who lacked the spellbinding gifts and electoral appeal of his predecessor. Although an able and energetic executive, Stanley had thrown the state into a turmoil with his wartime policies. His veto of a bill banning the teaching of German in the public schools had set the patriotic pack baying on his trail, while his appointment, at Wilson's request, of an interim senator pledged to vote for the Nineteenth Amendment had antagonized the potent Bourbon element, headed by Senator James C. H. Beckham, a bitter foe of enfranchising southern women.[16] The Republicans profited from all this to the extent of increasing their vote 24 per cent, but it was not quite enough to offset the 5 per cent increase that Wilson's appeal garnered for the Democrats.

Senator James Hamilton Lewis made a surprisingly good showing in Illinois in view of the wealth and influence of the McCormick connection arrayed against him.[17] Although the total vote declined slightly from that of the three-party 1914 senatorial contest, not all the Progressives reverted to the Republican standard. The 1918 Democratic vote increased 18 per cent, but the Republicans gained 20 per cent, and Lewis lost by only 53,000 ballots in a total of nearly a million. Since Wilson had lost Illinois by 200,000 in 1916, the result was a tribute not only to Lewis' local popularity but to the tremendous effort on his behalf by the administration, which placed important patronage and other perquisites freely at his disposal. The President's appeal might have carried the day had not the sectional issue intervened to minimize Democratic gains.[18]

Another surprisingly close contest occurred in Michigan, normally a Republican stronghold which seldom deviated from its fealty to the party that had saved the Union. Yet Henry Ford reduced a normal Republican plurality of 100,000 to one of 7,500 in losing to Newberry after a campaign given such prolonged and intense publicity that hardly any literate citizen could remain unaware of the issues at stake. The creator of the Model T was peculiarly the candidate of Wilson and known to represent the President's hopes for the future of mankind. Whether or not Wilson was wise in attaching such hopes to a man like Ford, the Republicans had to work hard and spend much money to defeat him. Ford carried Detroit by a substantial margin and did well in other industrial centers, but the rural voters would not desert their old allegiance. Nearly a third fewer voters went to the polls than in the 1916 senatorial contest, and the Republican decline was an astonishing 40 per cent. Had the Democrats been able to hold their 1916 level, Ford would have won, but the Democratic vote dropped 17 per cent, or just under the total amassed by Newberry. There was no outpouring of Michigan voters to rebuke the President for his appeal. If Wilson failed to elect his man, his party came much closer to it than on many previous occasions.

Historians of the conjectural school have made much of the fact that but for the defeat of Ford, generally and erroneously attributed to Newberry's purchase of the election, Democratic control of the Senate would have remained unchanged and the President spared much of the unpleasantness that followed. Such speculation is meaningless. While it is obvious that a shift of 4,000 votes, or about 1 per cent in a total of 432,000, would have given Ford the Senate seat, the result was equally close and equally disappointing to the administration in a number of other states where Democratic prospects were brighter than in Michigan. A shift of fewer than 600 out of 41,600 ballots cast in Delaware would have prevented the defeat of Senator Saulsbury, who fell a victim to the restoration of Republican harmony in a state long ruled by the Du Pont dynasty. In New Mexico a change of approximately 900 votes in a total of 46,700 would have eliminated Senator Fall and done much to improve the subsequent moral tone of the government. In New Hampshire a change of 500 votes in a total of 70,000 would have deprived the Republican "irreconcilables" of the invaluable services of Senator Moses in the fight against the Versailles Treaty. On the other hand, a shift of only 250 votes out of a total of 96,000 in one of the Idaho contests would have given the seat to another reactionary Republican and thereby placed the Democrats further in the minority. The extreme closeness of the result in most states indicated a Democratic disinclination or inability to meet successfully at the local level issues which Wilson's appeal at the national level failed to take into consideration.

The most astonishing result of all occurred in Massachusetts, where the defeat of Senator Weeks afforded the administration such solace as could be gleaned from the general situation. The senator's malignant and frequently senseless opposition to Wilson boomeranged in a manner that might have meant disaster for the party generally but for the skill of Chairman Hays in finding other issues to occupy the voters' attention. By ignoring the advice of Hays, who kept strictly out of the Massachusetts contest, and following instead the precepts of Lodge, the junior senator badly overreached himself and ruined his prospects for the 1920 presidential nomination. The blow stunned Lodge and his friends, whose gloom was not lightened by the easy victory in the gubernatorial election of the close-mouthed Coolidge over another Wilson-backed candidate.[19] "I am, like you," Lodge told Major General Wood, "bitterly disappointed over the election in Massachusetts. Weeks was beaten by the treachery of McCall and by the fact that we have an element of Republicans who feel it their duty to vote for Wilson and against everything else."[20] One of Weeks's State Street associates summed up the tragedy more poignantly. "Massachusetts," he said, "has covered herself with infamy by defeating a splendid senator like Weeks and electing in his place a slacker like Walsh. For Weeks' defeat I blame the apostate McCall, the grotesque Lawson, the woman suffragists, and such weak-kneed idolators [of Wilson] as Ellery Sedgwick, John F. Moors, Henry B. Cabot, and other long-haired men and short-haired women."[21]

The total Bay State vote was about 20 per cent under the record vote of 1916, when Mayor John F. Fitzgerald of Boston gave Lodge a stiff battle and lost by only 33,000 votes out of a half-million cast. The 1918 Democratic vote was down 12 per cent, but Weeks polled 30 per cent fewer votes than had Lodge, which cost him the election by a 16,000-vote margin. The "grotesque" Lawson's chivalrous sally into politics netted him about 22,000 votes, not all of which in a two-way contest would necessarily have gone to Weeks. The decisive factor was the shift of the independent element — the "long-haired men and short-haired women" — who might support Lodge out of a snobbish regard for his Brahmin ancestry or his intellectual attainments but found nothing stimulating in Weeks's purblind partisanship and indifference to developments outside of his State Street financial interests.[22]

Elsewhere in New England the Republicans had little to grieve them, although the vote was nowhere as one-sided as the disappointing outcome for Wilson's party might indicate. Republican congressional pluralities declined about 10 per cent in Connecticut, where the party carried four of the five districts by emphasizing the familiar theme that "no Northern Democrat amounts to anything in Congress but to vote to endorse the program laid down for him by his Southern associates.''[23] In the Hartford district, however, the Democratic representative nearly trebled his 1916 margin, while Governor Marcus Holcomb saw his state-wide plurality slashed 30 per cent despite the Republican fanfare about his splendid wartime services to the state. Labor unrest which had threatened Republican dynasties in Rhode Island and New Hampshire had subsided in the face of higher wages and full employment. With textile mills making profits of 300 per cent and paying out dividends of 100 per cent or more, wages had risen a modest 65 per cent, but it was beyond anything dreamed of in the pre-war era. As labor discontent faded in Rhode Island, so did the Democratic vote, which fell off 20 per cent. A Republican gain of 7 per cent enabled Senator Colt to edge out Representative George F. O'Shaunessy by 4,300 votes in about 80,000 cast. The Republicans also annexed O'Shaunessy's congressional seat in the Providence district. New Hampshire sent Governor Keyes to the Senate by about the same margin accorded Gallinger in 1914. For Gallinger's vacant seat, however, a very close vote gave the edge to George H. Moses, who displayed a more rancorous brand of Republicanism than the amiable Keyes. While Keyes led his opponent by 5,000 votes, Moses ran well behind his ticket and pulled through by about 1,000. Republican propaganda depicting the administration's fondness for the South hurt the Democrats in the mill towns, where there was little concern for Wilson's aspirations about a new world order.

The Democrats made a much stronger showing in New York than had been the case in 1916. Interest centered chiefly on the gubernatorial struggle because of its presidential overtones. Governor Charles S. Whitman's ambition in that direction, however, made him many Republican enemies and cooled off many erstwhile friends, including Colonel Roosevelt, who had his own interests in the matter to consider. Although the governor came down to New York City with an upstate lead of nearly a quarter of a million votes, it was not enough to overcome the mighty effort Tammany put forth on behalf of Al Smith, Boss Murphy's belated concession to the spirit of the

new age, and Whitman lost by a margin of 11,000 votes. Smith
was one of the very few Democrats to run without active administration support, which would have been no recommendation in New York City. McAdoo and Lansing alone in the
White House circle warmly endorsed the Happy Warrior, whose
victory was of small solace to Wilson, who never overcame his
repugnance for Tammany or any of its minions.[24] Tammany
also redeemed four of the metropolitan congressional seats it
had lost by cutting Wilson in the 1916 presidential election.
Upstate, however, one of the President's good friends and warm
admirers, Representative George R. Lunn, former Socialist
mayor of Schenectady, met defeat as a Democrat in the Thirty-
second District, his radical record proving too much of a handicap in the superheated atmosphere of 1918.

The Nugent organization, Tammany's New Jersey counterpart, also recovered sufficiently from its 1916 sulks to recapture
two congressional seats in its Hudson County stronghold. Although the machine was unable to elect its senatorial candidate,
La Monte made a very good showing against Governor Edge
and cut the Republican 1916 plurality by two thirds. The Republican vote declined 28 per cent, compared with an 11 per
cent Democratic recession, indicating some resurgence of support
for the President. Delaware, however, reversed its political position for the first time in a decade. A 20 per cent dip in the
Democratic vote, while the Republicans held their loss to 10 per
cent, proved fatal to Senator Saulsbury. Delaware was another
industrial state where Republican propaganda successfully neu-
tralized the effects of wartime prosperity by raising fears that
the good times would disappear in consequence of Wilson's
harebrained international adventures.

The West Virginia coal-mining industry had suffered severely
from governmental interference with production and prices,
and the state seethed with resentment against the administration. Organized labor refused to rally to Wilson's cause or
follow President Frank J. Hayes of the United Mine Workers
and many local union officials in endorsing the senatorial candidacy of Colonel Clarence W. Watson, who widely advertised
himself as a paragon among mineowners. Wilson himself, who

had endorsed Watson's opponent in the primary, steadfastly refused to speak for the ticket despite appeals from the state committee and the urging of Tumulty.[25] Consequently the Democratic vote fell off sharply, some 41,000 from 1916, compared with a Republican decrease of 29,000. While the ratio of defection was not great, it worked to the disadvantage of Watson, whose margin of defeat was less than 18,000 in a total of 213,000 votes.

Governor James M. Cox of Ohio was more successful in his third-term bid than was Governor Whitman. Whereas Whitman's defeat eliminated him from the 1920 presidential possibilities, Cox's victory put him in the front rank of Democratic favorite sons. The political eclipse of ex-Governor Frank B. Willis, who had again lost to Cox, also left Senator Harding without serious competition for Ohio's choice at the next Republican national convention. The vicissitudes of Ohio politics, moreover, enabled the Republicans to redeem the five congressional seats lost in 1916 when the Harding-Daugherty faction decamped after Daugherty's defeat in the senatorial primary. The districts were mostly in rural areas where prejudice had been whipped up against the administration's handling of the price-control situation. Ohio workers, on the other hand, remained loyal to the President's party, which managed to hold its eight seats in the industrial areas around Cleveland, Toledo, and Akron.

IV

WHEN ALL the returns were in and the dust had settled, a loud outcry arose against the President for his foolish appeal. The press, regardless of party, united in ascribing the Democratic defeat to this factor alone. Among themselves, however, the Democratic leaders displayed more candor in assessing the causes of the disaster. William J. Bryan not unnaturally detected the hand of big business in the debacle, but to this complaint Senator Thomas J. Walsh replied that "it would still remain debatable whether it [big business] accomplished the result by misrepresenting the President's letter or by the resurrection of the bloody shirt.''[26] Reviewing the shambles to which his party had been reduced in the West, Walsh felt that the bloody shirt was a sounder explanation. ''The President's letter,'' he said, ''was unfortunately phrased. If he had contented himself with asking for the return of those members, Democrat and Republican, who had earnestly and conscientiously supported the administration it would have been much better. Still I cannot believe that it resulted as disastrously as it is claimed. I am satisfied that the people generally accepted the argument that the south is running the Government and running it selfishly. The complaint about two-dollar wheat would have had little effect were it not for the fact that it was coupled with the accusation that the price of wheat had been fixed while that of cotton was not.''[27]

The vice-chairman of the Democratic National Committee attributed the defeat to three controlling factors: better Republican organization, sectionalism, and the poor caliber of the Democratic leadership in Congress. The country, said Cummings, had lost confidence in these leaders, many of whom had ''disclosed invincible provincialism in almost all matters of national consequence, and it was generally believed that the Selective Draft Law would have failed utterly had it not been for Republican support. The fact that many of these leaders were from the south did not help the situation any.''[28] Throughout the campaign, said a prominent western Democrat, ''the argument we had to meet everywhere was 'the south is in the saddle; it has the legislative and the executive, and laws are being enacted and enforced which are discriminating against the people of the north.' Not only was this proclaimed upon the stump, but the republican press bureau had it constantly before the people's eyes in season and out of season. Nothing was done to combat it. . . . Unquestionably, this argument defeated us in the last election and it lost us a great many eastern states in 1916.''[29] Representative Carter Glass, a member of the party's Executive Committee, supported this conclusion. ''The only remaining, as it is the most effective, asset of the Republican Party,'' he said, ''is sectionalism. This came near defeating us in 1916, and was primarily, if not solely, responsible for the overturn in Congress in 1918.''[30]

In view of the unanimity of expert opinion on the principal cause of his defeat, the question arises as to why Wilson had done nothing to combat this pernicious propaganda before it reached dangerous proportions. Fixing the price of cotton at thirty cents a pound, which was roughly equivalent to the price imposed upon the wheat farmer, would have harmed neither the administration, the country, nor the cotton grower. It would have served to stabilize the entire industry and put an end to the flagrant profiteering in textiles which irritated not only the cotton growers but consumers everywhere. Stabilization was possible as late as September, when cotton prices were in the doldrums and southern resistance at a low ebb over the prospect of an unmanageable new crop. Wilson, however, no longer considered price-fixing necessary, or else he felt nothing was to be gained by reopening the troublesome issue with Congress. In any case, he ignored repeated warnings from his worried western followers about the agitation spreading throughout their section of the country in favor of controls.[31] ''I was asked many times,'' one Ohio congressman told him, ''why the price of wool and wheat was regulated and the price of cotton permitted to soar. I will frankly confess, I was unable to give any satisfactory explanation.'' The farmers of his district, he added, would cheerfully submit to controls ''provided they do not believe that they have been discriminated against.''[32] The President apparently saw nothing particularly dangerous in the situation and vouchsafed no reply.

The War Industries Board sanctioned his attitude on economic grounds inasmuch as cotton, unlike wool and other commodities, was not in short supply.[33] The experts maintained that the Treasury would incur an intolerable burden if it attempted to carry the unsalable surplus from the huge 1918 crop and paid the growers a fixed price for what they could not sell on the open market.[34] This argument lost its pertinency after a severe drought that summer destroyed a third of the crop and presented despondent growers with a financial bonanza instead of an unmarketable product.[35] The rejoicing in Dixie at the prospect of a short crop and 40-cent cotton raised a loud outcry in the northern press for immediate government action to check skyrocketing cotton prices.[36] The uproar sent agitated Dixie congressmen rushing pell mell to the White House to demand a hands-off policy from Wilson, who hastened to assure them that he had no intention of interfering in the matter. Nevertheless, he thought it expedient to pacify the North by agreeing to appoint two committees to look into the situation and report upon the feasibility of price-fixing at some unspecified future date.[37] This quieted the excitement to the extent that McAdoo could assure his southern friends in the Senate late in September that "the cotton matter is going to work out all right and you need feel no more concern about it."[38]

Sympathy for the interests of the people among whom he was born and raised did not account solely for Wilson's equivocal behavior. Of more importance to him than the undignified and sordid squabble over price-fixing was the fate of the war revenue act, which he deemed vital to the financial welfare of the nation. The measure had made disappointingly slow progress through the legislative mill since his speech of May 27 had forced its consideration upon the attention of Congress. Only steady pressure from the White House, aided by a blistering press campaign against congressional irresponsibility, had finally overcome the dilatory tactics of the Democratic leadership and gotten the bill through the House on September 20.[39] Favorable Senate action before the rapidly approaching end of the session depended upon the support of at least a few southern senators. With the frenzy over government regulation reaching a peak at that moment, for Wilson to have recommended price-fixing on cotton would have ended all hope for the tax law in that session, a catastrophe he hoped to avoid at all costs.

Ironically, the Senate never got around to acting upon the bill. Wilson's peace negotiations so distracted the attention of that body in the closing days of the session that the revenue measure failed to emerge from the Finance Committee. In their preoccupation with Wilson's dickering with the Germans, the senators ignored the pleas and warnings of the Treasury Department that adjournment without provision being made for new taxes and more revenues would "disorganize and endanger the national finances."[40] Thus the President paid a high price for nothing, a price that cost his shortsighted party control of the government and wrecked his plans for the better ordering of world affairs.

V

CREDIT for unhorsing Wilson in 1918 must be allocated in about equal measure between Democratic ineptitude and Republican astuteness. Especially noteworthy in the latter respect was the success of Lodge, Roosevelt, and their followers in and out of Congress in keeping the party spirit alive at considerable risk during the difficult days of the war by a running attack on every phase of the war program. The supreme accolade, however, must go to the wily and indefatigable Hays. The dapper, little national chairman performed prodigies in knitting together the shattered fabric of the organization and in developing controversial issues only indirectly connected with the prosecution of the war but capable of inflaming sentiment against the administration over a wide area.

The Democrats, indifferent to the warnings of the 1916 election and to all the obvious signs in the 1918 campaign, allowed their opponents to manufacture a bogus economic issue out of the price-fixing situation and to use it in such a way as to undermine confidence in the impartiality of the government at a critical juncture in the nation's history. Over-all price stabilization might have had little or no economic justification; on the other hand, it could have done little harm financially or otherwise. From a political point of view, it would have silenced a great deal of harmful clamor throughout the North and West, deprived the Republicans of their most effective argument, and strengthened the administration in states or congressional districts where the President was more popular than his party.

In the last analysis, it was not Wilson's belated appeal, into which he finally allowed himself to be prodded by the antics of his adversaries, who had been hoping all along for such a reaction, that encompassed his defeat. The crucial mistake was his stubborn refusal to believe that the public temper had soured on some of his domestic policies to the extent that his party stood in peril of reprisals at the polls. His unalterable conviction that the voters shared his passionate interest in, and exalted concern for, world affairs and would not therefore let him down in the crisis sealed the fate of the party on November 5 and tragically altered the course of history, at least for those whose hopes he had aroused by his vision of the possibility of better things ahead for mankind than a perpetual recourse to war and devastation.

Whether or not the Versailles Treaty would have fared better at the hands of a Democratic Senate, the transfer of power to his enemies left Wilson in a hopeless position. Congress had come out of the war bruised and embittered by its experiences with an unbending and imperious Chief Executive. Released now from the compulsion of following him, however reluctantly, as a patriotic duty, the Republicans were even less inclined to endorse his aspirations for the future. When Congress reconvened shortly after the election, Senator Thomas J. Walsh observed that ''partisanship has never run so high in Congress since I have been here,'' and he found the Republicans willing to nullify the peace negotiations ''if only some political advantage can be secured by attacking Wilson and his principles.''[41] Concerned henceforward solely with re-establishing their primacy in national affairs by any means that came to hand, the Republican leaders did not fully achieve this objective until they brought forth the amiable Harding in 1920 from the obscurity of a smoke-filled room. This supremacy they continued to enjoy until brought low once more in their pride by the onset of the Great Depression.

A Democratic victory in 1918 would certainly have delayed this upward trend, or at least minimized its harsher aspects. Relieved from the necessity of making his disastrous western trip on behalf of the peace treaty, Wilson might have fought off any unpalatable compromises thrust upon him by his vindictive but untriumphant foes, much as he had repelled their earlier efforts to take the conduct of the war out of his hands and place it under the control of "instrumentalities" of their own choosing. In retrospect, it would seem that Wilson's mistakes, no less than the blind partisanship of his adversaries, contributed with the inexorability of a Greek tragedy to the catastrophe of Versailles and after.

NOTES

CHAPTER I: *The Politics of Preparedness*

1. Ray S. Baker, *Woodrow Wilson,* VIII, 513. Ray S. Baker and William E. Dodd, eds., *War and Peace,* I, 286–87.

2. Herbert Agar, *The Price of Union,* 69–70, makes Wilson guilty of issuing "the most unwise appeal in American history" despite the complete support given him by both parties in Congress during the war. Malcolm C. Moos, *The Republicans,* 306, follows the traditional pattern of abusing Wilson for reviving partisan warfare, which "took up where it had left off a year and a half before." Such views are derived from Frank R. Kent, *The Democratic Party,* 431–33; William S. Myers, *The Republican Party,* 431–32; Wilfred E. Binkley, *American Political Parties,* 370; and a host of other works of a similar character. George H. Mayer, *The Republican Party, 1854–1964,* 350–53, examines the election in some detail but misrepresents Wilson's motives and reaches wrong conclusions. The only adequate recognition of the subject is John M. Blum, *Joe Tumulty and the Wilson Era,* 157–68.

3. John A. Garraty, *Henry Cabot Lodge,* 336–42. New York *Times,* editorial, September 5, 1918. Lodge to John T. Morse, September 11, 1918; Lodge Papers.

4. Henry A. Wise Wood to McAdoo, June 3, 1918, enclosing pamphlet; McAdoo Papers. A Vermont Republican congressman, responding to a suggestion to omit a political campaign in 1918, rejected the idea on the ground that Wilson had to be stopped or Yankee civilization would disappear. (Frank L. Greene to Walter H. Crockett, March 30, 1918; Greene Papers.)

5. New York *Journal of Commerce,* May 23, 1917. Boston *Evening Transcript,* May 15, 1917, called Congress "a sorry spectacle" for wasting the first forty days of the war in "unseemly wrangling." The Virginia Council of Defense adopted a resolution condemning Congress for delaying "beyond reason" the enactment of vital war legislation. (W. M. Hunley to Carter Glass, May 16, 1917; Glass Papers.)

6. Borah called the militia lobby's fight against the General Staff proposals "a nauseating affair" and a "terrific raid upon the treasury"; Borah to W. H. Cowles, April 7, 23, 1916; to Thomas J. Jones, April 15, 1916; to Edward R. Kirby, April 18, 1918; Borah Papers. *Literary Digest,* Vol. 52, January 29, February 26, 1916. New York *Times,* April 26, May 5, 1916. Arthur S. Link, *Wilson,* IV, 328–34.

7. Chicago *Tribune,* May 10, 1916. New York *Times,* May 17, 1916, called the defeat of the Continental Army provision a "national calamity." Wilson saved his party from the stigma of having sabotaged the entire defense program by persuading the House to accept the Senate naval bill, which it grudgingly did on August 15, 1916.

8. Albert S. Burleson to Ray S. Baker, February 25, 1931, that the President telephoned the Postmaster General, read the McLemore resolution to him, and wanted it defeated. Burleson feared that if they lost this fight, the party would lose control of the House; Ray S. Baker Papers. Arthur S. Link, *Wilson,* IV, 188–94, sees no politics in the situation.

9. Greene to Frank E. Howe, March 10, 1916, protesting the attack on him in Howe's Bennington *Evening Banner;* Greene Papers. William Kent of California, one of the 33 Democrats to support the resolution, defended his vote on the ground that "I cannot follow the President in his demand that we should not notify American citizens that a merchant-man armed for defense is not a safe place for innocent bystanders." (Kent to H. A. George, March 6, 1916; Kent Papers.)

10. Quoted in New York *World,* September 28, 1916. Milwaukee *Journal,* October 9, 11, 1916. New York *Times,* November 6, 1916.

11. William Kent, who gave up his California congressional seat to organize the Wilson League of Independents in 1916, felt otherwise. "To my surprise and grief," he wrote, "Johnson, in his senatorial fight, strenuously advocated Hughes, thereby cutting down materially a larger Wilson majority." (Kent to William G. McAdoo, November 21, 1916; Kent Papers.)

12. J. E. Barnes to Poindexter, October 13, 1916; Poindexter to John T. Jones, October 6, 1916; to C. B. Kegley, November 8, 1916; Poindexter Papers. In many of the sparsely settled western states, where the railroad vote bulked large, the Adamson act establishing an eight-hour day for railroad workers probably helped Wilson's party as much as, or more than, the peace argument.

13. Ex-Senator Obadiah Gardner to Wilson, September 15, 1916; Wilson Papers. New York *World,* August 22, 1916. Portland *Daily Eastern Argus,* August 22, 24, 1916.

14. Frederic E. Kip to Frank B. Kellogg, September 29, 1916, enclosing pamphlet and form letter from Ralph Cole, chairman of the speakers bureau; Kellogg Papers.

15. David F. Houston to Wilson, September 15, 1916; Wilson Papers. George Creel to Harry A. Garfield, September 22, October 4, 1916; Garfield Papers.

16. "Sectionalism Rampant" (editorial), Reno *Evening Gazette,* September 20, 1916; cf. October 16, 1916. Wilmington (Del.) *Evening Journal,* October 10, 13, 1916. Boston *Herald,* November 6, 1916. Hartford *Daily Courant,* November 1, 1916, reproached Senator George P. McLean for raising the sectional issue in his Connecticut re-election campaign. In Vermont, Representative Frank L. Greene also did some bloody-shirt waving. (H. L. Hindley to Greene, November 24, 1916; Greene Papers.)

17. Edward M. House, Diary, XIII, 130–31, entry for May 17, 1918; House Papers.

18. McLemore supporters P. Davis Oakey of Connecticut and Ernest W. Roberts of Massachusetts, both Republicans, lost their seats for "flaunting the white feather of cowardice," according to Boston *Herald,* November 6, 1916. For the Ohio situation, see Cincinnati *Enquirer,* November 6, 8, 1916. The Democrats lost seven seats in Indiana, four in Illinois, four in New York, and three in Wisconsin besides a scattering elsewhere in Pennsylvania, New Jersey, Maine, Maryland, Iowa, Kansas, Oklahoma, and Montana.

19. New York *Tribune,* January 26, 1917. Gallinger to Benjamin W. Couch, February 8, 1917; Gallinger Papers. Gallinger was annoyed at the action of the New Hampshire legislature in passing a resolution urging the people to stand behind Wilson as they had stood behind Lincoln.

20. Lodge to Roosevelt, January 28, 1917; Roosevelt to Lodge, February 5, 1917; Lodge Papers. Roosevelt to Lodge, March 13, 1917; Roosevelt Papers.

21. Lodge feared that there might be no "sufficiently flagrant case of the destruction of an American ship and American lives to compel war." (Lodge to Roosevelt, February 13, 1917; Lodge Papers.)

22. Lodge believed that the Zimmermann note had aroused the country more than any other outrage. (Lodge to Roosevelt, March 2, 1917; *ibid.*)

23. *Congressional Record,* 64th Cong., 2d Sess., 4691. New York *Tribune,* March 2, 1917.

24. Roosevelt demanded an early session because "to leave Wilson alone in the face of a foreign crisis is like leaving Pierce or Buchanan or Tyler alone in the presence of secession. If Congress is in session, then at least we shall be sure to have some brave and honorable men to point out the nation's duty." (Roosevelt to Lodge, February 28, 1917; Lodge Papers.)

25. Washington *Post,* March 7, 1917. Lodge to Roosevelt, March 20, 1917; Lodge Papers.

26. House to Wilson, March 30, 1917; Wilson Papers.

27. Philadelphia *Public Ledger,* April 2, 3, 1917. Clark was re-elected April 2 on the first ballot, 217 to 205, with several Roosevelt followers refusing to vote for Mann.

28. New York *Tribune,* March 22, April 2, 1917. Washington *Post,* March 26, 31, 1917.

29. Representative Frank L. Greene of Vermont observed that while everybody hated the Kaiser, there was no great enthusiasm for the war or the Liberty loan or any other feature of it, in striking contrast to the popular enthusiasm of Spanish-American War days. (Greene to Walter H. Crockett, May 5, 1917; Greene Papers.)

CHAPTER II: *The Roosevelt Volunteer Controversy*

1. "He is a mean soul," wrote Lodge, "and the fact that he delivered a good message on April 2d does not alter his character." (Lodge to Roosevelt, April 23, 1917; Lodge Papers.)

2. Washington *Evening Star,* April 9, 1917. *Congressional Record,* 65th Cong., 1st Sess., 459. Ray S. Baker, *Woodrow Wilson,* VII, 24.

3. Gideon Welles, *Diary,* II, 198, 226. On the other hand, John G. Nicolay, and John Hay, *Abraham Lincoln,* V, 150–51, admit that the Committee assumed "a great range of prerogative" and was often hasty and unjust in its judgments, but conclude that it was earnest and patriotic and merited more praise than blame.

4. New York *Tribune,* April 10, 1917. Washington *Post,* April 15, 1917.

5. Senator J. S. Williams to D. D. Colcock, April 27, 1917; Williams Papers. Williams called Kitchin "a chronic dashboard kicker like a mare I once had."

6. Secretary of War Newton D. Baker to General Hugh L. Scott, June 7, 1917; Newton D. Baker Papers. Georgia vigilantes took to stopping and searching all strangers for smuggled weapons, while in Alabama federal agents were reported to have uncovered a German plot to send armed Negroes to Mexico as part of an invasion army. (San Francisco *Chronicle,* April 15, 1917. Baltimore *Sun,* May 16, 1917.)

7. Pou to Tumulty, April 11, 1917; Wilson Papers.

8. Philadelphia *Public Ledger,* April 19, 1917.

9. Washington *Post,* April 19, 1917.

10. *Congressional Record,* 65th Cong., 1st Sess., 995, 1001.

11. Borah, who led the Republican opposition to the draft, complained that "they are overriding and browbeating and insulting everybody who is opposed to conscription." (Borah to Frank R. Gooding, April 16, 1917; Borah Papers.)

12. Roosevelt to Emperor William II, December 26, 1908, quoted in Elting E. Morison, ed., *The Letters of Theodore Roosevelt,* VI, 1441–42.

13. House to Wilson, March 30, 1917; Wilson Papers. Washington *Post,* April 22, 1917. New York *World,* cited in Boston *Evening Transcript,* May 18, 1917, put Roosevelt's "paper army" at 1,175 men instead of the reported 200,000. The Roosevelt correspondence makes the *World* estimate seem nearer the mark.

14. Roosevelt to Leonard Wood, March 13, 1917; Roosevelt Papers.

15. Roosevelt to Judge Robert Grant, April 10, 1917; *ibid.* Gutzon Borglum to Newton D. Baker, April 13, 1917; Baker to Borglum, April 16, 1917; Newton D. Baker Papers.

16. Roosevelt to E. A. Koehr, April 10, 1917; to Emmett J. Scott, May 17, 1917; Roosevelt Papers.

17. Roosevelt to Lieutenant Colonel Robert Howze, April 11, 1917; *ibid.*

18. Roosevelt statement disbanding his volunteer force, no date, but probably late May; *ibid.*

19. Roosevelt to F. C. Walcott, March 7, 1917; *ibid.*

20. Baker to Roosevelt, March 20, 1917; Lodge Papers.

21. Roosevelt to Lodge, March 22, 1917; Roosevelt Papers.

22. Lodge to Roosevelt, March 23, 1917; Lodge Papers.

23. John J. Leary, Jr., *Talks with T. R.*, 93–99.

24. Roosevelt to J. C. O'Loughlin, April 13, 1917; Roosevelt Papers.

25. Joseph P. Tumulty, *Woodrow Wilson As I Know Him*, 285. George Creel, *The War, the World, and Wilson*, 78–80.

26. Roosevelt to Senator George E. Chamberlain, to Representative S. Hubert Dent, April 12, 1917; Roosevelt Papers.

27. Many newspapers supporting the draft argued that an exception could be made for Roosevelt without harming the war effort. (Baltimore *Sun*, April 10, 1917.) Tumulty to Wilson, April 12, 1917, regarding the "panic" in the congressional ranks over conscription; Tumulty Papers.

28. Baker to Roosevelt, April 13, 1917; Wilson Papers.

29. Roosevelt to Baker, April 22, 1917; Lodge Papers.

30. Roosevelt to John Nichols, March 5, 1917; to H. D. English, April 16, 1917; Roosevelt Papers.

31. Roosevelt to John Parker, April 10, 1917; *ibid.*

32. Roosevelt to Baker, May 8, 1917; Newton D. Baker Papers.

33. Lodge to Roosevelt, April 22, 1917; Lodge Papers.

34. Lodge to Roosevelt, April 23, 1917; *ibid.*

35. Lodge to Roosevelt, April 27, 30, 1917; *ibid.* Major General Wood, who canvassed his senatorial friends on behalf of the amendment, got a promise of support from Nelson of Minnesota, but Underwood of Alabama felt that the matter should be left to the decision of the General Staff. (Wood to Knute Nelson, April 26, 1917; to Oscar W. Underwood, April 27, 1917; Underwood to Wood, April 28, 1917; Nelson to Wood, May 2, 1917; Wood Papers.)

36. A member of the Farm Loan Board traveling through the West at this time found the average citizen strongly in favor of the Roosevelt division but most newspapers against it. (Frank R. Wilson, Memorandum, May 31, 1917; McAdoo Papers.)

37. Paul O. Husting to Wilson, April 27, 1917; Gilbert M. Hitchcock to Wilson, May 18, 1917; Wilson Papers.

38. Roosevelt to Harding, April 30, 1917; Roosevelt Papers.

39. New York *Times*, April 28, 1917.

40. Philadelphia *Public Ledger,* April 29, 1917.
41. Bismarck (N.D.) *Tribune,* June 15, 1917. Memphis *Commerical Appeal,* June 16, 1917.
42. *Congressional Record,* 65th Cong., 1st Sess., 1489, 1500.
43. Roosevelt to Joseph Leiter, April 27, 1917; Roosevelt Papers.
44. Roosevelt to Joseph Leiter, May 8, 1917; to Victor Heintz, May 11, 1917, that my opponents "have found a prize jackass in Joe Leiter to front for them"; *ibid.*
45. Roosevelt to Irvine Lenroot, April 30, 1917; to Julius Kahn, May 3, 1917; *ibid.*
46. Lodge to Roosevelt, May 4, 1917; Lodge Papers.
47. Lodge to Roosevelt, April 30, 1917; *ibid.*
48. Roosevelt to Lodge, May 10, 1917; *ibid.*
49. Roosevelt telegram in New York *Times,* May 12, 1917.
50. Washington *Post,* May 13, 1917.
51. Frank L. Greene to Frank E. Howe, May 16, 1917; Greene Papers. "The T.R. business," he added, "is all being done for political effect."
52. New York *Tribune,* April 20, 1917.
53. Roosevelt to Henry Warden, May 2, 1917; to Richard H. Edmonds, May 12, 1917; Roosevelt Papers.
54. Roosevelt to William Allen White, May 5, 1917; *ibid.*
55. Roosevelt to John C. Greenway, May 12, 1917; *ibid.*
56. Ray S. Baker, *Woodrow Wilson,* VII, 72.
57. Wilson to Baker, May 18, 1917; Newton D. Baker Papers.
58. Baker to Wilson, July 3, 1918; Wilson to Baker, July 5, 1918; *ibid.*

CHAPTER III: *The Political Pot Keeps Boiling*

1. Tumulty to Wilson, May 8, 1917; Wilson Papers.
2. Washington *Post,* March 11, 1917.
3. Frank I. Cobb to Col. E. M. House, August 21, 1917; Wilson Papers. The Wilmington (Del.) *Evening Journal,* September 10, 1918, protested that Creel's *Official Bulletin,* posted daily in 56,000 post offices, was a "sheet of the most partisan type" devoted to publicizing the Democratic party.
4. Thomas W. Gregory to Wilson, April 14, 1917; Wilson to Senator Charles A. Culberson, April 14, 1917; Wilson Papers.
5. New York *Times,* April 15, 1917.
6. *Ibid.,* April 29, 1917, published a letter from Wilson to Arthur Brisbane of the Washington *Times* defending his motives for seeking press controls.
7. McAdoo to Wilson, April 16, 1917, protesting the overlapping of the various security services; Burleson to Wilson, April 17, 1917, objecting to the intrusion of other government agencies on the work

of his post-office inspectors; Gregory to Wilson, April 17, 1917, that
the Treasury Department was interfering with the FBI; McAdoo to
Wilson, June 2, 1917, criticizing the Attorney General's undercover
activities; Gregory to McAdoo, June 14, 1917, defending his operations;
Wilson Papers.

8. New York *Times,* May 7, 1917. Tumulty to Wilson, May 8,
1917; Tumulty Papers.

9. *Congressional Record,* 65th Cong., 1st Sess., 1816.

10. *Ibid.,* 1785–86. New York *Times,* May 7, 1917. Tumulty to
Wilson, May 5, 1917; Tumulty Papers.

11. *Congressional Record,* 65th Cong., 1st Sess., 2165–66. Harding
said censorship was "utterly repugnant" to American principles and
dangerously augmentative of executive power. A few Republicans, like
Colt of Rhode Island and Nelson of Minnesota, supported censorship
because of the mischief created by northern newspapers during the
Civil War.

12. *Ibid.,* 2265.

13. Borah to Edward H. Dewey, May 9, 1917; Borah Papers.

14. Baltimore *Sun,* May 23, 24, 1917. New York *Times,* May 23,
1917.

15. The trading-with-the-enemy act of October 6, 1917, set up a
five-man censorship board, of which Creel was a member, with complete control over foreign cables and the foreign-language press. (James
R. Mock and Cedric Larsen, *Words that Won the War,* 44.)

16. New York *World,* June 2, 1917.

17. House to Wilson, April 10, 1917; Wilson Papers. McAdoo to
Wilson, April 17, 1917; McAdoo Papers.

18. Ray S. Baker, *Woodrow Wilson,* VII, 17. Rabbi Stephen S.
Wise to Wilson, April 24, 1917; House to Wilson, May 2, 1917; Wilson
Papers.

19. Cincinnati *Enquirer,* May 8, 1917. Baltimore *Sun,* May 18,
1917.

20. Senator Key Pittman to Wilson, June 22, 1917; Wilson
Papers.

21. New York *Journal of Commerce,* May 18, 1917. William
McAdoo, chief city magistrate of New York, to W. G. McAdoo, June
11, 1917; McAdoo Papers.

22. Lodge to Roosevelt, May 18, 1917; Lodge Papers.

23. Boston *Evening Transcript,* June 4, 1917.

24. Wilson to Vance McCormick, July 2, 1917; McCormick to
Wilson, June 28, 1917; Wilson Papers.

25. "Democratic Manual, 1918, or Help Wilson Win the War,"
forty-eight-page pamphlet; copy in Daniels Papers.

26. A. Mitchell Palmer to Baker, August 25, 1917; Newton D.
Baker Papers.

27. Boston *Evening Transcript*, June 12, 1917. Indianapolis *News*, June 12, 1917. Daniels to Baker, July 14, 1917; Daniels Papers.

28. D. B. Lucey, U.S. Attorney, northern district of New York, to Tumulty, November 19, 1917; Wilson Papers. Representative William H. Carter, Thirteenth Massachusetts District, to Daniels, February 22, 1918; Daniels Papers. A. Mitchell Palmer to Wilson, July 9, 1917; Baker to Palmer, August 9, 1917; Newton D. Baker Papers. Senator John Sharp Williams of Mississippi to Thomas A. O'Herin, December 27, 1918; Williams Papers.

29. Hoover to Wilson, June 28, 1917; Wilson Papers.

30. Harry A. Garfield to Wilson, October 3, 1917; *ibid.*

31. Vance McCormick to Wilson, October 4, 1917, enclosing telegram from Governor Simon Bamberger of Utah to J. H. Covington, September 12, 1917; *ibid.*

32. Philadelphia *Public Ledger*, April 4, 19, 1917.

33. Harry D. Westcott to Daniels, January 23, 1918; Daniels Papers.

34. Boston *Christian Science Monitor*, March 16, 18, 19, 20, 21, 23, 1918, ran a series of articles on these Councils.

35. George W. Jones to Borah, July 6, 1918, protesting against the threat of the Idaho Defense Council to levy $40 against every family in the state for Red Cross contributions; Borah Papers.

36. Jones to McAdoo, June 29, 1918; McAdoo Papers.

37. Wilson to Baker, December 6, 1917; Newton D. Baker Papers.

38. O. L. Husting to Tumulty, October 11, 1917; Wilson Papers.

39. Wilson to Tumulty, October 11, 1917; Creel to Wilson, October 19, 1917; *ibid.*

40. W. R. Hollister to Baker, December 10, 1917; Newton D. Baker Papers. See also Will H. Hays, *Memoirs* 116–18.

41. Indianapolis *News*, June 29, 1917.

42. W. R. Hollister to Burleson, December 3, 1917; Wilson Papers.

43. Baker to Wilson, December 9, 1917; *ibid.*

44. Indianapolis *News*, July 18, 1917. Cincinnati *Enquirer*, July 20, 1917.

45. Wilson to Baker, June 1, 1917; Newton D. Baker Papers. Baker to Wilson, June 2, 1917; Wilson Papers.

46. Baker to Wilson, July 5, 1917; *ibid.*

47. Wood to Representative Samuel J. Nicholls of South Carolina, May 28, 1917; Nicholls to Wood, May 31, 1917; Wood to Gordon Johnston, July 17, 1917; to M. W. Jacobi, August 3, 1917; Wood Papers.

48. Baker to Representative William G. Adamson of Georgia, July 11, 1917, repudiating Wood's "theory" and rejecting his recommendation for a camp site at Columbus, Georgia; Adamson to Baker,

July 12, 1917, vigorously contesting this decision; Diary, entries for June 5, June 14, 1917; Wood Papers.

49. Representative Hubert F. Fisher of Tennessee to Wilson, July 10, 1917; Wilson to Baker, July 12, 1917; Newton D. Baker Papers. Baker to Wilson, July 13, 1917; Wilson Papers. McKellar to McAdoo, July 27, 1917; McAdoo Papers.

50. Fletcher to Wilson, July 11, 1917; Wilson to Baker, July 12, 1917; Newton D. Baker Papers. Baker to Wilson, July 14, 1917; Wilson Papers.

51. McKellar sponsored one of the two anti-Baker bills in the next session of Congress; he had already authored anti-draft and anti-food control resolutions in the Senate. For Wood's abrupt transfer to Camp Funston, Kansas, in August, see Wood to Harold M. Harvey of the New York *Tribune*, August 18, 1917; to Russell B. Harrison, August 28, 1917; Diary, entry for August 14, 1917, said the transfer was "a piece of crooked work" and that he would let his southern friends know of Baker's animus toward him; Wood Papers. Camp Joseph E. Johnston, a $6 million unit, was built in October 1917. (U.S. Department of Defense, *Order of Battle*, III, 832.)

CHAPTER IV: *The Committee on the Conduct of the War*

1. Henry L. Higginson to Lodge, June 19, 1917; Lodge Papers.

2. With 1913 = 100, price indices for December 1917 were: food, 185; clothing, 206; fuel, 153; drugs, 230; household furnishings, 175; all, 181. (Simon Litman, *Prices and Price Control*, 181–2.)

3. Washington *Post*, May 26, 27, 1917. New York *Journal of Commerce*, May 15, 22, 1917. Joseph N. Teal to McAdoo, May 10, 1917; Leo J. Rountree to McAdoo, May 24, 1917; McAdoo Papers. Thomas C. Leslie to Borah, May 3, 1917; Borah Papers.

4. Lodge claimed the bill disregarded economic and natural laws (Springfield *Republican*, July 11, 1917). Senators Gore and Reed insisted that huge Allied purchases, not speculators, forced up food prices (*Congressional Record*, 65th Cong., 1st Sess., 2870, 3772).

5. David F. Houston to Wilson, May 14, 1917; Wilson Papers.

6. Washington *Post*, May 14, 1917. V. E. Howard to Carter Glass, May 15, 1917; Glass Papers. Hoover to Wilson, June 12, 1917; Wilson Papers.

7. *Congressional Record*, 65th Cong., 1st Sess., 4190.

8. Indianapolis *News*, June 25, 1917. New York *World*, July 2, 1917.

9. Hollis to Tumulty, June 1, 1917; Wilson Papers.

10. Washington *Post*, June 17, 1917.

11. J. S. Shortwell, of the National Council of Farmers' Cooperative Associations, to Senator Miles Poindexter, July 14, 1917; Poindexter to Shortwell, July 17, 1917; Poindexter Papers. Borah to Frank

R. Gooding, June 25, 1917; Borah Papers. New York *Journal of Commerce,* June 10, 1917, reported that farmers wanted to delay price-fixing until they could enjoy huge profits on at least one crop, since there had been no profit on the 1916 crop.

12. *Congressional Record,* 65th Cong., 1st Sess., 4610, 4702. New York *Tribune,* July 3, 1917. McAdoo to Wilson, June 2, 1917, strongly urging the necessity of legislative price-fixing; McAdoo Papers.

13. Borah to F. A. David, February 6, 1918; to A. L. Trenan, June 17, 1918, explaining that his amendment to fix the price of farm implements, steel, cotton, wool, and other commodities was adopted, but "twenty-four hours later by reason of some change of view difficult to describe but not hard to understand, reconsideration was had and it was defeated." Borah Papers.

14. Hoover to Wilson, June 29, July 12, 1917, complaining that so many radical alterations had rendered the food control bill "nugatory"; Wilson to Senator Thomas S. Martin, July 13, 1917, pointing out that the bill had been emasculated and robbed of all effective features; Wilson to McKellar, July 6, 1917, begging him to withdraw his crippling amendment to the bill; Wilson Papers.

15. *Congressional Record,* 65th Cong., 1st Sess., 5363-67.

16. Ray S. Baker, *Woodrow Wilson,* VII, 72. New York *Times,* July 20, 21, 1917.

17. Lodge, determined to "keep down the excessive power for which Wilson is grasping with a view to electing himself or McAdoo," felt confident that "a feeling of hostility is so growing in both parties that we may be able to do something." (Lodge to Roosevelt, May 28, 1917; Lodge Papers.) New York *Times,* August 19, 1917, criticized the growing hostility to the President among certain senators.

18. Owen to Wilson, June 15, 1917; Wilson to Owen, July 23, 1917; Wilson Papers.

19. Borah to Joseph L. Bristow, June 25, 1917, that "in my judgment, no country ever witnessed such a riot of extravagance"; Borah Papers.

20. McAdoo to Wilson, May 12, 1917, protested that he was not consulted with respect to the Shipping Board's expenditure of a billion dollars and pointed out "grave weaknesses" in the agency; McAdoo Papers. Senator Benjamin R. Tillman to Wilson, July 17, 1917; Wilson Papers.

21. Wilson to Goethals, July 24, 1917; to Denman, July 24, 1917; Wilson Papers. Denman to McAdoo, July 30, 31, 1917, giving his side of the controversy; McAdoo Papers. New York *Times,* July 25, 26, 1917.

22. *Congressional Record,* 65th Cong., 1st Sess., 5363-64, 5553-54.

23. Chicago *Tribune,* July 23, 1917. Indianapolis *News,* July 25, 26, 1917. Springfield *Republican,* July 23, 24, 1917. New York *Times,*

August 9, 1917, said that "Congress needs a rest if for no other purpose than to set right . . . statesmen who seem to think this is not a war but a political campaign."

24. Lodge to Roosevelt, August 14, 1917; Lodge Papers.
25. Chicago *Tribune,* July 24, 1917. New York *Tribune,* July 24, 1917. Ray S. Baker, *Woodrow Wilson,* VII, 185.
26. *Congressional Record,* 65th Cong., 1st Sess., 5838–46, 5862–66.
27. The New York *Times,* August 6, 1917, published an editorial, "Politics and the War," criticizing Weeks's threat.
28. Wilson to Representative John J. Fitzgerald, September 4, 1917; Wilson Papers.
29. New York *World,* September 6, 1917.
30. McAdoo to Kitchin, April 30, 1917, that 50 per cent of the cost of the war should be raised by taxes; McAdoo Papers. The Treasury estimated the cost of the war for the first year at $3.6 billion; it turned out to be $12 billion.
31. J. P. Morgan to McAdoo, April 27, 1917; Higginson to McAdoo, May 4, 1917; *ibid.*
32. New York *Journal of Commerce,* May 12, 1917. Baltimore *Sun,* May 17, 1917. Cincinnati *Enquirer,* May 17, 1917, reported the presence in Washington of representatives of four thousand midwestern business firms to protest against raising revenue by taxes.
33. G. R. Cooksey to McAdoo, May 18, 1917, regarding Republican hostility to the bill and efforts to recommit it; McAdoo Papers.
34. Lodge to Frank L. Higginson, May 22, 1917; Lodge Papers. New York *Times,* May 22, 1917. C. B. Watkins to Carter Glass, May 11, 1917; Glass to D. B. Ryland, May 23, 1917; Glass Papers.
35. McAdoo to Senator William J. Stone, June 6, 1917; to Senator Furnifold M. Simmons, June 6, 1917; McAdoo Papers.
36. The Republican press roundly denounced McAdoo for falling so far short in his estimate. (Wheeling *Intelligencer,* July 25, 1917, clipping in William L. Brice to McAdoo, July 27, 1917; McAdoo Papers.) Referring to rumors that the Cabinet had split over his financial policies, McAdoo wrote: "The craze of the partisan newspapers to injure the administration has led them to give wide currency to this unfortunate story." (McAdoo to E. F. Sweet, August 10, 1917; *ibid.*)
37. Borah to W. J. McConnell, September 11, 1917; Borah Papers. Circular letters put out on July 27 and August 3 by the Illinois Manufacturers' Association urged members to "keep on pounding" their congressmen until taxes were lowered. Unless they acted quickly, said the Association, most of the $17 billion would be saddled on the manufacturers. (Copy in McAdoo Papers.)
38. *Congressional Record,* 65th Cong., 1st Sess., 6469–74.
39. Lodge to Roosevelt, September 6, 1917; Lodge Papers. Senator

Frank B. Kellogg also took Roosevelt to task, pointing out that the British tax allowed for certain exemptions to business and that Britain had never raised more than 25 per cent of its war costs by taxes alone, compared to the 36 per cent in the McAdoo bill. (Kellogg to Roosevelt, September 6, September 8, 1917; Kellogg Papers.) Many liberals, however, came out in support of the Johnson amendment. (E.g., Professor John R. Commons to McAdoo, August 27, 1917; F. F. Ingram to McAdoo, September 4, 1917; McAdoo Papers.)

40. Borah to ex-Governor W. J. McConnell of Idaho, September 11, 1917; Borah Papers. *Congressional Record*, 65th Cong., 1st Sess., 6503, 6621, 6727.

41. Sacramento *Union,* September 4, 13, 1917.

42. Henry L. Doherty to McAdoo, September 8, 1917. Jacob H. Schiff to Wilson, September 23, 1917, that the revenue bill was economically unsound and would strike at the very roots of our prosperity; McAdoo to John A. Sleicher, September 24, 1917; to S. R. Berton, September 27, 1917; McAdoo Papers.

43. M. H. Coffin to Borah, September 3, 1917, expressing his conviction that the farmer had been "double-crossed"; Borah Papers. Minneapolis *Tribune,* September 11, 1917. New York *World,* November 15, 1917. New York *Times,* editorials, December 4, 11, 1917, decrying the injustice of the tax law and urging its revision. Ervin Wardman to McAdoo, October 10, 1917, that the "average citizen" was "outraged" by the revenue act; McAdoo Papers.

CHAPTER V : *The Gathering Storm*

1. New York *World,* November 9, 1917. Senator Hiram W. Johnson to Philander C. Knox, November 2, 1917; Knox to Johnson, November 9, 1917; Knox Papers. Thomas N. Page to Wilson, November 4, 1917; House to Wilson, November 9, 1917; Wilson Papers.

2. Wilson to Baker, July 26, 1917; Wilson Papers. New York *World,* July 25, 1917. New York *Sun,* November 19, 20, 1917.

3. "The official view in Washington," said one newspaper correspondent, "is that the public ought to know as little as possible about what their government is doing to make the world safe for democracy." (H. N. Rickey to McAdoo, August 30, 1917; McAdoo Papers.)

4. Wilson to Josephus Daniels, June 4, 1917; Daniels Papers. House to Wilson, June 7, 1917; C. S. Hamlin to Wilson, October 22, 1917; Wilson Papers.

5. Chicago *Tribune,* September 28, 1917, rebuked Roosevelt for "digging into the rubbish heap of past mistakes to assail the Administration" and urged him to moderate his criticism.

6. E. H. Collier to McAdoo, October 2, 1917; McAdoo to W. L. Saunders, November 2, 1917; McAdoo Papers.

7. A prominent Chicagoan warned the Secretary of War that

"Colonel Roosevelt will find a fruitful state of mind to listen to his criticisms because there is a widespread feeling that we are not accomplishing all in getting ready that might be accomplished." (William H. Carter to Baker, September 28, 1917; Newton D. Baker Papers.)

8. New York *World*, November 18, 1917.

9. Diary, entry for December 9, 1917; Wood Papers. For the official reaction see: Walter H. Page to Lansing, November 30, 1917; Franklin K. Lane to Wilson, December 3, 1917; Wilson Papers. The noted Liberal scholar and diplomat, James Bryce, insisted there was much truth and good sense in Lansdowne's letter. (Bryce to Lodge, December 24, 1917; Lodge Papers.)

10. Lodge to William S. Bigelow, December 14, 1917; Lodge Papers. Lodge had already advised Roosevelt that, although Baker's incompetence and the resultant confusion in the War Department were well-known in Congress, he hesitated to expose the situation because of the hue and cry that criticism of the President would raise. (Lodge to Roosevelt, September 17, 1917; *ibid.*)

11. Wood to Major Frank R. McCoy, November 15, 1917, that Senator James W. Wadsworth of New York had spent a couple of days looking over Camp Funston, "especially our wooden artillery, horses and guns"; Wood Papers.

12. Lodge to Roosevelt, September 17, 1917; Lodge Papers. Roosevelt to J. E. Steward, November 16, 1917; Roosevelt Papers.

13. Ray S. Baker and William E. Dodd, eds., *War and Peace,* I, 128–29.

14. New York *Sun,* December 12, 1917. New York *Times,* December, 12, 1917.

15. Lodge to Roosevelt, December 13, 18, 1917; Lodge Papers.

16. December 13, 1917.

17. New York *Sun,* December 18, 20, 1917. New York *Times,* December 14, 1917.

18. William R. Thayer to Lodge, January 4, 1918; John T. Morse, Jr., to Lodge, February 5, 1918; Lodge Papers. New York *World,* December 15, 22, 1917. Boston *Evening Transcript,* December 11, 17, 1917.

19. H. A. Garfield to Robert S. Lovett, December 24, 1917; Wilson Papers.

20. The Fuel Administration informed a Philadelphia businessman (who had asked where Garfield had learned anything about the coal or any other business) that Garfield, before joining the Princeton University law faculty in 1904, had had sixteen years' experience as a lawyer in Cleveland, organizing and developing various enterprises including the Piney Fork Coal Company and the Cleveland Trust Company. (Unsigned copy of letter to Norman B. Hafleigh, January 24, 1918; Garfield Papers.)

21. Lodge to Roosevelt, November 19, 1917; Lodge Papers. Roosevelt to Dix W. Smith, December 12, 1917; Roosevelt Papers.

22. New York *Times,* December 29, 30, 1917. During the first cold snap the *Times* reported on December 21, 1917, 24 deaths from cold and 32 cases of frostbite at the Essex County Asylum in New Jersey, which housed 1,800 inmates.

23. Boston *Evening Transcript,* December 31, 1917, reported the coldest weather in 105 years. New York *Times,* January 8, 1918, said floating ice in New York harbor sank 24 loaded coal barges and immobilized 150 ships.

24. Lodge to Roosevelt, September 17, 1917; Lodge Papers. New York *World,* December 13, 1917. John J. Pershing, *My Experiences in the World War,* I, 183. "The Bureau Chiefs," Wood noted, "are having the time of their lives and are drunk with authority and reveling in inefficiency." Diary, entry for December 7, 1917; Wood Papers.

25. Lodge to Roosevelt, December 18, 1917; Lodge Papers. As a result of the delay, contracts for the Browning gun were not let until October 1917, production did not begin until May 1918, and American troops did not receive the weapon until July. The Ordnance bureau turned out 2,959 Lewis guns in 1917 and 591 in 1918; no Browning guns in 1917 and 56,608 in 1918. (U.S. Department of Defense, *Order of Battle,* III, 358. Benedict Crowell and Robert F. Wilson, *The Giant Hand,* xvii–xxi.)

26. New York *World,* December 23, 1917. U.S. Congress, "Investigation of War Department," II, 705. (These hearings, which cover 2,560 pages of testimony, are hereafter referred to as "Investigation.") Wood later admitted that the Browning was a good weapon, but said it was folly to adopt it untested, Diary, entry for June 18, 1918; Wood Papers.

27. *Congressional Record,* 65th Cong., 2d Sess., 976.

28. Boston *Evening Transcript,* December 21, 1917.

29. New York *World,* December 19, 1917. "Investigation," II, 345–47. McCormick to Roosevelt, November 17, 1917; Roosevelt Papers. McCormick to Wood, November 1, 1917; McCormick to Clark Howell, November 24, 1917; Wood Papers.

30. General Tasker H. Bliss to Baker, December, 4, 1917; U.S. Department of Defense, *United States Army in the World War, 1917–1919,* II, 94–95.

31. Representative Tom Stout of Montana to Carter Glass, February 12, 1918; Glass Papers.

32. Camp Funston, Kansas, on a mudflat between two rivers, was flooded at high water and damp at all times. The recruits had neither rifles nor heavy clothing; when snow came, only four of the twenty heating units had been completed. (Wood to Henry L. Stimson, October 30, 1917; Wood to Brigadier General E. St. J. Greble, September 6, 1917; Wood Papers.)

33. New York *World,* November 11, 21, 1917.
34. *Ibid.,* November 29, 1917.
35. Augustus P. Gardner to Tumulty, December 1, 1917, in Constance Gardner, ed., *Some Letters,* 121–25. Gardner, a nephew of Senator Lodge and close friend of Roosevelt, had resigned his Massachusetts congressional seat to accept a major's commission in the Army. His death from pneumonia on January 14, 1918, at Camp Wheeler greatly embittered both Lodge and Roosevelt, who held Wilson and Baker to blame.
36. Spokane Chamber of Commerce to Senator Poindexter, December 29, 1917; Poindexter to Major General William C. Gorgas, January 28, 1918; Poindexter Papers. Des Moines *Evening Tribune,* December 12, 1917.
37. New York *World,* December 13, 1917.
38. Boston *Evening Transcript,* December 19, 1917.
39. New York *World,* December 22, 27, 1918. "Investigation," II, 794–98.
40. New York *Times,* December 28, 1917; clipping in Wilson Papers.
41. New York *World,* December 29, 1917. "Investigation," II, 955–68.
42. New York *World,* December 30, 1917. Borah to A. J. Dunn, January 5, 1918; Borah Papers. E. O. Savage to Knute Nelson, January 12, 1918; Nelson Papers.
43. Tumulty to Wilson, December 29, 1917; Wilson Papers.
44. Lodge to Roosevelt, December 29, 1917; Lodge Papers.
45. Cobb to House, December 21, 1917; Wilson to Willcox, January 18, 1918; Wilson Papers. New York *World,* January 19, 1918.
46. New York *Times,* January 19, 1918.
47. "Minutes of the Executive Committee of the Democratic National Committee," January 14, 1918; Glass Papers.
48. Brisbane to Wilson, December 18, 1917; Wilson to Tumulty, December 18, 1917; Wilson Papers.
49. Boston *Evening Transcript,* December 28, 1917. Lodge to Roosevelt, December 29, 1917; Lodge Papers. "The whole thing," said Lodge, "is at bottom being planned to re-elect the present President. The war is being used primarily for personal advancement and secondarily for party purposes; I may say very secondarily, because Wilson's interest in himself far surpasses his interest in his party."

CHAPTER VI: *"Tantrums on the Hill"*
1. Chicago *Tribune,* December 29, 1917. Memphis *Commercial Appeal,* December 27, 1917.
2. Creel to Wilson, January 3, 1918; Wilson Papers.
3. Boston *Evening Transcript,* December 24, 1917.
4. Minneapolis *Tribune,* December 21, 1917.

5. Boston *Evening Transcript,* December 18, 1917. Chicago *Tribune,* December 21, 1917. Charles L. West to Knute Nelson, December 28, 1917; John M. Gillette to Nelson, January 11, 1918; Nelson Papers.

6. New York *World,* January 4, 1918. Boston *Evening Transcript,* January 5, 7, 1918. *Congressional Record,* 65th Cong., 2d Sess., 557–58.

7. Diary, XIII, 11, entry for January 9, 1918; House Papers.

8. *Ibid.,* 10. "Baker seems to be getting deeper into the mire," said House, "and the President cannot see it." One of Baker's confidential advisers warned him that the existence of "a widespread and growing dissatisfaction with the administration of the War Department cannot be truthfully denied by anyone who is following opinion throughout the country, nor by one who is in intimate contact with men who know, or who are part of, affairs in Washington." (Quoted in Felix Frankfurter, "Memorandum on the Necessary Reorganization of the Functions Exercised by the Secretary of War," January 7, 1918; Newton D. Baker Papers.) According to House, Baker was "dumbfounded" upon receiving this memorandum. (Diary, XIII, 10; House Papers.)

9. Joseph P. Tumulty, *Woodrow Wilson As I Know Him,* 264–65.

10. A. C. Barrow, a Lynchburg, Virginia, manufacturer, and several other local businessmen to Carter Glass, January 21, 1918, demanding Baker's removal and creation of a War Cabinet; Glass Papers. Similarly, Charles I. Dean to Poindexter, January 23, 1918; J. J. Donovan to Poindexter, January 25, 1918; Poindexter Papers. Charles S. Cairns to Knute Nelson, January 22, 1918; W. H. Williams to Nelson, January 31, 1918; Nelson Papers.

11. New York *World,* January 5, 1918. New York *Times,* January 4, 5, 1918. House Republicans held a caucus on the Chamberlain bill on January 8 but deferred a decision. (Washington *Times,* January 9, 1918. Boston *Evening Transcript,* January 9, 1918.)

12. Wilson to Chamberlain, January 11, 1918; Wilson Papers.

13. Wilson to Gilbert M. Hitchcock, March 7, 1914; Bryan to Wilson, August 21, 1914; Wilson Papers. On August 21, 1918, House noted a visit from Hitchcock, who discussed his feud with Bryan at some length; Diary, XIV, 214–15, House Papers.

14. Wilson opposed Hitchcock's becoming chairman of the Foreign Relations Committee upon Stone's death in April 1918. Thereafter the President refused to consult with the new chairman or trust him with any information. House, Diary, XIII, 131, entry for May 17, 1918; *ibid.*

15. Baker to Wilson, October 4, 1917; Newton D. Baker Papers. Baker to Wilson, November 12, 1917; Wilson Papers.

16. Chamberlain to Wilson, October 1, 1917, that he was recover-

ing from a serious illness; *ibid.* New York *Times,* February 20, 1918, reported an operation for appendicitis.

17. R. Coleton Blackford to Carter Glass, March 4, 1918; Glass Papers.

18. Boston *Evening Transcript,* January 12, 1918. New York *World,* January 13, 1918. "Investigation," III, 1781–83.

19. Boston *Evening Transcript,* January 11, 1918. New York *Tribune,* January 13, 1918.

20. The New York *Times,* January 14, 1918, editorially condemned Baker's "complacency" with present conditions and said he had given a "false impression" of his efficiency. Grosvenor Clarkson, secretary of the Council of National Defense, to Baker, February 7, 1918, regarding a luncheon at Delmonico's on February 1 with a number of New York newspaper editors who said they disliked Baker simply because he was "too debonair when he should have been serious." McAdoo Papers.

21. Savannah *Morning News,* January 12, 1918. New York *Times,* January 13, 1918. Portland *Morning Oregonian,* January 13, 1918.

22. New Orleans *Times-Picayune,* January 12, 1918.

23. J. M. Klinglesmith to McAdoo, January 24, 1918; McAdoo Papers.

24. Quoted in Boston *Evening Transcript,* January 24, 1918. "Baker as a Campaign Issue for the Republicans," New York *Times Magazine,* February 3, 1918.

25. Tumulty to Wilson, January 17, 1918; Tumulty Papers.

26. McAdoo to Wilson, December 24, 1917; Memorandum from the British Embassy, January 3, 1918; Wilson Papers.

27. Diary, XIII, 23, entry for January 17, 1918; House Papers. A Boston businessman said that "shutting down everything for lack of coal was . . . just what the Germans wanted." (Stephen M. Weld to Charles S. Hamlin, January 17, 1918; McAdoo Papers.) Newspaper publishers protested the Monday closing order as disastrous for the press, which had to discontinue Sunday advertising, and for merchants, who thereby lost the most profitable day of the week. (Arthur Brisbane to Wilson, January 20, 1918; Garfield Papers.)

28. New York *World,* January 18, 1918. D. A. Reynolds, a New York business executive, to McAdoo, January 18, 1918, deploring the effect of the Garfield order on labor and industry; McAdoo Papers. See also Empire Milling Company of Minneapolis to Nelson, January 17, 1918; Nelson Papers.

29. Boston *Evening Transcript,* January 19, 1918.

30. C. R. Gray to McAdoo, January 20, 1918, "Memorandum for the Director General of Railroads," on the progress made despite the weather in clearing freight congestion and restoring normal traffic movements; McAdoo Papers.

31. New York *World*, January 23, 1918.

32. Diary, XIII, 24, entry for January 17, 1918; House Papers.

33. *Congressional Record*, 65th Cong., 2d Sess., 1077. Washington *Times*, January 18, 19, 1918.

34. New York *Times*, January 24, 1918. Portland *Morning Oregonian*, January 23, 1918.

35. Boston *Evening Transcript*, January 22, 1918.

36. New York *World*, January 28, 1918.

37. Clark to Wilson, January 23, 1918; Wilson to Clark, January 24, 1918; Wilson Papers. New York *Tribune*, January 25, 1918, published a letter from Wilson to Senator Ollie M. James of Kentucky expressing the President's surprise at hearing of a "War Cabinet of a type unknown to our practice or institutions."

38. Chamberlain, a native of Mississippi, moved to Oregon as a young man. He became governor in 1903 and senator in 1908. Some Democrats asserted that he had imbibed too much champagne at the luncheon in his honor before the speech and referred caustically to his "alcoholic ravings." (Tom Stout to Carter Glass, February 12, 1918; A. Coleton Blackford to Glass, March 4, 1918; Glass Papers.) Others called Chamberlain a Copperhead. (Richard C. Derby to Glass, February 8, 1918; *ibid.*)

CHAPTER VII: *The Badgering of Baker*

1. New York *World*, January 20, 1918.

2. *Ibid.*, January 23, 1918. Roosevelt was a leading light in the American Defense Society. Largely supported by businessmen and financiers popularly considered to have more than an ordinary stake in the war, both groups pursued chauvinistic policies and methods highly offensive to liberal opinion. (W. L. Saunders to Wilson, January 24, 1918; McAdoo Papers.)

3. Brisbane to Wilson, January 22, 1918; Wilson to Brisbane, January 24, 1918; Wilson Papers.

4. Taylor Kennedy to Tumulty, January 21, 1918; *ibid.*

5. Roosevelt to Owen Wister, January 23, 1918; Roosevelt Papers.

6. Roosevelt to Senator William M. Calder, July 25, 1918; *ibid.* Roosevelt had already planned to come to Washington about this time to discuss party strategy for the 1918 campaign. (Roosevelt to George W. Perkins, December 3, 1917; *ibid.* Henry Wallace to Gifford Pinchot, December 31, 1917; Pinchot Papers.)

7. "It was a wild day in the Senate yesterday," House noted in his Diary on January 22, 1918. (XIII, 30; House Papers.) Cleveland *Plain Dealer*, January 23, 1918, ran the front-page headline: WILSON READY TO BATTLE ROOSEVELT, PRESIDENT IN HOT FIGHT FOR WAR CONTROL. The Senate debate is in *Congressional Record*, 65th Cong., 2d Sess., 1087–98.

8. New York *World,* January 22, 1918.

9. Boston *Evening Transcript,* January 22, 1918.

10. E. S. Kinsley to H. L. Hindley, January 25, 1918; Greene Papers. The Vermont representative also said that on July 12 he had warned Baker to take Congress into his confidence or an investigation would follow; however, he had been "civilly but jauntily" dismissed.

11. Frank L. Greene to Walter H. Crockett, February 2, 1918; *ibid.*

12. New York *World,* January 24, 1918.

13. Borah to George Turner, January 24, 1918; Borah to Frank E. Johnesse, February 1, 1918; Calvin Keller to Borah, February 16, 1918; Borah Papers.

14. House, Diary, XIII, 33, entry for January 27, 1918; House Papers.

15. Poindexter to J. J. Donovan, January 23, 1918; Poindexter Papers.

16. Representative George R. Lunn, a New York Democrat, condemned Chamberlain's "patent insincerity" and urged the War Department to make all the facts known without delay. (Lunn to Baker, January 26, 1918; Newton D. Baker Papers.) New Orleans *Times-Picayune,* January 24, 25, 1918. *Congressional Record,* 65th Cong., 2d Sess., 1194–1211.

17. New York *World,* January 25, 1918. *Literary Digest,* Vol. 56, February 2, February 9, 1918.

18. New York *World,* January 29, 1918.

19. Washington *Times,* January 25, 1918.

20. New York *World,* January 25, 1918.

21. Boston *Evening Transcript,* January 16, 1918.

22. New York *Tribune,* January 26, 1918.

23. Diary, XIII, 33, entry for January 27, 1918; House Papers.

24. *Ibid.,* pp. 26–28, entries for January 19, 20, 1918.

25. New York *Tribune,* February 3, 1918. Baker to Wilson, January 24, 1918; Newton D. Baker Papers.

26. Overman to Borah, April 29, 1918; Borah to C. C. Cavanah, August 15, 1918; Borah Papers.

27. Milwaukee *Sentinel,* April 30, 1918. Gallinger to James O. Lyford, May 6, 1918; Gallinger Papers.

28. Washington *Times,* February 5, 1918. New York *Tribune,* February 6, 1918. Senator John S. Williams to Wilson, February 8, 1918; Williams Papers. *Congressional Record,* 65th Cong., 2d Sess., 1842–45.

29. New York *Tribune,* February 7, 1918. This canard gained considerable currency; Supreme Court Justice Louis Brandeis told House that Baker's mind did not function properly. (Dairy, XIII, 69, entry for February 23, 1918; House Papers.)

30. Portland *Oregon Daily Journal,* January 23, 1918. Cleveland *Plain Dealer,* January 23, 1918.

31. John S. Cohen, editor of the Atlanta *Journal,* to Josephus Daniels, January 24, February 4, 1918; Daniels Papers.

32. Lodge to William S. Bigelow, February 21, 1918; Lodge Papers.

33. *Congressional Record,* 65th Cong., 2d Sess., 2136–49. New York *Tribune,* February 16, 1918. Glass of Virginia set forth the administration's position in a House speech on February 7, to which the War Department contributed the facts and figures. The Democratic National Committee had the speech distributed throughout the country, 100,000 copies being sent to Indiana alone. (Ralph Hayes to Glass, January 23, 1918; Glass to Woodburn Mason, February 27, 1918; Glass to A. S. Thompson, April 12, 1918; Glass Papers.)

34. Lodge to William S. Bigelow, January 10, 1918; Lodge Papers. Greene of Vermont, on the other hand, felt the War Department had been "abused worse than it deserves," and he reproached his colleague Porter H. Dale for "running around Vermont making speeches attacking the Administration." (Greene to F. E. Howe, February 24, 1918; Greene to H. L. Hindley, February 6, 1918; Greene Papers.)

35. For instance, Democratic papers like the Houston *Post,* January 24, 25, 26, 1918, strongly disapproved of Wilson's partisan handling of the investigation and urged him to call a "free conference" of leaders on both sides to settle the matter.

36. Brooks Adams to Lodge, February 3, 1918; Lodge Papers. The Massachusetts legislature, however, endorsed the war attitude of Lodge and Weeks with only three dissenting votes. (Boston *Evening Transcript,* March 8, 1918.)

37. Roosevelt to Senator Joseph S. Frelinghuysen of New Jersey, February 2, 1918; Roosevelt Papers.

38. Roosevelt to Kermit Roosevelt, February 18, 1918; *ibid.*

39. Roosevelt to Sir Arthur Lee, February 21, 1918; *ibid.*

40. Wilson to Baker, March 4, 1918; Newton D. Baker Papers.

41. Roosevelt to Sir Arthur Lee, February 21, 1918; Roosevelt Papers.

42. Henry Wallace, the Iowa farm journal editor, urged Roosevelt to temper his criticisms somewhat because Republican newspapers in the Middle West were turning against him. (Wallace to Gifford Pinchot, December 31, 1917; Pinchot Papers.)

CHAPTER VIII: *Overhauling the Party Machinery*

1. Indianapolis *News,* June 20, 22, 1917. In six congressional by-elections the Republicans lost one seat to the Democrats in Pennsylvania and one to the Nonpartisan League in North Dakota.

2. House to Burleson, September 13, 1917; Tumulty to Burleson, September 15, 1917; House to Wilson, September 19, 1917; Tumulty Papers. Wilson to Matthew Hale, October 2, 1917; Wilson Papers. Boston *Evening Transcript,* October 3, 1917.

3. New York *Sun,* November 1, 4, 1917. Tammany's Hylan polled 297,282 votes, Mitchel 149,307, and the Socialist Hillquit 142,178.

4. Mark Eisner to McAdoo, October 11, 1917; Samuel Untermyer to McAdoo, November 1, 1917; William H. Edwards to McAdoo, October 19, 1917; McAdoo Papers. Colonel House, however, worked hard for Mitchel. (J. H. O'Neil to McAdoo, September 27, 1917; *ibid.*)

5. Representative Daniel J. Riordan threatened to inform the President that instead of having the loyalty of the twenty Tammany congressmen on all questions, "he could depend upon this number opposing his program, as he [Riordan] would be obliged to do, unless the National Administration kept out of local politics." (W. J. Martin, memorandum [of Riordan's visit] for the Secretary of the Treasury, September 17, 1917; *ibid.*)

6. W. J. Martin to McAdoo, October 11, 1917; W. J. Martin to Stuart G. Gibboney, October 18, 1917; William H. Edwards, collector of the Port of New York, to McAdoo, October 19, 1917; *ibid.*

7. R. B. Van Cortland to McAdoo, November 15, 1917; Byron R. Newton to McAdoo, October 24, 1917; *ibid.*

8. New York *World,* November 19, 1917.

9. New York *Tribune,* January 7, 1918.

10. *Ibid.,* January 17, 1917.

11. Roosevelt to Goodrich, January 31, 1918; to King, February 5, 1918; to Adams, February 5, 1918; Roosevelt Papers.

12. Roosevelt to Hays, February 6, 1918; *ibid.*

13. Borah to Hart, January 20, 1918; Hart to Borah, February 2, 1918; Borah Papers.

14. Hays to Borah, February 19, 1918; Borah to Hart, February 26, 1918; *ibid.* Hays in his *Memoirs* omits this episode in keeping with his general denial of any political activity during the war.

15. Chicago *Tribune,* February 12, 1918. New York *Tribune,* February 13, 1918. Of the eleven committeemen who deserted Adams, six voted for Hays and five abstained. Penrose replaced W. Murray Crane of Massachusetts, Adams' chief supporter, as party boss.

16. Chicago *Tribune,* February 16, 1918.

17. Hays to Senator Knute Nelson, April 1, 1918, that he was going West to meet "the working Republicans of all factions, including former Progressives"; Nelson Papers.

18. Hays to Frank L. Greene, April 1, 1918; Greene Papers. Miles Poindexter to Horace Kimball, March 18, 1918; Kimball to Poindexter, June 20, 1918; Poindexter Papers. Hart to Borah, April 10, 1918; Borah Papers.

19. Diary, XIV, 220, entry for August 27, 1918; House Papers.

20. J. Henry Goeke, treasurer of the Democratic National Committee, to Carter Glass, June 14, 1917; Glass Papers.

21. Neal Brewster, collector of internal revenue at Syracuse, New York, to W. J. Martin, August 16, 1918, protesting a $500 assessment

toward paying off the committee's deficit; McAdoo Papers. Hays to Poindexter, October 2, 1918, enclosing the Democratic National Committee letter of September 18, 1918; Poindexter Papers. Lloyd C. Whitman to Tumulty, September 18, 1918, protesting this method of fund-raising; Wilson Papers. New York *World,* September 25, 1918.

22. Representative Richard W. Austin of Tennessee, chairman of the congressional committee's finance committee, to Frank L. Greene, October 15, 1916, and May 28, 1917; Greene Papers.

23. Austin to Fred H. Babbitt, a Bellows Falls, Vermont, paper manufacturer, December 10, 1917, soliciting funds for the 1918 campaign; Greene to Babbitt, January 21, 1918, advising against any contribution at that time; Greene Papers.

24. Philadelphia *Record,* July 3, 1918. A copy of the July 3 letter signed by Woods and Kahn of the congressional committee is in the Burleson Papers.

25. *Official Report of the Proceedings of the Democratic National Committee . . . June, 1920* (Indianapolis, 1920), 488–93.

26. New York *Times,* November 5, 1918. The League admitted to spending $235,667 on the campaign. (U.S. Congress, "Investigation of the National Security League," I, p. 11.)

27. W. R. Hollister to Glass, June 1, 1917; Glass Papers.

28. W. D. Jamieson to Glass, October 5, 1917; *ibid.*

29. "Minutes of the Executive Committee Meeting," January 14, 1918; *ibid.*

30. Hollister to Glass, February 1, 1918; *ibid.*

31. Roosevelt to John T. King, February 28, 1918; Roosevelt Papers.

32. New York *World,* January 9, 1918.

33. Wausau *Record-Herald,* quoted in Milwaukee *Journal,* October 24, 1917.

34. C. G. Pearse to Wilson, November 3, 1917; Wilson Papers. Milwaukee *Journal,* January 9, March 14, 1918.

35. Lodge to Roosevelt, March 5, 1918; Roosevelt to Lodge, March 5, 1918; Lodge Papers. Knute Nelson to Alfred A. Norton, March 16, 1918; Nelson Papers.

36. Charles McCarthy to Tumulty, March 5, 1918; Joseph P. Martin to Burleson, February 25, 1918; Wilson Papers. New York *Times,* March 22, 1918. Davies to McAdoo, March 14, 1918, seeking help from the National Committee; McAdoo to Benjamin J. Rosenthal, March 26, 1918, that he is doing all he can to bring about Davies' election; McAdoo Papers.

37. Davies to Wilson, March 12, 1918; Wilson Papers.

38. Wilson to Burleson, March 13, 1918; Burleson Papers.

39. Wilson to Marshall, March 15, 1918; Wilson Papers. Ray S. Baker, *Woodrow Wilson,* VIII, 30.

40. Wilson to Davies, March 18, 1918; quoted in *ibid.* In an in-

correct footnote Baker states that the letter was to assist Davies in his campaign against La Follette.

41. Poindexter to Hugh T. Halbert, April 11, 1918, denying press charges of partisan animus in the airplane controversy; Poindexter Papers.

42. Boston *Evening Transcript*, March 26, 1918. Minneapolis *Tribune*, March 27, 1918. St. Paul *Pioneer Press*, March 27, 1918.

43. *Congressional Record*, 65th Cong., 2d Sess., 4058–66, 4133–39.

44. New York *Times*, March 29, 1918.

45. John W. Burke to McAdoo, May 4, 1918; McAdoo Papers.

46. New York *Times*, March 29, 1918.

47. Milwaukee *Journal*, April 10, 1918. Official returns gave Lenroot 163,980 votes, Davies 148,714, and Berger 110,487.

48. *Ibid.*, April 3, 1918.

49. Vicksburg *Herald*, April 7, 1918.

50. Cleveland *Plain Dealer*, April 7, 1918. Baltimore *Sun*, April 7, 1918.

CHAPTER IX: *"Politics Is Adjourned"*

1. Ralph M. Easley, director of the League for National Unity, to McAdoo, February 1, 1918, enclosing the League's appeal to the voters to return congressmen "only with unequivocal war records"; McAdoo Papers.

2. McAdoo to Wilson, May 8, 1918; *ibid.* New York *World*, May 6, 1918.

3. G. R. Cooksey, "Memorandum for the Secretary," May 20, 1918; McAdoo Papers.

4. Representative Henry T. Rainey of Illinois to McAdoo, May 21, 1918; *ibid.*

5. Tax Legislation Memorandum, May 20, 1918; *ibid.*

6. G. R. Cooksey, "Memorandum for the Secretary," May 20, 1918; *ibid.* New York *Times*, May 21, 1918.

7. Fordney of Michigan, representing the Republicans, agreed to the special session, but his Democratic colleagues refused. (Wilson to McAdoo, May 23, 1918; McAdoo Papers.) Illness kept McAdoo away from these conferences.

8. Boston *Evening Transcript*, June 7, 14, 1917. Washington *Post*, June 13, 1917. Baker to Wilson, June 21, 1917; Newton D. Baker Papers. The idea of selling this preposterous program to the public originated at a luncheon at Delmonico's attended by a group of prominent industrialists and government officials. (Grosvenor Clarkson to McAdoo, July 31, 1917; McAdoo Papers.) Frank L. Greene to H. L. Hindley, May 5, 1918, recalling the extravagant outburst of newspaper publicity which "clouded the sky with airplanes" and led the people to expect "miracles"; Greene Papers.

9. William F. Durand, chairman of the National Advisory Committee on Aeronautics, to Wilson, January 24, 1918, denying the serious charges of confusion and delay in the airplane program published in *The Outlook,* January 16, 1918; Wilson Papers. The New York *World* ran a series of articles on this subject. (Frederick Upham Adams to Josephus Daniels, April 9, 1918; Daniels Papers.)

10. New York *Tribune,* March 28, 1918.

11. Diary, entry for March 25, 1918; Wood Papers. New York *Tribune,* March 26, 27, 1918.

12. Springfield *Republican,* April 11, 1918.

13. Chicago *Tribune,* May 3, 1918. St. Louis *Globe-Democrat,* May 3, 1918. Baker to Wilson, May 3, 1918, asking for an investigation of the Senate charges; Wilson Papers.

14. Wood to Senator Charles S. Thomas, May 4, 1918; Thomas to Wood, May 15, 1918; Wood Papers. *Literary Digest,* Vol. 57, April 27, May 25, 1918.

15. New York *Times,* May 7, 1918. Chicago *Tribune,* May 7, 1918.

16. Borglum to Wilson, November 22, 1917; Wilson Papers. Mary Borglum and Robert J. Casey, *Give the Man Room,* 137–50, 238.

17. Baker to Tumulty, November 28, 1917; Borglum to Wilson, December 25, 1917; Wilson to Borglum, January 2, 1918; Wilson Papers.

18. Stanley King, "Memorandum for the Secretary of War," January 23, 1918; Baker to Wilson, January 21, 1918; Newton D. Baker Papers. Tumulty to Wilson, January 24, 1918, that Borglum, an intimate friend of Roosevelt, was "getting ready to make an attack upon us in some way helpful to T. R."; Tumulty Papers.

19. H. Snowden Marshall, "Report to the President," April 12, 1918; Newton D. Baker Papers. Charles D. Walcott to Wilson, April 15, 1918; Wilson Papers.

20. For Squier's limitations, see Major General James G. Harbord to Wood, March 12, 1918; Senator Charles S. Thomas to Wood, May 8, 1918; Wood Papers. Coffin to Wilson, April 18, 1918; Wilson to Coffin, April 20, 1918; Wilson Papers. Wilson offered the job to Henry Ford, who declined but requested the retention of Colonel Edward A. Deeds, against whom serious charges were made. (Ford to Tumulty, April 22, 1918; Wilson Papers.)

21. Borglum to Wilson, April 13, 1918; Wilson to Borglum, April 15, 1918; Wilson to Borglum, January 2, 1918 (italics supplied); *ibid.*

22. John Wilson to Wilson, April 3, 1918; Wilson to Tumulty, May 6, 1918; *ibid.*

23. Wilson to Tumulty, no date but probably May 8, 1918, Tumulty Papers.

24. Senator Charles S. Thomas to Wilson, May 3, 1918; Wilson Papers.

25. Tumulty to Wilson, May 8, 1918; Tumulty Papers. Wilson to Baker, May 7, 1918; Wilson Papers.

26. New York *Tribune,* May 7, 1918.

27. New York *Times,* May 8, 1918. *Congressional Record,* 65th Cong., 2d Sess., 6642.

28. New York *Tribune,* May 10, 1918.

29. Tumulty to Thompson, May 17, 1918; Wilson Papers.

30. Boston *Evening Transcript,* May 15, 1918. Milwaukee *Sentinel,* May 16, 1918.

31. Major General Wood and his Republican friends filled the press with their clamor about the deplorable situation. (Wood to John A. Sleicher, editor of *Leslie's,* April 9, April 18, May 11, 1918; Wood to James T. Williams, editor of the Boston *Evening Transcript,* April 14, 1918; Wood to Robert Collier of *Collier's Weekly,* April 16, 1918; Wood to Colonel George Harvey, May 10, 1918, enclosing Salina, Kansas, *Evening Journal* article on the airplane fiasco, the material for which he had inspired; Wood to Thomas L. Masson, editor of *Life,* May 13, 1918; Wood to Charles Munn, editor of *Scientific American,* May 16, 1918; Wood Papers. On the other hand, Representative Frank L. Greene, a former Vermont newspaper editor, defended the War Department and sought unsuccessfully to get the Vermont Republican press to moderate its violent criticism of Wilson and Baker. (Greene to Howard L. Hindley, May 5, May 26, 1918; Greene Papers.)

32. House approached Hughes on May 4 through Richard Washburn Child, a mutual friend. (Diary, XIII, 119, 124, 128, entries for May 4, May 12, May 15, 1918; House Papers.)

33. House to Wilson, May 9, 1918; Wilson Papers.

34. Wilson to Winthrop M. Daniels, February 4, 1918; *ibid.*

35. Wilson to Hughes, May 13, 1918; Hughes to Wilson, May 15, 1918; *ibid.* Baltimore *Sun,* May 16, 1918. Philadelphia *Inquirer,* May 16, 1918.

36. Quoted in Milwaukee *Sentinel,* May 17, 1918. New York *Tribune,* May 17, 1918.

37. Lodge to William S. Bigelow, May 20, 1918; Lodge Papers.

38. Milwaukee *Sentinel,* May 24, 1918.

39. New York *World,* May 23, 1918.

40. U.S. Department of Justice, *Report of the Hughes Aircraft Inquiry,* 181. Borglum was especially indignant that Henry Ford had been let off the hook in view of the strong evidence against him. For a whitewash of the airplane industry at this period, see Isaac F. Marcosson, *Colonel Deeds, Industrial Builder.* Deeds was the official against whom criminal proceedings had been recommended. Merlo J. Pusey, *Charles Evans Hughes,* I, 374–82, summarizes the investigation without comment.

41. Borglum to Wood, July 10, December 4, 1918; Wood Papers.

42. Philadelphia *Public Ledger,* August 23, 1918. Boston *Evening Transcript,* August 23, 1918. New York *Tribune,* August 25, 1918.

43. The New York *World* said the report would carry no weight with the public because the Committee was composed of "professional critics of the conduct of the war." Quoted in "Why American Airplanes Are not Winning the War," *Literary Digest,* Vol. 58, September 7, 1918.

44. McAdoo to Representative John N. Garner of Texas, June 3, 1918; McAdoo Papers.

45. Simmons to Wilson, May 25, 1918; Wilson Papers. New York *Times,* May 25, 1918. Philadelphia *Public Ledger,* May 25, 1918.

46. Senator Henry F. Hollis of New Hampshire, one of the few Democrats to support the Treasury's position, suggested that the crisis warranted another visit by Wilson to Congress. (Hollis to Wilson, May 21, 1918; Hollis to McAdoo, May 21, 1918; McAdoo Papers.) McAdoo to Wilson, May 27, 1918, urging a personal appearance, suggests that the Secretary was not consulted about the President's intention beforehand; *ibid.*

47. Ray S. Baker, *Woodrow Wilson,* VIII, 171. New York *Times,* May 28, 1918. McAdoo was "very glad to see the President take such a strong stand on profiteering in his speech" and promised to make information on profiteers directly available to the press. (McAdoo to John Skelton Williams, June 4, 1918; McAdoo Papers.)

48. Springfield *Republican,* June 8, 1918.

49. New York *Evening Post,* June 6, 1918.

50. McAdoo to Daniel C. Roper, June 2, 1918; McAdoo Papers.

51. New York *Times,* May 30, 1918.

52. Roper to McAdoo, June 4, 1918; McAdoo Papers. Roper, the internal revenue commissioner and a former congressman, served as a liaison between the Treasury and Congress. On June 5 McAdoo sent Kitchin a statement of what the Treasury wanted in the revenue bill and hoped the hearings might be completed in two weeks. The Committee dragged them out for fourteen weeks before reporting out the bill on September 10.

53. Representative William Gordon of the Twenty-first Ohio District complained to Secretary of War Baker, who was also chairman of the Democratic Executive Committee of Cuyahoga County, in which Gordon's Cleveland district lay, of the "libelous and slanderous" reports circulated in that area regarding his poor "acid test" record. (Gordon to Baker, June 15, 1918; Newton D. Baker Papers.) Cleveland *Plain Dealer,* August 1, 7, 11, 1918, bitterly opposed Gordon's renomination on patriotic grounds.

54. San Francisco *Chronicle,* July 14, 15, 1918.

CHAPTER X: *Primaries and Platforms*

1. New York *Times,* July 26, 1917, editorially condemned the war records of both Hardwick and Hoke Smith. Hollins N. Randolph, an Atlanta lawyer, wrote to McAdoo, August 20, 1917, that he could not understand "what has gotten into our two senators. Up to the present time they have been in open and active hostility to all of the administration's policies"; McAdoo Papers.

2. Tumulty to Wilson, July 10, 1917; Tumulty Papers. Harris to Tumulty, December 31, 1917; Wilson Papers. New York *World,* August 19, 1917. Vicksburg *Herald,* January 2, 1918. Atlanta *Constitution,* January 5, 9, 1918.

3. Aldine Chambers to McAdoo, October 20, 1917; Clark Howell to McAdoo, December 20, 1917; McAdoo Papers. Harris to Tumulty, December 5, 1917; S. M. Howard to Wilson, February 21, 1918; Clark Howell to Wilson, July 24, 1918; Wilson Papers.

4. Roosevelt to John T. King, July 15, 1918; Roosevelt Papers.

5. Wilson to Colonel Edward T. Brown, March 29, 1918; Wilson Papers.

6. John S. Cohen to Wilson, April 1, 1918; John B. Gamble to Wilson, June 15, 1918; *ibid.* John J. Hunt to McAdoo, March 28, 1918; McAdoo Papers.

7. Senator John Sharp Williams to Wilson, August 20, November 8, December 20, 1917; Wilson Papers. Vicksburg *Herald,* April 14, 18, 1918.

8. Thomas W. Gregory to Wilson, August 21, 1917; John S. Williams to Wilson, August 28, 1917; Wilson to Winthrop M. Daniels, February 1, 1918; Wilson Papers. John S. Williams to George L. Donald, August 14, 1917; to T. H. Brown, August 29, 30, 1917; W. L. Pryor to Williams, July 28, 1918; Williams Papers. Albert D. Kirwan, *Revolt of the Rednecks,* 279–84.

9. Washington *Times,* March 5, 1918. Tillman to Daniels, no date but probably February 1918, asking administration help because the "Bleasites are already organizing their forces for the purpose of downing everyone of the eight Congressmen, including myself for the Senatorship, if I allow my name to be used." Tillman to Daniels, May 2, 1918, repeating the request; Daniels Papers. Representative James F. Byrnes to Carter Glass, July 24, 1918, asking for Wilson's help in the primary; Glass Papers.

10. Columbia *State,* May 30, June 2, 1918. Glass to James F. Byrnes, August 3, 1918; Glass Papers.

11. Governor Frederick D. Gardner to A. M. Dockery, June 29, July 18, 1918; Wilson Papers. St. Louis *Globe-Democrat,* July 5, 14, 1918. Nicholas M. Bell to McAdoo, April 6, 1918, voicing the "profound contempt" of loyal Missourians for Reed's conduct; McAdoo Papers.

Wilson to Tumulty, May 22, 1918; Tumulty to Wilson, May 29, 1918; Tumulty Papers.

    12. House to Wilson, August 12, 1918; Wilson Papers.

    13. Edward F. Goltra, national committeeman from Missouri, to McAdoo, June 10, 1918, urging administration support for Wilfley, since otherwise the machine could not elect Folk in the fall; McAdoo Papers.

    14. Boston *Evening Transcript,* September 14, 25, 1918.

    15. New York *Tribune,* May 26, 1918.

    16. David Baird, a wealthy Camden contractor, typified the party boss from whose clutches Wilson had sought to free the state during his governorship. (Washington *Times,* February 23, 25, 1918. Philadelphia *Public Ledger,* February 27, 1918.)

    17. New York *Times,* March 21, 1918.

    18. Tumulty to Wilson, July 16, 1918, opposing the senatorial candidacy of Congressman Tom Scully because a Roman Catholic could not be elected in New Jersey; Tumulty Papers. Wilson to Tumulty, August 8, 1918; ex-Governor James F. Fielder to Tumulty, August 15, 1918; Wilson Papers. Newark *Evening News,* September 2, 6, 17, 20, 1918. New York *Times,* September 22, 1918. John M. Blum, *Joe Tumulty and the Wilson Era,* 156–57, is an excellent summary of the New Jersey situation.

    19. Wilmington *Morning News,* May 10, June 1, July 9, 1918.

    20. Colonel J. P. Bass, editor of the Bangor *Daily Commercial,* to Daniels, August 31, 1918, that his is the only newspaper in the state of Maine to support the administration; Daniels Papers. James T. Williams, editor of the Boston *Evening Transcript,* the bitterest of all the anti-Wilson papers, was a close friend of Major General Leonard Wood, who kept him well supplied with information derogatory to the government's war preparations. (Wood to Williams, October 1, 1917; August 22, 1918; Williams to Wood, April 9, June 11, July 8, 1918; Wood Papers.)

    21. Lodge to Roosevelt, October 14, 1918; Lodge Papers.

    22. Springfield *Republican,* June 27, 1918. Lodge to W. F. Craig, December 4, 1917; to Fred L. Atkinson, December 19, 1917; Lodge Papers.

    23. Boston *Evening Transcript,* August 6, 8, 12, 1918.

    24. Springfield *Republican,* May 26, June 1, August 10, 18, 20, 1918.

    25. Michael O'Leary to Daniels, May 6, 24, 1918; Daniels Papers.

    26. Boston *Evening Transcript,* May 20, 1918. Springfield *Republican,* July 14, 20, 1918.

    27. Sioux City *Journal,* June 3, 1918.

    28. James F. Kirby to Baker, May 17, 1918; Newton D. Baker Papers.

29. Sioux City *Journal,* July 12, 1918, quoting Waterloo *Courier.* Roosevelt to Maurice Leon, July 23, 1918, on the imperative need to get rid of Woods; Roosevelt Papers.

30. William R. King to McAdoo, April 10, 1918; McAdoo to King, April 15, 1918; T. S. Myers, Portland postmaster, to McAdoo, May 1, 1918, asking patronage help for a candidate who has "absolutely no use for Senator Chamberlain and has never been a Chamberlain supporter"; McAdoo Papers.

31. West to Josephus Daniels, May 28, 1918; Daniels Papers.

32. Wilson to Tumulty, June 5, 1918; Tumulty Papers.

33. New York *World,* June 21, 1918. The Democratic National Committee ran a full-page advertisement in the newspapers hailing Wilson's gesture as reducing partisan discord to a minimum. Wilson had already endorsed Nelson's re-election back in December. (Victor L. Stephenson to Nelson, December 13, 1917, enclosing New York *Evening Post,* December 13, 1917, clipping; Nelson Papers.) This may have been done to win Republican support on the eve of the Senate investigation.

34. Baltimore *Sun,* May 17, June 7, 1918.

35. "I am by no means satisfied," said Borah, "that the narrow, personal and more or less picayunish and constant faultfinding upon the part of some prominent Republicans at this time is either wise politically or the patriotic thing to do from the standpoint of the nation's interest." (Borah to Frank R. Gooding, April 27, 1918; Borah Papers.)

36. Lodge to Roosevelt, March 5, 1918; Lodge Papers.

37. Roosevelt to Lodge, March 8, 1918; *ibid.*

38. Portland *Daily Eastern Argus,* March 29, 1918.

39. Scott Ferris to Carter Glass, May 3, 1918, that a careful inventory was being made of all congressional districts in which the Democrats were considered to have a fighting chance; Glass Papers.

40. Milwaukee *Sentinel,* May 28, 1918.

41. Near the end of May, a "confidential conference committee" of three House members, three senators, and three national committeemen met with Hays to map Republican campaign plans. (Frank L. Greene to W. H. Crockett, June 26, 1918; Greene Papers.)

42. "Platform Adopted by the Indiana Republican State Convention, May 29, 1918," pamphlet in Poindexter Papers. Cincinnati *Enquirer,* May 30, 1918. Milwaukee *Journal,* May 30, 1918. Indianapolis *News,* May 30, 1918.

43. Indianapolis *News,* June 6, 1918.

44. Roosevelt to Hamlin Garland, June 5, 1918; Roosevelt Papers.

45. Roosevelt to Henry L. Stimson, June 5, 1918; *ibid.* (Italics in original.)

46. Burleson to Tumulty, May 11, 1918; Burleson Papers. The re-

visions in Wilson's handwriting were made about the time he composed his "Politics Is Adjourned" address. (Undated draft in Wilson Papers.) On August 15, Wilson told Colonel House that he had written the platform and given Secretary of War Baker a six-page draft to take to Indianapolis. (Diary, XIV, 204; House Papers.)

47. Indianapolis *News,* June 19, 20, 1918.

48. New York *Times,* June 21, 1918.

49. Milwaukee *Journal,* June 24, 1918.

50. Washington *Post,* June 29, 1918. In July the Republicans staged another massive demonstration of party enthusiasm at their New York state convention at Saratoga. New York *Tribune,* July 18, 1918, hailed it as a challenge to the notion "that partisanship is tabu in time of war." Roosevelt gave the keynote speech, and Taft created a sensation with an equally savage attack on Wilson and Baker. (New York *Times,* July 21, 1918.) New York *World,* July 21, 1918, considered the "win the war" eloquence at Saratoga mere camouflage for the 1920 presidential contest and ridiculed the demand for a Republican Congress since the Republicans had no program that the American people would accept in place of Wilson's.

CHAPTER XI: *The "Acid Test"*

1. Frank Cobb of the New York *World* considered the public reaction to the President's course in the primaries "highly unfavorable" and counter-productive of the effect Wilson wanted. (Cobb to House, August 14, 20, 1918; House Papers.)

2. F. W. McLean to John W. Burke, December 6, 1917; Fred B. Lynch to McAdoo, December 8, 1917; Charles W. Ames to McAdoo, December 5, 13, 1918; McAdoo Papers.

3. Charles W. Ames to McAdoo, December 2, 1917; *ibid.* Ames was a member of the Minnesota Public Safety Commission.

4. Representative John M. Baer to Wilson, February 7, 1918; Wilson Papers.

5. Wilson to Baer, February 18, 1918; Louis Seibold to Wilson, February 14, 1918; Wilson to Creel, February 18, 1918; *ibid.* A series of articles in the New York *World,* December 20-27, 1917, by Seibold, a correspondent close to the White House, on the situation in the Northwest and Townley's potentiality for mischief, may have made Wilson somewhat more cautious.

6. Kent to A. B. Bielaski, July 3, 1918; Kent Papers. The *Non-Partisan Leader,* April 8, 1918, printed Kent's St. Paul speech and editorially eulogized him as "A Millionaire Who Plays Straight." His membership card in the League, dated April 23, 1918, is in the Kent Papers.

7. Roosevelt to Willis C. Cook, Republican national committeeman

from South Dakota, January 23, 1918, that "Wilson is trying to secure the friendship of Townley, La Follette, and others of the same type"; Roosevelt Papers. Creel to Tumulty, July 12, 1918; Wilson Papers.

8. St. Paul *Dispatch,* March 18, 20, 22, 1918.

9. N. A. Grevstad to Knute Nelson, March 8, 1918; Nelson Papers. Dixon C. Williams to Wilson, April 3, 1918; E. S. Nichols to Wilson, April 8, 1918; Wilson Papers. Creel had already enraged the patriots by allowing League speakers to defend La Follette at the rallies held by the Committee on Public Information to counteract the bad effects of the senator's celebrated "Lusitania" speech at St. Paul on September 20. (Creel to Robert W. Hagardine, November 4, 1917; Charles Patterson to Charles W. Ames, December 3, 1917; McAdoo Papers.)

10. Nelson to Gregory, March 16, 1918; Nelson to Creel, April 8, 1918; George A. Heisey to Nelson, March 30, 1918; Nelson Papers.

11. Wilson to Creel, April 1, 1918; Creel to Wilson, April 2, 1918; Wilson Papers. The press release, dated April 9, 1918, is in the Nelson Papers.

12. Houston to Wilson, March 28, 1918; Wilson Papers.

13. Wilson to Kent, May 1, 1918; *ibid.*

14. Kent to Wilson, April 22, 1918; *ibid.*

15. Crane to Wilson, April 29, 1918; Wilson to Crane, May 1, 1918; *ibid.*

16. Wilson to Tumulty, March 22, 1918, that "I don't feel at all safe in the hands of Mr. Townley or the Non-Partisan League and would like to proceed rather carefully in dealing with them." See, however, Wilson to Gregory, June 12, 1918, saying "the League has rendered consistent assistance and very effective assistance where it could to the cause of the war"; *ibid.*

17. St. Paul *Dispatch,* June 26, 1918.

18. Fred E. Wheaton, Democratic state chairman, to McAdoo, November 30, 1918, that Nelson's decision to run had healed the factional rift which had long disrupted the party; McAdoo Papers.

19. Portland *Oregon Voter,* April 6, 1918, asserted Wilson was behind the League, which was using his letter to Baer to help in collecting the $16 membership dues; clipping in John A. Sleicher to Wilson, April 16, 1918; J. W. Rice to Representative Dan V. Stephens of Nebraska, July 6, 1918, that the Republicans were using Wilson's interview with Townley to discredit the Democratic party in Nebraska; Wilson Papers. In August the President issued instructions that "under no circumstances" was the administration to be drawn into the "very savage partisan fight" in the Northwest. (Wilson to Tumulty, August 3, 1918; *ibid.*)

20. Daniels to E. G. Liebold, Ford's secretary, December 22, 1917; Daniels to E. W. Rice, April 4, 1918; Daniels Papers. Boston *Christian Science Monitor,* April 15, 1918.

21. Memorandum by Katherine E. Brand of interview with Josephus Daniels, August 8, 1936; Ray S. Baker Papers. Josephus Daniels, *The Wilson Era,* 293–305.

22. Ray S. Baker, *Woodrow Wilson,* VIII, 209. New York *Times,* June 14, 1918. McAdoo to Henry Ford, June 15, 1918, that Ford had shown himself a "real patriot" and the kind of man needed in Congress; McAdoo Papers.

23. New York *Times,* June 13, 28, 1918. The Republican state central committee voted 8 to 1 against a proposal for a non-partisan coalition that would have left the field clear for Ford.

24. New York *World,* June 15, 1918.

25. Wilson to Daniels, September 6, 1918; Daniels to Wilson, September 9, 1918; Daniels Papers.

26. Roosevelt to the Newberry Volunteer Committee, September 13, 1918; Roosevelt Papers.

27. Charleston *News and Courier,* August 16, 29, 1918.

28. Ray S. Baker, *Woodrow Wilson,* VIII, 189. Tumulty to Wilson, September 18, 1918; Tumulty Papers.

29. Shields, said the President's brother, "never has been and will not be a cause for satisfaction in administration circles"; J. R. Wilson to McAdoo, November 16, 1917; McAdoo Papers.

30. Wilson to McAdoo, March 13, 1918. Wilson to Josephus Daniels, July 31, 1918; Wilson Papers.

31. Nashville *Tennessean,* July 18, 24, 31, August 20, 1918. Memphis *Commercial Appeal,* July 28, August 5, 17, 20, 1918.

32. Dallas *Morning News,* July 20, 26, 1918.

33. New York *Times,* July 31, 1918.

34. Dallas *Morning News,* July 25, 1918.

35. *Ibid.,* July 29, 1918.

36. Burleson wanted a telegram sent saying that Wilson could not support Slayden in view of his record, "as no one can claim that he has given support to the administration"; Tumulty to Wilson, July 23, 1918; Tumulty Papers.

37. Wilson to Glass, July 31, 1918; Wilson Papers.

38. Birmingham *Age-Herald,* August 10, 1918.

39. *Ibid.*

40. Vicksburg *Herald,* August 11, 1918.

41. New York *Times,* September 1, 1918. Kansas City *Journal,* September 1, 1918. Chicago *Tribune,* September 2, 1918. Washington *Post,* September 2, 1918. *Literary Digest,* Vol. 58, August 24, 1918.

42. Franklin Remington to Pinchot, June 6, 1918, enclosing National Security League form letter urging prominent people to cooperate in this patriotic work; Pinchot Papers.

43. U.S. Congress, "National Security League," II, 1641–44.
44. Orth to Borah, October 9, 1918; Borah Papers.
45. U.S. Congress, "National Security League," I, 664.
46. Albany *Evening Journal,* August 23, 1918.
47. U.S. Congress, "National Security League," II, 1825.
48. *The Nation,* LX (August 24, 1918), 1918. Indianapolis *News,* September 7, 1918. Denver *Rocky Mountain News,* September 10, 1918.
49. Madison *Wisconsin State Journal,* August 26, September 4, 1918.
50. U.S. Congress, "National Security League," I, 991–93; II, 1491–1569.
51. Lodge to Roosevelt, August 31, 1918; Roosevelt to Lodge, September 4, 1918; Lodge Papers. Foss, as chairman of the Naval Affairs Committee, had done much to help Roosevelt put his Big Navy program across.
52. Chicago *Tribune,* October 4, 1918.
53. Washington *Post,* July 14, 1918.
54. *Congressional Record,* 65th Cong., 2d Sess., 10219–20, 10530–36, 10663–68, 10683–84.

CHAPTER XII: *The Issues*

1. Vernon Kellogg, "Patriotism and Food," *Atlantic Monthly,* CXX (November 1917) 582. H. C. Connelly to McAdoo, June 11, 1917, asking how people could buy Liberty Bonds with potatoes selling for $1.20 a peck; McAdoo Papers. The Treasury Department estimated that 31,500 of the nation's 51,000 corporations were engaged in profiteering. (War Revenue Act Memorandum, August 14, 1918; *ibid.*)
2. John W. Burke to McAdoo, August 29, 1917; *ibid.* Hoover to Wilson, November 15, 1917; Wilson Papers.
3. Hoover to Wilson, December 1, 1917; *ibid.*
4. *Congressional Record,* 65th Cong., 2d Sess., 821–25. F. E. Hadley, president of the Minnesota Editorial Association, to Nelson, November 30, 1917; W. S. Gordland to Nelson, January 14, 1918; Nelson to J. Burgesse of the *Minneapolis Daily News,* January 15, 1918; Nelson Papers.
5. David F. Houston to Baker, January 11, 1918; Wilson to Baker, January 16, 1918; Newton D. Baker Papers.
6. Gifford Pinchot to Will H. Hays, February 15, 1918, regarding his propaganda campaign for higher farm prices; Tiffany Blake to Pinchot, February 19, 1918; Pinchot Papers. (Blake, a Chicago *Tribune* editor, wrote: "What you told me about the farmer's condition and present mood gives me more encouragement than anything I heard in Washington concerning the prospects of a revival of the Republican party.") Washington *Post,* February 24, 1918.
7. Red River Development Association to Nelson, February 23, 1918; William G. Crocker to Nelson, February 28, 1918; Nelson to

Hoover, February 25, 1918; Hoover to Nelson, February 26, 1918; Nelson Papers.

8. Ferris to Wilson, May 16, 1918; Wilson to Ferris, May 20, 1918; Wilson Papers. Ferris to McAdoo, April 4, 1918; McAdoo Papers.

9. Lord Reading to McAdoo, July 11, 1918; Wilson Papers.

10. Scott Ferris to Wilson, July 9, 1918; *ibid.*

11. Borah to W. S. Parkhurst, July 18, 1918; Borah Papers.

12. Frank R. Wilson, "Memorandum for the Secretary of the Treasury," May 31, 1917; McAdoo Papers.

13. Senator John W. Weeks to Wilson, April 11, 1918; Wilson Papers. New York *Tribune*, March 23, 26, 1918. New York *Times*, April 10, 1918.

14. Springfield *Republican*, April 8, 1918. Theodore H. Price to McAdoo, March 22, 1918; Stuart W. Cramer to McAdoo, May 6, 1918; McAdoo Papers.

15. Houston *Post*, April 21, 1918. Memphis *Commercial Appeal*, May 18, 1918.

16. Robert W. Brookings to Wilson, March 22, March 27, 1918; Wilson Papers. Houston *Post*, April 11, 17, 1918. Columbia (S.C.) *State*, April 6, 8, 13, 1918. Philadelphia *Public Ledger*, April 18, 20, 1918.

17. Indianapolis *News*, June 1, 1918. New York *Sun*, May 29, June 17, 1918. Boston *Herald*, June 3, 26, 1918. Buffalo *Morning Express*, June 4, 25, 1918.

18. *Congressional Record*, 65th Cong., 2d Sess., 8792. Indianapolis *News*, July 8, 10, 1918.

19. Natchez *Democrat*, July 3, 1918. New Orleans *Times-Picayune*, July 6, 1918.

20. "Memorandum Regarding Cotton," July 20, 1918; copy in McAdoo Papers.

21. Harding to Wilson, July 20, 1918; Wilson to Harding, July 24, 1918; Wilson Papers. Houston *Post*, July 18, 1918. Natchez *Democrat*, July 18, 1918.

22. Houston *Post*, July 21, 22, 1918. Vicksburg *Herald*, July 21, 1918.

23. Knoxville (Iowa) *Journal*, quoted in Sioux City *Journal*, July 20, 1918.

24. Lincoln *Nebraska State Journal*, July 31, 1918.

25. Cleveland *Plain Dealer*, August 29, 1918. Kansas City *Journal*, August 27, 1918. Helena *Montana Record-Herald*, September 10, 1918. Denver *Rocky Mountain News*, September 26, 1918. Salt Lake City *Tribune*, October 5, 1918. New York *Times*, September 27, 1918.

26. Prior to the fourth Liberty Loan drive, the Treasury Department recommended fixing cotton prices in order to put the public in a

better frame of mind. (Memorandum for Secretary McAdoo from Assistant Secretary of the Treasury Leffingwell, September 20, 1918; McAdoo Papers.)

27. Wilson's candidate, Harris, won the Georgia primary on September 13 after the President had publicly repudiated Senator Hardwick and assured Harris by telegram that the government had no intention of fixing cotton prices as Hardwick alleged in his campaign. (Savannah *Morning News,* August 13, September 12, 14, 1918. Harris to Tumulty, September 6, 1918; Wilson to Harris, September 6, 1918; Wilson Papers.)

28. *Congressional Record,* 65th Cong., 2d Sess., 9601–06, 9656, 9856–62.

29. There were only 2,400,000 Class I men, of whom 800,000 had been exempted. (New York *World,* June 26, 1918.)

30. Richard M. Hurd, chairman of the American Defense Society, to Wood, March 27, 1918: "Your call for five million men . . . has electrified Congress and the Nation"; Wood to Roosevelt, April 18, May 11, June 20, 1918; Wood Papers. Boston *Evening Transcript,* May 3, 1918, reported a Boston speech by Roosevelt assailing the War Department's "absurd" draft policy, which ignored the advice of patriots like Major General Wood. On May 8, the paper endorsed Senator Weeks's demand for an army of five million men. See also New York *Times,* April 13, 26, June 25, 27, 29, 1918.

31. Springfield *Republican,* June 29, 1918. Wood to Senator Porter J. McCumber, July 6, 1918; McCumber to Wood, July 11, 1918; Wood Papers.

32. Indianapolis *News,* August 24, 26, 1918. Kansas City *Star,* August 26, 1918. Philadelphia *Public Ledger,* August 25, 1918.

33. New York *Times,* September 8, 1918. Chicago *Tribune,* September 12, 1918.

34. Frank P. Woods to Poindexter, August 27, 1918; Poindexter Papers.

35. Ray S. Baker, *Woodrow Wilson,* VIII, 389. Indianapolis *News,* September 11, 1918. Newark *Evening News,* September 13, 14, 1918.

36. New York *Times,* September 13, 1918. Cf. *ibid.,* September 14, 1918.

37. See Chapter XIV for a fuller discussion of this issue.

38. Borah to Shad L. Hodges, October 23, 1918; Borah Papers.

39. Cincinnati *Enquirer,* October 16, 1918.

40. Scott Ferris to McAdoo, October 7, 1918, that "the Louisville district is a very dangerous one and it will only be by the hardest work and the best strategy of all of us that Sherley can be elected"; Wilson and McAdoo were asked to help at "the earliest possible moment in order to hold things in line down there"; McAdoo Papers.

41. Frank E. Morrison to Wilson, September 25, 1918; Wilson to Patrick M. Gorman, October 4, 1918; Wilson Papers. Sherley, however, attributed his defeat to the fact that the Republicans got out a large Negro vote, antagonized by Wilson's racist views. (Sherley to McAdoo, November 8, 1918; McAdoo Papers.)

42. James F. O'Conner to Walsh, November 7, 1918; Walsh Papers. The National Legislative and Information Bureau of the Big Four Brotherhoods ordered all its members to vote for Walsh. (H. E. Wells to Walsh, September 30, 1918; *ibid.*)

43. E. Ben Johnson to Poindexter, September 26, 1918; Horace Kimball to Poindexter, October 4, 1918; Poindexter Papers. Dan Kelleher to McAdoo, November 2, 1918; McAdoo Papers.

44. William J. Bryan to McAdoo, September 20, 1918, regarding the "diabolical plot" in California to name a "wet" Democratic candidate for governor; *ibid.* For the bizarre situation in Nevada, see Samuel W. Belford to Pittman, September 16, September 27, 1918; Pittman Papers. In Pennsylvania the administration repudiated the "wet" Democratic candidate for governor.

45. Burleson to Wilson, September 17, 1918; Wilson Papers. The states specifically mentioned were Rhode Island, Massachusetts, Delaware, Ohio, and New York, where "now the result is involved in gravest doubt."

46. The Montana branch of the Anti-Saloon League sent out six thousand letters urging Walsh's re-election. The Idaho branch performed a similar service for Borah. (Joseph Pope to Walsh, October 30, 1918; Walsh Papers. E. E. Hunt to Borah, November 9, 1918; Borah Papers.)

47. Senator Wesley Jones of Washington, an Anti-Saloon League spokesman, emphasized the close relationship between the United States Brewers' Association and the German-American Alliance and said the government had evidence of a huge slush fund raised by the beer barons to pervert the elections. (Newark *Evening News*, September 20, 1918.)

48. Indianapolis *News*, August 2, 1918. Wilson to Governor Augustus O. Stanley of Kentucky, August 30, 1918; Wilson Papers. McAdoo also wrote several hostile Democratic senators urging them to support the amendment. (McAdoo to E. B. Craig, August 6, 1918, referring to Wilson's letters of June 26 and 27 to Senator Shields of Tennessee and asking Craig to intercede with Shields; to Governor Richard I. Manning of South Carolina, October 1, 1918, asking him to use his influence with Senator Benet; to Senator Claude A. Swanson of Virginia, October 1, 1918; McAdoo Papers.)

49. Toledo *News-Bee*, August 24, 1918.

50. Carrie Chapman Catt to McAdoo, August 30, 1918; McAdoo Papers.

51. Indianapolis *News,* September 7, 14, 16, 1918.

52. Samuel W. Belford to Pittman, August 12, 1918, that Anne Martin of the National Woman's Party was conducting a "rather dangerous campaign" and lining up the women against Senator Henderson; Pittman Papers.

53. *Congressional Record,* 65th Cong., 2d Sess., 10984.

54. Walsh to ex-Governor Edwin L. Norris, October 4, 1918; Walsh Papers. McAdoo to Governor Richard I. Manning, October 5, 1918, that "I think it most unfortunate that so many Democrats failed to support the President in this important matter"; McAdoo Papers.

55. Newark *Evening News,* October 2, 1918.

CHAPTER XIII: *The Campaign*

1. McAdoo to Lord Cunliffe, October 20, 1918, that the success of the loan was "really a great achievement in the face of a nation-wide epidemic of influenza which stopped all meetings, a political campaign for a new Congress, the indeterminate revenue bill which has been pending in Congress since last May . . . and the German peace drive"; McAdoo Papers.

2. Hays to Poindexter, October 2, 1918, that "immediately upon the conclusion of this Liberty Loan drive the entire Republican organization must be put in high speed"; Poindexter Papers.

3. Roosevelt to Hays, October 17, 1918; Roosevelt Papers.

4. New York *Tribune,* August 17, 1918.

5. George H. Mayer, *The Republican Party,* 238, 396.

6. *Congressional Record,* 65th Cong., 2d Sess., 10147.

7. Told that Weeks's defeat was possible, Wilson was "unable to express the great gratitude he felt upon receiving this cheering information." (Pittman to Mrs. John E. Crowley, November 9, 1918; Pittman Papers.)

8. Boston *Evening Transcript,* November 6, 1918, also said that the Democrats feared Weeks more than any other Republican.

9. *Ibid.,* August 8, 1918.

10. Ralph D. Redfern, secretary of the Fitchburg Chamber of Commerce, to G. R. Cooksey, September 3, 1918, that "the impression obtains quite generally throughout New England that this section is not especially favored in connection with anything of a Government nature"; McAdoo Papers.

11. Representative Samuel E. Winslow of Massachusetts to Frank L. Greene, July 27, 1918; Greene Papers.

12. Boston *Post,* November 1, 1918. Boston *Evening Transcript,* November 1, 1918.

13. Lodge to Roosevelt, October 7, 19, 24, 1918; Lodge Papers. Roosevelt to the Republican State Committee, October 17, 1918; Roosevelt Papers.

14. Boston *Daily Globe,* October 26, 31, 1918. William A. White, *A puritan in Babylon,* 134, says that Coolidge considered Weeks a handicap and cut him as much as possible in the 1918 campaign.

15. Manchester *Union,* September 19, 20, October 5, 11, 1918. Merrill A. Symonds, *George Higgins Moses,* 32–33.

16. Wilson to La Monte, October 22, 1918; Wilson Papers.

17. Newark *Evening News,* September 17, 20, October 18, 23, 1918. New York *Tribune,* October 18, 20, 1918.

18. Tumulty to Wilson, October 9, 1918; Wilson Papers. Philadelphia *Record,* October 7, 1918. Newark *Evening News,* October 15, 1918. La Monte to J. A. Edgerton, October 29, 1918; McAdoo Papers.

19. F. W. Oliver to Wilson, July 5, 1918; Wilson to Oliver, July 9, 1918; Wilson Papers.

20. Kansas City *Times,* August 27, 1918. St. Louis *Globe-Democrat,* September 23, 1918.

21. Ferris to Wilson, September 27, 1918; Wilson to Folk, October 3, 1918; Wilson Papers.

22. Roosevelt to Selden P. Spencer, October 15, 1918; Roosevelt Papers.

23. Minneapolis *Journal,* October 2, 1918.

24. David F. Houston to Wilson, September 4, 1918; Wilson to Creel, September 4, 1918, asking the Committee on Public Information to assemble the facts to demonstrate that the price of wheat had advanced more rapidly and to a higher level than the cost of the things which the farmer bought ("If we can get these facts properly established and lucidly set forth," he said, "it will be of great service and will guide editorial opinion throughout the country.") George P. Hampton, secretary of the National Wheat Growers' Association, to Wilson, September 19, 1918; Houston to Wilson, October 7, 1918; Wilson to Hampton, October 9, 1918; Wilson Papers.

25. Pinchot to Will H. Hays, September 24, 1918; Pinchot to Henry Wallace, October 17, 1918; Pinchot Papers.

26. Cincinnati *Enquirer,* September 22, 1918. Indianapolis *News,* September 27, 1918. Columbus *Ohio State Journal,* October 6, 1918, reported that the Republican state committee was sending out 25,000 pieces of campaign literature daily.

27. McCormick to Scripps, September 10, 1918; Scripps to Wilson, September 14, 1918; Wilson to Scripps, September 18, 1918; Wilson Papers.

28. Topeka *State Capital,* September 14, 1918.

29. Governor Arthur Capper to Wood, June 29, 1918; Wood to Capper, November 2, 1918; Capper to Wood, November 8, 1918; Wood Papers.

30. Roosevelt to George W. Perkins, August 30, 1918; Roosevelt Papers. Fred Robertson to Wilson, August 31, 1918; Wilson Papers.

31. Ferris to Tumulty, September 16, 1918; Wilson to Tumulty, September 16, 1918; *ibid.*

32. Lincoln *Nebraska State Journal,* October 17, 1918. *Wallaces' Farmer,* Vol. 43 (October 11, 18, 25, 1918), Henry C. Wallace to Pinchot, September 14, October 8, 1918; Pinchot Papers.

33. Roosevelt to George Harvey, September 3, 19, 1918; Roosevelt Papers.

34. Kent to Borah, September 11, 1918; Borah to Kent, September 12, 1918; Kent Papers.

35. Edgar Howard to Newton D. Baker, October 19, 1918; Wilson Papers.

36. Arthur F. Mullen to Tumulty, October 24, 1918; Wilson to Tumulty, October 25, 1918; *ibid.* Mullen, the state chairman, Governor Keith Neville, and Senator Hitchcock ran the machine, which the Bryan faction detested.

37. Wilson to Mayor Edward P. Smith of Omaha, October 28, 1918; *ibid.*

38. W. J. Sheldon to Nelson, June 19, 1918, reporting that Douglas county had "gone over the top for the Kaiser"; Nelson Papers.

39. W. G. Calderwood to John Lind, October 23, 1918; Democratic National Committee to John Lind, October 23, 1918; E. E. Smith to Nelson, October 23, 1918, regarding the ample funds at Calderwood's disposal; *ibid.*

40. George B. Safford, superintendent of the Minnesota Anti-Saloon League, to Nelson, October 22, 1918; *ibid.*

41. Nelson to Rev. J. A. O. Stub, December 17, 1917, regarding disloyalty among the Norwegians, particularly the Lutheran pastors, who were "saturated" with pro-German propaganda; N. A. Grevstad to Nelson, March 9, 1918, saying something should be done to rouse the patriotic cooperation of the Sons of Norway, whose fifteen thousand members were among the least Americanized elements in the state; Nelson to D. S. Hall, October 22, 1918; *ibid.*

42. R. G. Leffingwell to McAdoo, July 20, 1918; McAdoo to William P. G. Harding, July 21, 1918; Harding to McAdoo, August 7, 1918; William Kent to McAdoo, September 4, 1918; McAdoo Papers.

43. The Latah County Defense Council suppressed a logging camp strike in July 1917 and detained sixty-one I.W.W. agitators in the Moscow State Fair Grounds until lack of evidence and the approach of winter compelled their release. Governor Moses Alexander denied press reports of a reign of terror in Idaho. (Alexander to Borah, July 10, July 12, 1918; W. J. McConnell to Representative Burton L. French of Idaho, August 11, 1917; M. E. Lewis to Borah, December 15, 1917; Borah Papers.) For mob violence against the Washington State Grange for alleged disloyal activities, see William Bouck to Wilson, June 11, 1918; Wilson Papers.

44. Borah to Daniel Dean, November 16, 1917; Borah to F. E. Springs, January 9, 1918; Borah Papers.

45. Miles Cannon to Borah, January 28, 1918; Borah to W. G. Schultz, February 28, 1918; *ibid.* Cannon and Schultz were League organizers.

46. Boise *Capital News,* July 3, August 2, 10, 1918. James H. Hawley to Burleson, September 5, 1918; Burleson Papers.

47. Edward J. Barber to Borah, September 24, 1918; David Burrell to Borah, October 21, 1918; Borah Papers. The edge of Gooding's attack was somewhat blunted when the Nugent forces published a letter from Gooding soliciting a League endorsement prior to the primaries.

48. W. R. Hamilton to Wilson, August 28, 1918; Nugent to Wilson, October 5, 1918; Wilson Papers. D. W. Davis to Borah, October 22, 1918; Borah Papers. Boise *Idaho Daily Statesman,* October 20, 1918.

49. Borah to David Burrell, October 26, 1918; Borah Papers.

50. Y. C. Mansfield to Borah, August 2, 1918; *ibid.* Spokane *Spokesman-Review,* October 27, 1918, estimated that the League controlled twenty of Montana's forty-three counties. H. S. McGinley to Walsh, August 7, 1918, estimating that 60 per cent of the farm vote was Nonpartisan; Walsh Papers.

51. Secretary of Labor William B. Wilson to Wilson, June 26, 1917; Wilson Papers. Burton K. Wheeler to McAdoo, May 3, 1918, regarding the hysteria in Montana and the shameful treatment of Miss Rankin and everyone else who did not agree with the "Company"; McAdoo Papers.

52. David Hilger to Walsh, March 22, 1918; Walsh Papers.

53. Burton K. Wheeler to Walsh, July 9, 1918; Walsh to Hugh R. Wells, July 26, 1918; Walsh to Wheeler, August 29, 1918; *ibid.*

54. Governor Sam V. Stewart of Montana to Walsh, August 31, October 16, 1918; Walsh to Wilson, October 11, 1918; Richard C. Purcell to Walsh, October 2, 1918; J. M. Kennedy to Walsh, October 20, 1918; *ibid.*

55. A. J. King to Walsh, May 3, October 17, 1918; W. H. Woodridge to Walsh, October 14, 1918; *ibid.* Anaconda *Standard,* August 30, 1918.

56. A. S. Pettit to Walsh, July 3, 1918; Walsh Papers.

57. George L. Ramsey to Walsh, September 5, 1918; *ibid.*

58. Reno *Evening Gazette,* August 16, 1918. For her picketing exploits, see Pittman to Mrs. H. H. Clark, May 22, 1917; Pittman Papers.

59. New York *Tribune,* March 5, 1918, ran an article on her senatorial candidacy. Governor Emmet D. Boyle of Nevada to Pittman, April 16, 1918; Samuel W. Belford to Pittman, August 12, 1918; T. A. Brandon to Pittman, October 13, 1918; Pittman Papers.

60. Joe McEachin to Pittman, April 23, 1918; Vail Pittman to Pittman, April 28, 1918; *ibid.* Boston *Evening Transcript,* April 20, 1918.

61. A. B. Gray to Pittman, July 1, 1917; George B. Ackerman to Pittman, October 6, 1917; Pittman Papers.

62. Boyle to Pittman, October 17, 1918; *ibid.* Reno *Evening Gazette,* September 21, 1918.

63. Cheyenne *State Leader,* August 12, 18, 20, 1918.

64. *Ibid.,* September 20, 25, 1918.

65. Denver *Rocky Mountain News,* September 10, 1918.

66. Scott Ferris to Wilson, October 23, 1918; Tumulty to Wilson, October 25, 1918; Wilson Papers. Keating received the general endorsement sent to most candidates after the October 25 appeal, enabling him to boast in his *A Gentleman from Colorado,* 438–40, that he was the only anti-war congressman Wilson endorsed for re-election.

67. Caesar A. Roberts to McAdoo, November 14, 1918; T. J. O'Donnell to McAdoo, November 16, 1918; McAdoo Papers. William N. Vaile to Simeon D. Fess, September 28, 1918; Greene Papers. Vaile, Hilliard's Republican opponent in the Denver district, asked the congressional campaign committee for information on "Government taxes and spending in favor of the South" to support allegations that Texas received $100 per capita in war contracts compared to forty-seven cents per capita for Colorado.

68. Denver *Rocky Mountain News,* May 3, October 18, 1918.

69. H. K. Tammen, editor of the Denver *Post,* to McAdoo, October 29, 1918; McAdoo Papers.

70. A. B. McGaffey to McAdoo, October 7, 1918; McAdoo to Wilson, October 19, 1918; Wilson Papers.

71. Sante Fe *New Mexican,* September 28, 1918.

72. A. B. McGaffey to McAdoo, October 7, 1918; Wilson Papers.

73. Sante Fee *New Mexican,* October 21, 25, 1918.

74. *Ibid.,* October 30, 1918. Boston *Evening Transcript,* November 1, 1918.

75. New York *Times,* November 2, 1918.

CHAPTER XIV: *The Appeal*

1. McAdoo to J. H. O'Neil, October 14, 1918, that "the President will do the right thing in spite of partisan, captious or hysterical criticism. He has to deal with very grave issues and it is a pity that partisanship at least cannot be silenced at this time"; McAdoo Papers.

2. Pittman to John F. Kunz, chairman of the Nevada Democratic central committee, October 12, 1918, that Wilson often talked about the need for a Democratic Congress and that "he is under great strain because of fear of this"; Pittman Papers. Charles H. Randall to

McAdoo, October 17, 1918, asking for Wilson's help in Randall's Ninth California District; McAdoo Papers.

3. Scott Ferris to Wilson, October 12, 1918; Wilson Papers.

4. Roosevelt to A. J. Ewing, July 8, 1918, that "if Mr. Baker had done his duty, we would have had a million men in France by March last, when the great drive began"; Wood Papers.

5. Tumulty to Wilson, June 18, 1918; Wilson Papers. Many people urged Wilson to participate in the Liberty Loan campaign. (C. A. Hinsch to McAdoo, August 5, 1918; C. R. Bliss to McAdoo, August 8, 1918; McAdoo Papers.)

6. Wilson to Jouett Shouse, August 14, 1918; Wilson to Governor F. D. Gardner of Missouri, August 20, 1918; Wilson Papers. House noted on August 18 that Wilson wanted McAdoo to avoid another Liberty Loan speaking trip because of a chronic sore throat "and will make a more limited tour of the country himself." (Diary, XIV, 212; House Papers.)

7. McAdoo to Wilson, August 27, 1918; McAdoo Papers.

8. Boston *Evening Transcript,* August 5, 1918. New York *Evening Post,* September 3, 1918. Topeka *Daily State Journal,* September 9, 1918.

9. Diary, XIV, 226, entry for September 8, 1918; House Papers. Spokane *Spokesman-Review,* September 7, 1918.

10. Garfield to Wilson, September 5, 1918; Wilson to Garfield, September 6, 1918; Garfield Papers.

11. Indianapolis *News,* September 10, 1918.

12. Tumulty to Wilson, September 4, 1918; Wilson Papers.

13. House to Tumulty, July 26, 1918; *ibid.* John M. Blum, *Joe Tumulty and the Wilson Era,* 160–61.

14. McAdoo to George W. Wheeler, November 6, 1918; McAdoo Papers. McAdoo added that Chairman Hays during the third Liberty Loan campaign had "organized a speaking tour for himself and in that guise held political conferences with State and county chairmen in the different States he visited and on the same dates that he spoke for the Liberty Loan. I received many complaints about this."

15. George L. Ramsey to Senator Thomas J. Walsh, September 3, 1918, asking for material to refute Republican propaganda in Montana about the airplane scandal; Walsh to Ramsey, September 19, 1918, on how best to handle the problem; Walsh Papers. To counteract the bad impression created by the scandal, the Committee on Public Information had a Flying Squadron of American military planes tour the West that summer. (Boston *Evening Transcript,* August 29, 1918.)

16. See, for instance, Karl Schriftgiesser, *The Gentleman from Massachusetts,* 300, and Gerald W. Johnson, *Incredible Tale,* 75–76. This morbid myth is given currency in Gene Smith, *When the Cheering Stopped,* 56.

17. Indianapolis *News,* May 29, 1918.

18. *Congressional Record,* 65th Cong., 2d Sess., 9392–94.

19. Lodge to Roosevelt, August 31, 1918; Lodge Papers.

20. Boston *Evening Transcript,* August 24, 1918.

21. Springfield *Republican,* August 25, 1918.

22. Roosevelt to Albert J. Beveridge, July 18, August 14, 1918; Roosevelt Papers.

23. Chicago *Tribune,* August 27, 1918. Roosevelt renewed the attack at the Lafayette anniversary ceremonies in New York on September 6. (New York *Times,* September 7, 1918.)

24. New York *Tribune,* September 16, 1918.

25. Boston *Evening Transcript,* September 17, 1918.

26. Diary, XIV, 244; House Papers.

27. Newark *Evening News,* September 28, 1918.

28. Overman to Wilson, October 4, 1918; Wilson to Overman, October 5, 1918; Hitchcock to Wilson, October 23, 1918; Wilson Papers. *Congressional Record,* 65th Cong., 2d Sess., 10838–42. Burlington (Vt.) *Free Press and Times,* October 24, 1918, editorial praising the Weeks resolution. Chicago *Tribune,* October 7, 1918, editorial denouncing the Overman resolution as "partisan and sectional."

29. Roosevelt to William Flinn, September 3, 1918; to Truman H. Newberry, September 19, 1918; Roosevelt Papers.

30. Kansas City *Journal,* October 4, 1918.

31. Roosevelt to H. H. Kohlsaat, October 17, 1918; Roosevelt Papers.

32. Ray S. Baker, *Woodrow Wilson,* VIII, 474, 477–79.

33. *Congressional Record,* 65th Cong., 2d Sess., 11156–63.

34. Wood to Bishop William T. Manning, October 12, 1918; to J. St. Loe Strachey, October 23, 1918; Wood Papers. Nelson to Charles H. Wheeler, October 21, 1918; to John R. H. Pratt, October 28, 1918; Nelson Papers.

35. Richard M. Bissell to McAdoo, October 9, 1918; F. T. Bonfils to McAdoo, October 11, 1918; McAdoo Papers. Chicago *Tribune,* October 14, 1918. In the Senate, Brandegee of Connecticut said that an armistice now would lose the war. (Newark *Evening News,* October 14, 1918.)

36. *Congressional Record,* 65th Cong., 2d Sess., 11205–36. Pittman to Governor Emmet D. Boyle of Nevada, October 12, 1918; Pittman Papers. John Sharp Williams to Wilson, October 14, 1918; Wilson Papers.

37. Roosevelt to John H. Bartlett, October 18, 1918; Roosevelt Papers.

38. McAdoo to Wilson, October 9, 1918; Wilson Papers. McAdoo to Newton D. Baker, October 14, 1918; to General John J. Pershing, October 14, 1918; McAdoo Papers. Boston *Globe,* October 22, 1918.

39. Governor Sam V. Stewart of Montana to Walsh, October 13, 1918; Walsh to J. M. Kennedy, October 10, 1918; Walsh Papers.

40. Philadelphia *Record,* October 12, 1918. New York *World,* October 19, 1918.

41. Tumulty to Wilson, September 18, 23, October 16, 1918; Tumulty Papers.

42. Cordell Hull, *Memoirs,* I, 98–99. For press rumors, see Toledo *News-Bee,* August 16, 1918. Indianapolis *News,* September 16, 1918. New York *Evening Post,* October 3, 1918. Lincoln *Nebraska State Journal,* October 10, 1918.

43. Diary, XIV, 237, entry for September 24, 1918; 4 (second), entry for October 25, 1918; House Papers. (House started numbering the remaining pages of Volume XIV from 1 again after he left the United States on October 17.)

44. *Ibid.,* 261, entry for October 15, 1918. House considered Lansing "stupid." (*Ibid.,* 246, entry for September 27, 1918.) Arthur D. Howden Smith, *Mr. House of Texas,* 272–74, says that House, alerted by newspapermen on October 14 to Wilson's intent, telephoned the White House to advise against it. The Diary mentions no such call, and the author gives no citation.

45. Ray S. Baker, *Woodrow Wilson,* VIII, 421.

46. New York *Sun,* September 26, 1918. Spokane *Spokesman-Review,* October 5, 1918. Chicago *Tribune,* October 16, 1918.

47. Ralph Pulitzer to Wilson, October 14, 1918; Wilson Papers.

48. Ray S. Baker, *Woodrow Wilson,* VIII, 469.

49. Cummings to Ray S. Baker, November 21, 1928; Ray S. Baker Papers.

50. Lane to Wilson, October 17, 1918; Wilson to Lane, October 18, 1918; Wilson Papers.

51. Memorandum in the House Papers, cited in Herbert C. Hoover, *The Ordeal of Woodrow Wilson,* 16, footnote 2.

52. Daniels memorandum, August 8, 1936; Ray S. Baker Papers. Daniels presents a mellower version of the episode in *The Wilson Era,* 308.

53. Herbert C. Hoover, *The Ordeal of Woodrow Wilson,* 15–16. Hoover also absolves the Republicans from any show of partisanship during the war. Curiously, his book opens (pp. 1–2) with an account of Senator Lodge's politically inspired attempt in 1915 to wreck the Commission for Relief in Belgium and Northern France, of which Hoover was the head.

54. Anne W. Lane and Louise H. Wall, eds., *The Letters of Franklin K. Lane,* 297–99. Josephus Daniels, *The Wilson Era,* 306–7.

55. Burleson memorandum, March 17, 1927; Ray S. Baker Papers.

56. "Memorandum of Conversation with Vance C. McCormick, July 15, 1928," *ibid.*

57. Scott Ferris to Ray S. Baker, March 2, 1936; *ibid.*
58. Key Pittman to John F. Kunz, October 21, 1918; Pittman Papers.
59. Diary, XIII, 10, entry for January 9, 1918; House Papers.
60. Ray S. Baker, *Woodrow Wilson,* VIII, 510.
61. John M. Blum, *Joe Tumulty and the Wilson Era,* 165.

CHAPTER XV: *The Verdict*

1. Memorandum from Scott Ferris, no date but probably early October; Wilson Papers.
2. The Socialists lost their New York City seat but elected Victor Berger in Milwaukee, where local patriots, in their zeal to purge Republican Representative William H. Stafford because of his poor "acid test" record, opened the way for Berger. A Republican congressman from Duluth with a satisfactory "acid test" record was upset by an Independent running with Nonpartisan League support.
3. One of Scott Ferris' campaign workers in the Middle West reported that "the biggest load we had to carry was the feeling over cotton" but stated somewhat prematurely that Wilson's appeal had been "wonderfully effective" in overcoming "all sorts of influences, open and secret, operating against us." (James K. McGuire to McAdoo, October 31, 1918; McAdoo Papers.)
4. Lodge to Roosevelt, November 15, 1918; Lodge Papers. The pre-election newspaper consensus was that the administration would hold the Senate by a narrow margin. (San Francisco *Chronicle,* September 19, 1918. New York *Sun,* October 21, 1918. Omaha *Bee-News,* November 3, 1918.)
5. Joseph P. Tumulty, *Woodrow Wilson As I Know Him,* 333.
6. Lodge to Sir George Otto Trevelyan, November 19, 1918; Lodge Papers.
7. Figures are based on election returns, not always complete, in *The World Almanac and Book of Facts* (New York: New York *World*) for the years 1914–20, and in various local newspapers.
8. G. W. A. Luckey to McAdoo, November 20, 1918; McAdoo Papers.
9. Portland *Morning Oregonian,* October 1, 8, 1918. John Burke to McAdoo, May 4, 1918, advising against administration support for West, a Chamberlain adherent; McAdoo Papers.
10. Shafroth to McAdoo, November 20, 1918; *ibid.*
11. E. E. Smith to Knute Nelson, November 15, 1918; Nelson Papers.
12. L. M. Willcuts to Nelson, November 9, 1918; Nelson to Willcuts, November 12, 1918; *ibid.* Nelson considered Miller, who was one

of Wilson's noisiest critics, "the ablest man in our House delegation by all odds." (Nelson to James T. McCleary, November 11, 1918; *ibid.*)

13. Reno *Evening Gazette,* November 7, 1918. Prince A. Hawkins to Pittman, November 8, 1918; Pittman Papers.

14. Anaconda *Standard,* November 8, 1918. Daniel L. O'Hearn to Walsh, November 12, 1918; Walsh Papers.

15. Boise *Idaho Daily Statesman,* November 26, 1918.

16. Wilson to Governor A. O. Stanley, August 30, 1918; Wilson to Polk Lafoon, October 7, 1918, explaining that Stanley's veto was not a disloyal act; Wilson Papers.

17. Arthur Brisbane to McAdoo, August 7, 1918; McAdoo Papers. Brisbane, whose *Herald and Examiner* was the only Democratic paper in Chicago, felt McCormick would win by a big margin because of disaffection in the party and the power of the *Tribune.*

18. J. Hamilton Lewis to McAdoo, June 14, 1918; Tumulty to McAdoo, July 12, 1918; *ibid.* Springfield *Illinois State Register,* September 19, 1918, said Republican candidates were emphasizing the "South is in the saddle" theme, while the principal Democratic issue was Republican opposition to Wilson and the war.

19. Lodge to Roosevelt, November 15, 1918; to James Bryce, November 16, 1918; to Sir George Otto Trevelyan, November 19, 1918; to William S. Bigelow, November 26, 1918; Lodge Papers.

20. Wood to Lodge, November 10, 1918; Lodge to Wood, November 16, 1918; Wood Papers.

21. Springfield *Republican,* November 8, 1918.

22. Boston *Post,* November 7, 1918.

23. Hartford *Daily Courant,* October 24, November 6, 1918.

24. Dwight Braman to Wood, July 2, September 9, December 4, 1918; Wood Papers. (Braman, a New York broker, claimed to have engineered the transfer of 175,000 Republican votes to Smith.) McAdoo to Smith, September 6, 1918; George W. Meade to McAdoo, September 11, 1918; Edward C. Heflin to McAdoo September 11, 1918; McAdoo Papers. New York *Times,* September 11, 1918.

25. John T. McGraw to Wilson, October 16, 1918; Wilson Papers. Tumulty to Wilson, October 24, 1918; Tumulty Papers. Charleston (W.Va.) *Gazette,* October 29, 1918. Wheeling *Register,* November 2, 1918.

26. Walsh to Bryan, November 19, 1918; Walsh Papers.

27. Walsh to W. M. Johnston, November 18, 1918; *ibid.*

28. Homer S. Cummings to Wilson, November 7, 1918; Wilson Papers.

29. John W. Burke to Tumulty, November 17, 1918; *ibid.* Burke, a former governor of North Dakota, was treasurer of the United States.

30. Glass to McAdoo, December 11, 1919; Glass Papers.

31. Memorandum for the President, January 23, 1918; Wilson to

Tumulty, no date but probably mid-January, to inform Senator Simmons of North Carolina that the President wanted controls over all articles necessary to the war; Wilson Papers.

32. William A. Ashbrook to Wilson, August 17, 1918; *ibid.* Ashbrook's plurality in his 17th Ohio District dropped from 8,038 in 1916 to 1,918 in 1918.

33. Domestic wool production of 290,000,000 pounds accounted for little more than half the government's requirements; the entire industry was taken over in May 1918 after the price of raw wool had soared to 58 cents a pound compared with 17 cents in 1914. Simon Litman, *Prices and Price Control,* 301.

34. Josephus Daniels, *Wilson Era,* 244–46.

35. New York *Times,* September 5, 1918. In one day the price shot up $11 per bale on some exchanges, $13 on others.

36. Lincoln *Nebraska State Journal,* September 11, 1918. Kansas City *Journal,* September 18, 1918. Sioux City *Journal,* September 18, 1918. Denver *Rocky Mountain News,* September 22, 25, 1918. St. Louis *Globe-Democrat,* September 23, 1918. Spokane *Spokesman-Review,* September 25, 1918. Newark *Evening News,* September 13, 1918. St. Paul *Dispatch,* September 26, 1918.

37. Wilson to Tumulty, September 19, 1918, to direct all cotton congressmen to Bernard M. Baruch at the War Industries Board in order to relieve the congestion at the White House; Wilson Papers.

38. McAdoo to Senator F. M. Simmons, September 27, 1918; McAdoo Papers. Wilson calmed Senator John Sharp Williams, who was obsessed by fears of price-fixing, by saying, "You have certainly expressed the right feeling as well as the right principle . . . I realize the delicacy and danger of the whole business and am trying to treat it with prudence and also, which is of the essence, with promptness." (Williams to Wilson, September 18, 19, 1918; Wilson to Williams, September 21, 1918; Wilson Papers.)

39. Assistant Secretary of the Treasury R. G. Leffingwell to McAdoo, August 7, 1918; McAdoo to House, August 13, 1918, regarding Kitchin's efforts to sabotage the bill; Leffingwell to McAdoo, September 30, 1918, that Senator Simmons, chairman of the Finance Committee, "is clearly procrastinating on the Tax bill and plans to put it off until after the election"; McAdoo Papers.

40. Cincinnati *Enquirer,* October 4, 1918. Boston *Evening Transcript,* October 4, 1918.

41. Walsh to Richard Purcell, December 6, 1918; Walsh Papers.

BIBLIOGRAPHY

I. Primary Sources

A. MANUSCRIPT COLLECTIONS

Each collection is in the Library of Congress, except where otherwise noted.

Newton D. Baker Papers
Ray Stannard Baker Papers
William E. Borah Papers
Albert Sidney Burleson Papers
Josephus Daniels Papers
Jacob H. Gallinger Papers (New Hampshire Historical Society, Concord, New Hampshire)
Harry A. Garfield Papers
E. Carter Glass Papers (Alderman Library, University of Virginia)
Frank L. Greene Papers
Edward M. House Papers (Yale University Library)
Frank B. Kellogg Papers (Minnesota Historical Society, St. Paul, Minnesota)
William Kent Papers (Yale University Library)
Philander C. Knox Papers
Henry Cabot Lodge Papers (Massachusetts Historical Society, Boston, Massachusetts)
William G. McAdoo Papers
Knute Nelson Papers (Minnesota Historical Society, St. Paul, Minnesota)
George W. Norris Papers
Gifford Pinchot Papers
Key Pittman Papers
Miles Poindexter Papers (Alderman Library, University of Virginia)
Theodore Roosevelt Papers
William H. Taft Papers
Joseph P. Tumulty Papers
Thomas J. Walsh Papers
John Sharp Williams Papers
Woodrow Wilson Papers
Leonard Wood Papers

B. GOVERNMENT DOCUMENTS (in chronological order)

U.S. Congress, *Congressional Record,* 64th and 65th Congresses (47 vols.; Washington, 1915–19).
U.S. Congress, "Defective Ammunition," *Hearings, September 5, 1917,*

U.S. Senate Military Affairs Committee, 65th Cong., 1st Sess. (Washington, 1917).

U.S. Congress, "Investigation of War Department," *Hearings for the purpose of inquiring from the different branches of the service of the War Department as to the progress made in the matter of providing for ordnance, small arms, munitions, etc., in connection with the present war and to ascertain the Government need thereof, December 12, 1917–March 29, 1918,* Senate Military Affairs Committee, 65th Cong., 2d Sess. (8 vols.; Washington, 1918).

U.S. Congress, "Aircraft Production in the United States," *Senate Report 555, August 22, 1918,* Senate Military Affairs Committee, 65th Cong., 2d Sess. (Washington, 1918).

U.S. Congress, "Investigation of the National Security League," *House Report 1173,* 65th Cong., 3d Sess. (Washington, 1918).

U.S. Department of Justice, *Report of the Hughes Aircraft Inquiry, October 25, 1918, to the Attorney General* (Washington, no date).

U.S. Congress, "National Security League," *Hearings before a Special Committee of the House of Representatives, 65th Congress, 3d Session, on House Resolution 476 to investigate and make report as to the officers, membership, financial support, expenditures, general character, activities, and purposes of the National Security League, a Corporation of New York, and of any associated organization* (2 vols.; Washington, 1919).

U.S. Department of Defense, *United States Army in the World War, 1917–1919* (17 vols.; Washington, 1931–49). I, *Organization of the American Expeditionary Forces;* II, *Policy-Forming Documents, American Expeditionary Force.*

U.S. Department of Defense, *Order of Battle of the United States Land Forces in the World War* (3 vols.; Washington, 1949). III, *Zone of the Interior.*

C. Newspapers (by area)

New England states

Connecticut: Hartford *Daily Courant,* Hartford *Times,* New Haven *Courier-Journal.*

Maine: Bangor *Daily Commercial,* Portland *Daily Eastern Argus.*

Massachusetts: Boston *Christian Science Monitor,* Boston *Daily Globe,* Boston *Herald,* Boston *Post,* Boston *Evening Transcript,* Springfield *Republican.*

New Hampshire: Manchester *Union.*

Rhode Island: Providence *Journal.*

Vermont: Bennington *Evening Banner,* Burlington *Free Press and Times,* Rutland *Daily Herald.*

Middle Atlantic states

Delaware: Wilmington *Morning News*, Wilmington *Evening Journal*.
District of Columbia: Washington *Post*, Washington *Evening Star*, Washington *Times*.
Maryland: Baltimore *Sun*.
New Jersey: Newark *Evening News*, Trenton *Evening Times*.
New York: Albany *Evening Journal*, Buffalo *Morning Express*, New York *Journal of Commerce*, New York *Evening Post*, New York *Sun*, New York *Times*, New York *Tribune*, New York *World*.
Pennsylvania: Philadelphia *Inquirer*, Philadelphia *Public Ledger*, Philadelphia *Record*, Pittsburgh *Post*.
West Virginia: Charleston *Gazette*, Wheeling *Register*.

Southern states

Alabama: Birmingham *Age-Herald*, Birmingham *News*, Mobile *Register*, Montgomery *Advertiser*.
Florida: Jacksonville *Times-Union*.
Georgia: Atlanta *Constitution*, Atlanta *Journal*, Savannah *Morning News*.
Kentucky: Louisville *Courier-Journal*.
Louisiana: New Orleans *Times-Picayune*.
Mississippi: Natchez *Democrat*, Vicksburg *Herald*.
Oklahoma: Oklahoma City *Daily Oklahoman*.
South Carolina: Charleston *News and Courier*, Columbia *State*.
Tennessee: Memphis *Commercial Appeal*, Nashville *Tennessean*.
Texas: Dallas *Morning News*, Houston *Post*.
Virginia: Richmond *Times-Dispatch*.

Middle Western states

Illinois: Chicago *Herald and Examiner*, Chicago *Tribune*, Springfield *Illinois State Register*.
Indiana: Indianapolis *News*.
Iowa: Des Moines *Evening News*, Des Moines *Register*, Sioux City *Journal*.
Kansas: Emporia *Gazette*, Leavenworth *Times*, Topeka *Daily State Journal*, Topeka *State Capital*.
Michigan: Detroit *Free Press*.
Minnesota: Minneapolis *Journal*, Minneapolis *Morning Tribune*, St. Paul *Dispatch*, St. Paul *Pioneer Press*.
Missouri: Kansas City *Journal*, Kansas City *Star*, Kansas City *Times*, St. Louis *Globe-Democrat*, St. Louis *Republic*.
Nebraska: Lincoln *Nebraska State Journal*, Omaha *Bee-News*, Omaha *World-Herald*.

North Dakota: Bismarck *Tribune,* Fargo *Non-Partisan Leader* (weekly).

Ohio: Cincinnati *Enquirer,* Cleveland *Plain Dealer,* Columbus *Ohio State Journal,* Toledo *News-Bee.*

South Dakota: Sioux Falls *Daily Argus-Leader.*

Wisconsin: Madison *Democrat,* Madison *Wisconsin State Journal,* Milwaukee *Sentinel,* Milwaukee *Journal.*

Western states

Colorado: Denver *Post,* Denver *Rocky Mountain News.*

Idaho: Boise *Capital News,* Boise *Idaho Daily Statesman.*

Montana: Anaconda *Standard,* Butte *Daily Post,* Helena *Independent,* Helena *Montana Record-Herald.*

Nevada: Reno *Evening Gazette.*

New Mexico: Albuquerque *Morning Journal,* Santa Fe *New Mexican.*

Utah: Salt Lake City *Deseret News,* Salt Lake City *Tribune.*

Wyoming: Cheyenne *State Leader.*

Pacific Coast states

California: Los Angeles *Times,* Sacramento *Union,* San Francisco *Chronicle.*

Oregon: Portland *Morning Oregonian,* Portland *Oregon Daily Journal.*

Washington: Seattle *Daily Times,* Seattle *Post-Intelligencer,* Spokane *Spokesman-Review.*

D. MAGAZINES

The Atlantic Monthly, Collier's Weekly, Forum, Literary Digest, The Nation, North American Review, Wallaces' Farmer.

II. General Sources

Agar, Herbert. *The Price of Union.* Boston: Houghton Mifflin Co., 1950.

Arnett, Alex M. *Claude Kitchin and the Wilson War Policies.* Boston: Little, Brown & Co., 1937.

Bailey, Thomas A. *Woodrow Wilson and the Lost Peace.* New York: The Macmillan Company, 1944.

Baker, Ray S., and Dodd, William E. (eds.) *War and Peace: Presidential Messages, Addresses, and Public Papers (1917–1924) by Woodrow Wilson.* 2 vols. New York: Harper & Brothers, 1927.

Baker, Ray S. *Woodrow Wilson: Life and Letters.* 8 vols. Garden City, N.Y.: Doubleday, Page & Co., 1927–39.

Baruch, Bernard M. *American Industry in the War: A Report of the War Industries Board (March, 1921).* New York: Prentice-Hall, Inc., 1941.

Bell, Herbert C. F. *Woodrow Wilson and the People.* Garden City, N.Y.: Doubleday, Doran & Co., 1945.

Belmont, Perry. *An American Democrat: The Recollections of Perry Belmont.* 2d ed. New York: Columbia University Press, 1941.

Binkley, Wilfred E. *American Political Parties, Their Natural History.* New York: Alfred A. Knopf, Inc., 1943.

Bishop, Joseph B. *Theodore Roosevelt and His Time Shown in his Own Letters.* 2 vols. New York: Charles Scribner's Sons, 1920.
———. *Goethals, Genius of the Panama Canal: A Biography.* New York: Harper & Brothers, 1930.

Blum, John M. *Joe Tumulty and the Wilson Era.* Boston: Houghton Mifflin Co., 1951.
———. *Woodrow Wilson and the Politics of Morality.* Boston: Little, Brown & Co., 1956.

Bolles, Blair. *Tyrant from Illinois: Uncle Joe Cannon's Experiment with Personal Power.* New York: W. W. Norton & Co., Inc., 1951.

Borglum, Mary, and Casey, Robert J. *Give the Man Room: The Story of Gutzon Borglum.* Indianapolis: Bobbs-Merrill Co., 1952.

Bowden, Robert D. *Boies Penrose, Symbol of an Era.* New York: Greenberg, 1937.

Brooks, Robert C. *Political Parties and Electoral Problems.* 3d ed. New York: Harper & Brothers, 1933.

Bryn-Jones, David. *Frank B. Kellogg, a Biography.* New York: G. P. Putnam's Sons, 1937.

Christianson, Theodore. *Minnesota: The Land of Sky-Tinted Waters, a History of the State and Its People.* 5 vols. New York and Chicago: The American Historical Society, Inc., 1935.

Clark, Champ. *My Quarter Century of American Politics.* 2 vols. New York: Harper & Brothers, 1920.

Crawford, Lewis F. (ed.). *History of North Dakota.* 3 vols. New York and Chicago: The American Historical Society, Inc., 1931.

Creel, George. *Rebel at Large: Recollections of Fifty Crowded Years.* New York: G. P. Putnam's Sons, 1947.
———. *The War, The World, and Wilson.* New York: Harper & Brothers, 1920.

Crighton, John C. *Missouri and the World War, 1914–1917: A Study in Public Opinion.* Columbia: University of Missouri Press, 1947.

Crowder, Enoch H. *The Spirit of Selective Service.* New York: The Century Company, 1920.

Crowell, Benedict, and Wilson, Robert F. *The Giant Hand: Our Mobilization and Control of Industry and Natural Resources, 1917–1918.* 6 vols. New Haven: Yale University Press, 1921.

Daniels, Josephus. *The Life of Woodrow Wilson, 1856–1924.* Philadelphia: The John C. Winston Company, 1924.
———. *The Wilson Era: Years of War and After, 1917–1923.* Chapel Hill: University of North Carolina Press, 1946.

Davenport, Walter. *Power and Glory: The Life of Boies Penrose.* New York: G. P. Putnam's Sons, 1931.

Diamond, William. *The Economic Thought of Woodrow Wilson*. Baltimore: The Johns Hopkins Press, 1943.

Doan, Edward N. *The La Follettes and the Wisconsin Idea*. New York: Rinehart & Company, 1947.

Dodd, William E. *Woodrow Wilson and his Work*. Garden City, N.Y.: Doubleday, Page & Co., 1920.

Dulles, Foster Rhea. *Twentieth Century America*. Boston: Houghton Mifflin Co., 1945.

Dunaway, Wayland F. *A History of Pennsylvania*. New York: Prentice-Hall, Inc., 1935.

Dunn, Arthur Wallace. *From Harrison to Harding: A Personal Narrative, Covering a Third of a Century, 1888–1921*. 2 vols. New York: G. P. Putnam's Sons, 1922.

Edge, Walter E. *A Jerseyman's Journal*. Princeton: Princeton University Press, 1948.

Ervin, Spencer. *Henry Ford vs. Truman H. Newberry, the Famous Senate Election Contest: A Study in American Politics, Legislation and Justice*. New York: R. R. Smith, 1935.

Essary, J. Frederick. *Covering Washington: Government Reflected to the Public in the Press, 1822–1926*. Boston: Houghton Mifflin Co., 1927.

Ewing, Cortez A. M. *Congressional Elections, 1896–1944: The Sectional Basis of Political Democracy in the House of Representatives*. Norman: University of Oklahoma Press, 1947.

Fite, Gilbert C. *Peter Norbeck, Prairie Statesman*. Columbia: University of Missouri Press, 1948.

Fitzpatrick, Edward A. *McCarthy of Wisconsin*. New York: Columbia University Press, 1944.

Fletcher, John C. *Arkansas*. Chapel Hill: University of North Carolina Press, 1947.

Flick, Alexander C. (ed.). *History of the State of New York*. 10 vols. New York: Columbia University Press, 1933.

Fyfe, Henry Hamilton. *Northcliffe, an Intimate Biography*. New York: The Macmillan Company, 1930.

Gardner, Constance (ed.). *Some Letters of Augustus Peabody Gardner*. Boston: Houghton Mifflin Co., 1920.

Garraty, John A. *Henry Cabot Lodge, a Biography*. New York: Alfred A. Knopf, Inc., 1953.

Gaston, Herbert E. *The Nonpartisan League*. New York: Harcourt, Brace and Howe, 1920.

Geiger, Louis G. *Joseph W. Folk of Missouri*. Columbia: University of Missouri Press, 1953.

Gompers, Samuel. *Seventy Years of Life and Labor, an Autobiography*. 2 vols. New York: E. P. Dutton & Co., Inc., 1925.

Grantham, Dewey W., Jr. *Hoke Smith and the Politics of the New South.* Baton Rouge: Louisiana State University Press, 1958.

Griffin, Solomon B. W. *Murray Crane, a Man and Brother.* Boston: Little, Brown & Co., 1926.

Groves, Charles S. *Henry Cabot Lodge, the Statesman.* Boston: Small, Maynard & Co., 1925.

Hacker, Louis M., and Kendrick, Benjamin B. *The United States Since 1865.* New York: F. S. Crofts & Co., 1939.

Hapgood, Norman. *The Changing Years, Reminiscences of Norman Hapgood.* New York: Farrar & Rinehart, Inc., 1930.

Hardy, Charles O. *Wartime Control of Prices.* Washington: The Brookings Institution, 1940.

Hays, Will H. *The Memoirs of Will H. Hays.* Garden City, N.Y.: Doubleday, Doran & Co., 1955.

Heaton, John L. *Cobb of "The World," a Leader in Liberalism; compiled from his Editorial Articles and Public Addresses.* New York: E. P. Dutton & Co., Inc., 1924.

Hechler, Kenneth W. *Insurgency: Personalities and Politics of the Taft Era.* New York: Columbia University Press, 1940.

Hennessy, Michael E. *Four Decades of Massachusetts Politics, 1890–1935.* Norwood, Mass.: The Norwood Press, 1935.

Herring, Edward P. *The Politics of Democracy: American Parties in Action.* New York: W. W. Norton & Co., Inc., 1940.

Hofstadter, Richard. *The Age of Reform; from Bryan to FDR.* New York: Alfred A. Knopf, Inc., 1955.

Holley, Irving B., Jr. *Ideas and Weapons: Exploitation of the Aerial Weapon by the United States during World War I. A Study in the Relationship of Technological Advance, Military Doctrine, and the Development of Weapons.* New Haven: Yale University Press, 1953.

Holthusen, Henry F. *James W. Wadsworth, Jr.: A Biographical Sketch.* New York: G. P. Putnam's Sons, 1926.

Hoover, Herbert C. *The Ordeal of Woodrow Wilson.* New York: McGraw-Hill Book Company, Inc., 1958.

Houston, David F. *Eight Years with Wilson's Cabinet, 1913–1920; with a Personal Estimate of the President.* 2 vols. Garden City, N.Y.: Doubleday, Page & Co., 1926.

Howard, Joseph K. *Montana: High, Wide and Handsome.* New Haven: Yale University Press, 1959.

Hull, Cordell. *The Memoirs of Cordell Hull.* 2 vols. New York: The Macmillan Company, 1948.

Jackson, William Rufus. *Missouri Democracy: A History of the Party and its Representative Members — Past and Present; with a Vast Amount of Informative Data.* 3 vols. Chicago: S. J. Clarke Publishing Co., 1935.

Jessup, Philip C. *Elihu Root.* 2 vols. New York: Dodd, Mead & Co., 1938.

Johnson, Claudius O. *Borah of Idaho.* New York: Longmans, Green & Co., 1936.

Johnson, Gerald W. *Incredible Tale, the Odyssey of the Average American in the Last Half Century.* New York: Harper & Brothers, 1950.

Johnson, Walter. *William Allen White's America.* New York: Henry Holt & Co., 1947.

Johnson, Willis F. *George Harvey, a "Passionate Patriot."* Boston: Houghton Mifflin Co., 1929.

Keating, Edward. *The Gentleman from Colorado, A Memoir.* Denver: Sage Books, 1964.

Kent, Frank R. *The Democratic Party, a History.* New York: The Century Co., 1928.

Kerney, James. *The Political Education of Woodrow Wilson.* New York: The Century Co., 1926.

Kirwan, Albert D. *Revolt of the Rednecks; Mississippi Politics, 1876–1925.* Lexington: University of Kentucky Press, 1951.

La Follette, Belle Case, and La Follette, Fola. *Robert M. La Follette: June 14, 1855–June 18, 1925.* 2 vols. New York: The Macmillan Company, 1953.

Lamont, Thomas W. *Across World Frontiers.* New York: Harcourt, Brace & Co., 1951.

Lane, Anne W., and Wall, Louise H. (eds.). *The Letters of Franklin K. Lane, Personal and Political.* Boston: Houghton Mifflin Co., 1924.

Lawrence, David. *The True Story of Woodrow Wilson.* New York: George H. Doran Co., 1924.

Lawrence, William. *Henry Cabot Lodge: A Biographical Sketch.* Boston: Houghton Mifflin Co., 1925.

Leary, John J., Jr. *Talks with T. R., from the Diaries of John J. Leary, Jr.* Boston: Houghton Mifflin Co., 1920.

Lief, Alfred. *Democracy's Norris: The Biography of a Lonely Crusade.* New York: Stackpole Sons, 1939.

Lindley, Harlow, and Wittke, Carl F. (eds.). *The History of the State of Ohio.* 6 vols. Columbus: Ohio State Archaeological and Historical Society, 1942.

Link, Arthur S. *Wilson,* Volume IV: *Confusions and Crises, 1915–1916.* Princeton: Princeton University Press, 1964.

———. *Woodrow Wilson and the Progressive Era.* New York: Harper & Brothers, 1954.

Litman, Simon. *Prices and Price Control in Great Britain and the United States During the World War.* New York: Oxford University Press, 1920.

Livermore, Seward W. "The Sectional Issue in the 1918 Congressional Elections," *Mississippi Valley Historical Review,* XXXV (June 1948), 29–60.

Lockard, Duane. *New England State Politics.* Princeton: Princeton University Press, 1959.

Lodge, Henry Cabot (ed.). *Selections from the Correspondence of Theodore Roosevelt and Henry Cabot Lodge, 1884–1918.* 2 vols. New York: Charles Scribner's Sons, 1925.

Longworth, Alice R. *Crowded Hours, Reminiscences of Alice Roosevelt Longworth.* New York: Charles Scribner's Sons, 1933.

McAdoo, Eleanor Wilson. *The Woodrow Wilsons.* New York: The Macmillan Company, 1937.

McAdoo, William Gibbs. *Crowded Years, the Reminiscences of William G. McAdoo.* Boston: Houghton Mifflin Co., 1931.

McKenna, Marian C. *Borah.* Ann Arbor, University of Michigan Press, 1961.

Marcosson, Isaac F. *Colonel Deeds, Industrial Builder.* New York: Dodd, Mead & Co., 1947.

Marshall, Thomas R. *Recollections of Thomas R. Marshall, Vice President and Hoosier Philosopher: A Hoosier Salad.* Indianapolis: Bobbs-Merrill Co., 1925.

Mayer, George H. *The Republican Party, 1854–1964.* New York: Oxford University Press, 1964.

Meriwether, Lee. *Jim Reed, "Senatorial Immortal." A Biography.* Webster Groves, Mo.: International Mark Twain Society, 1948.

Millis, Walter. *Road to War; America, 1914–1917.* Boston: Houghton Mifflin Co., 1935.

Milton, George Fort. *The Use of Presidential Power, 1789–1943.* Boston: Little, Brown & Co., 1944.

Minor, Henry A. *The Story of the Democratic Party.* New York: The Macmillan Company, 1928.

Mock, James R., and Larson, Cedric. *Words that Won the War: The Story of the Committee on Public Information, 1917–1919.* Princeton: Princeton University Press, 1939.

Moos, Malcolm Charles. *The Republicans: A History of Their Party.* New York: Random House, 1956.

Morison, Elting E. (ed.). *The Letters of Theodore Roosevelt.* 8 vols. Cambridge: Harvard University Press, 1951–54.

Mowry, George E. *Theodore Roosevelt and the Progressive Movement.* Madison: University of Wisconsin Press, 1946.

Mullendore, William C. *History of the United States Food Administration, 1917–1919.* Palo Alto: Stanford University Press, 1941.

Myers, William Starr. *The Republican Party, a History.* Rev. ed. New York: The Century Co., 1931.

Neuberger, Richard L., and Kahn, Stephen B. *Integrity: The Life of George W. Norris*. New York: The Vanguard Press, 1937.

Nicolay, John G., and Hay, John. *Abraham Lincoln: A History*. 10 vols. New York: The Century Co., 1917.

Nye, Russell B. *Midwestern Progressive Politics: A Historical Study of its Origins and Development, 1870–1950*. East Lansing: Michigan State College Press, 1951.

Odland, Martin W. *The Life of Knute Nelson*. Minneapolis: The Lund Press, 1926.

O'Keane, Josephine. *Thomas J. Walsh, a Senator from Montana*. Francestown, N.H.: M. Jones Co., 1955.

Osborn, George C. *John Sharp Williams, Planter-Statesman of the Deep South*. Baton Rouge: Louisiana State University Press, 1943.

Palmer, Frederick. *Newton D. Baker: America at War, Based on the Personal Papers of the Secretary of War in the World War; his Correspondence with the President and Important Leaders at Home and Abroad; the Confidential Cablegrams Between the War Department and Headquarters in France; the Minutes of the War Industries Board, and Other First-Hand Material*. 2 vols. New York: Dodd, Mead & Co., 1931.

Pershing, John J. *My Experiences in the World War*. 2 vols. New York: Frederick A. Stokes Co., 1931.

Plumb, Ralph G. *Badger Politics, 1836–1930*. Manitowoc: Brandt Printing and Binding Co., 1930.

Pollard, James E. *The Presidents and the Press*. New York: The Macmillan Company, 1947.

Powell, Walter A. *A History of Delaware*. Boston: The Christopher Publishing House, 1928.

Pringle, Henry F. *Alfred E. Smith; a Critical Study*. New York: Macy-Masius, 1927.

———. *The Life and Times of William Howard Taft; a Biography*. 2 vols. New York: Farrar & Rinehart, Inc., 1939.

———. *Theodore Roosevelt, a Biography*. New York: Harcourt, Brace & Co., 1931.

Pusey, Merlo J. *Charles Evans Hughes*. 2 vols. New York: The Macmillan Company, 1951.

Raney, William F. *Wisconsin: A Story of Progress*. New York: Prentice-Hall, Inc., 1940.

Reddig, William M. *Tom's Town, Kansas City and the Pendergast Legend*. Philadelphia: J. B. Lippincott Co., 1947.

Redfield, William C. *With Congress and Cabinet*. Garden City, N.Y.: Doubleday, Page & Co., 1924.

Rippy, James Fred. *F. M. Simmons; Statesman of the New South, Memoirs and Addresses*. Durham: Duke University Press, 1936.

Roper, Daniel C. *Fifty Years of Public Life*. Durham: Duke University Press, 1941.

Russell, Charles E. *The Story of the Nonpartisan League; a Chapter in American Evolution*. New York: Harper & Brothers, 1920.

Russell, John Andrew. *Joseph Warren Fordney, an American Legislator*. Boston: The Stratford Co., 1928.

Sait, Edward McC. *American Parties and Elections*. 3d ed. New York: D. Appleton-Century Co., 1942.

Saloutos, Theodore, and Hicks, John D. *Agricultural Discontent in the Middle West, 1900–1939*. Madison: University of Wisconsin Press, 1951.

Schriftgiesser, Karl. *The Gentleman from Massachusetts: Henry Cabot Lodge*. Boston: Little, Brown & Co., 1944.

Seymour, Charles. *The Intimate Papers of Colonel House Arranged as a Narrative*. 4 vols. Boston: Houghton Mifflin Co., 1930.

———. *Woodrow Wilson and the World War; a Chronicle of our Own Times*. New Haven: Yale University Press, 1921.

Simkins, Francis B. *Pitchfork Ben Tillman, South Carolinian*. Baton Rouge: Louisiana State University Press, 1944.

Sinclair, Andrew. *The Available Man, the Life Behind the Masks of Warren Gamaliel Harding*. New York: The Macmillan Company, 1965.

Smith, Arthur D. Howden. *Mr. House of Texas*. New York: Funk & Wagnalls Co., 1940.

Smith, Gene. *When the Cheering Stopped: The Last Years of Woodrow Wilson*. New York: William Morrow & Co., Inc., 1964.

Smith, Rixey, and Beasley, Norman. *Carter Glass: A Biography*. New York: Longmans, Green & Co., 1939.

Socolofsky, Homer E. *Arthur Capper, Publisher, Politician and Philanthropist*. Lawrence: University of Kansas Press, 1962.

Stephenson, George M. *John Lind of Minnesota*. Minneapolis: University of Minnesota Press, 1935.

Sullivan, Mark. *Our Times; the United States, 1900–1925*. 6 vols. New York: Charles Scribner's Sons, 1928–35.

Symonds, Merrill A. *George Higgins Moses of New Hampshire: The Man and the Era*. Ann Arbor: University of Michigan Microfilms, 1955. (Microfilm copy of Clark University thesis.)

Tansill, Charles C. *America Goes to War*. Boston: Little, Brown & Co., 1938.

Thomas, Charles M. *Thomas Riley Marshall, Hoosier Statesman*. Oxford, Ohio: Mississippi Valley Press, 1939.

Toole, K. Ross, and Burlingame, Merrill G. *A History of Montana*. 3 vols. New York: Lewis Historical Publishing Co., 1957.

Tucker, Ray T., and Barkley, Frederick R. *Sons of the Wild Jackass*. Boston: L. C. Page & Co., 1932.

Tumulty, Joseph P. *Woodrow Wilson as I Know Him.* Garden City, N.Y.: Doubleday, Page & Co., 1921.

Viereck, George S. *Spreading Germs of Hate.* New York: Horace Liveright, Inc., 1930.

Wallace, David D. *South Carolina: A Short History, 1520–1948.* Chapel Hill: University of North Carolina Press, 1951.

Washburn, Charles G. *The Life of John W. Weeks.* Boston: Houghton Mifflin Co., 1928.

Watson, James Eli. *As I Knew Them: Memoirs of James E. Watson.* Indianapolis: Bobbs-Merrill Co., 1936.

Welles, Gideon. *Diary of Gideon Welles, Secretary of the Navy under Lincoln and Johnson.* 3 vols. Boston: Houghton Mifflin Co., 1911.

White, William Allen. *The Autobiography of William Allen White.* New York: The Macmillan Company, 1946.

————. *A Puritan in Babylon, the Story of Calvin Coolidge.* New York: The Macmillan Company, 1938.

————. *Woodrow Wilson, the Man, his Times, and his Task.* Boston: Houghton Mifflin Co., 1929.

INDEX

Adams, John T., defeated for Republican national chairmanship, 107–109.

Aero Club of America, *see* Borglum, Gutzon.

Agriculture, 48–51, 81, 140, 148, 153–156, 158, 169–176, 181–182, 192–198, 201, 203, 204, 224. *See also* Food Administration; Hoover, Herbert; Lever, Asbury F.

Agriculture, Department of, 49–50, 181–182.

Aircraft Production Board, troubles of, 118–119; criticism of, 125–127; reorganization of, 128; investigation of, 129–133; reports on, 133–134; as campaign issue, 134.

American Defense Society, Chamberlain speech to, 9.

American Federation of Labor, attitude toward elections, 180.

Anthony, Daniel R., offers Roosevelt amendment, 28.

Anti-Saloon League, 182, 196. *See also* Prohibition.

Armed Neutrality, 12–13, 118, 165, 167. *See also* Cooper amendment.

Army cantonments, controversy over site of, 46–47, 53; bad conditions in, 66, 73–76; criticism of in press, 74, 79; in Congress, 74–76, 82, 96; defended by Baker, 85, 96.

Army League of the United States, Roosevelt resigns from, 27.

Austin, Richard W., sponsors Roosevelt amendment, 26.

Ayres, William A., on price-fixing, 174; wins in Kansas, 233.

Baer, John M., corresponds with Wilson on Nonpartisan League, 154, 158.

Baker, Newton D., hostility to, 14; rejects Roosevelt division, 21, 23; blasted by Roosevelt, 24,

102; on politics in Defense Councils, 45; in camp site controversy, 46–47; war management under attack, 66, 67, 70, 72; visits cantonments, 73; assailed by Penrose, 76; creates Supreme War Council, 79; ouster demanded, 80, 81, 82, 88–89; grilled by Chamberlain committee, 84–85; testimony derided, 86; criticized by House, 88; defended by Wilson, 93; answers Chamberlain camp death charges, 96; troop transport figures challenged, 99–100; tours battlefront, 120; accused of blocking airplane probe, 126; asks Borglum to investigate, 127; rejects his report, 128; request for War Department inquiry refused, 129; made issue by Indiana Republicans, 150; praised by Indiana Democrats, 151–152; presents new draft bill, 177–178. *See also* War Department.

Balfour, Arthur James, on British War Mission, 30, 37.

Beach, H. L., Wilson telegram to, 162.

Beckham, James C. H., opposes woman's suffrage, 235.

Berger, Victor L., Socialist candidate in Wisconsin election, 116–117, 121; wins House seat, 225.

Beveridge, Albert J., campaigns for Weeks, 188; advises Roosevelt on campaign issues, 211–212.

Blease, Coleman L., in South Carolina primary, 140; repudiated by Wilson, 161.

Borah, William E., denounces Hay-Chamberlain bill, 6–7; urges higher war taxes, 59, 61; opposes War Cabinet bill, 95; supports Overman bill, 98; backs Hays for national chairman, 107–108; favors moderation in campaign,

convention tactics denounced, 150, 152; attacks Wilson's peace aims, 178–179; raises sectional issue in campaign, 176; endorses Gooding in Idaho, 198; advises Roosevelt on western tour, 214; keeps out of Weeks campaign, 237; credit for Republican victory, 245.

Henderson, Charles B., in Nevada campaign, 200–201; elected, 233–234.

Herrick, Myron T., in 1916 Ohio campaign, 11.

Higginson, Henry L., opposes high war taxes on business, 58.

Hill, Ebenezer, opposes censorship, 34.

Hilliard, Benjamin C., in Colorado campaign, 202; defeated, 232.

Hitchcock, Gilbert M., supports Roosevelt amendment, 26; Weeks resolution, 53; refuses to heed Wilson, 82–83; attacks Baker, 84, 99–100; opposes Garfield order, 87; becomes issue in Nebraska campaign, 195, 231; opposes Republican post-war scheme, 214; supports Wilson's peace overtures, 215.

Holcomb, Marcus, reduced majority for in Connecticut, 239.

Hollis, Henry F., supports Roosevelt amendment, 26; criticizes Wilson's attitude, 50–51; declines renomination in New Hampshire, 144.

Hollister, W. R., 111.

Hoover, Herbert C., named temporary Food Administrator, 51; confirmation opposed in Senate, 52; denounced by Reed, 51, 68; urges price-fixing, 170; criticizes Wilson's appeal, 221; mentioned, 41, 175. *See also* Food Administration.

House, Edward M., suggests Root for Russian mission, 37; on Garfield order, 87–88; critical of Baker, 88, 98; of Wilson, 97; Republican criticism of, 65;

meddles in 1917 election, 105; reports Vance C. McCormick's views, 111; urges Hughes for airplane probe, 131–132; admires Folk, 141; opposes Wilson's trip, 208; approves Tumulty letter, 208; on Wilson's New York speech, 213; discusses campaign with Wilson, 217; disapproves of appeal, 218.

Houston, David F., on Nonpartisan League, 156; on wheat price agitation, 192.

Houston *Post*, 160.

Howell, Clark, on Georgia situation, 138–139.

Huddleston, George, attempted purge of by Wilson, 163–164.

Hughes, Charles E., in 1916 campaign, 8–9; backs Mitchel in New York, 106; sees Hays, 110; asked to probe airplane situation, 131–133; report on, 133–134; demands bigger draft army, 179; mentioned, 77, 109, 149.

Hughes, William, death of, 142.

Hull, Cordell, on rumors of a White House appeal, 217.

Husting, Paul O., supports Roosevelt amendment, 26; critical of Wisconsin Defense Council, 44; death of, 115–116.

Hylan, John F., elected New York mayor 1917, 105–106; mentioned, 185.

Industrial Workers of the World (I.W.W.), 196, 198, 199, 201.

Influenza, Spanish, 185–186, 227.

James, Ollie M., death of, 235.

Jameson, John B., in New Hampshire campaign, 189; defeated, 239.

Jamieson, W. D., 111.

Joffre, Joseph Jacques Césaire, on French War Mission, 30, 37.

Johnson, Charles F., loses 1916 Maine election, 9.

Johnson, Hiram W., in 1916 elec-